Keys
to Reading
and
Study Skills

	Date	Assignment			Date	assignment	
T I 7-8	2/8/76	✓ 2 - 7	7 ≠ 8	✓		32 - 40	pg 38
		✓ 9 - 11	pg 16	✓		50 - 57	pg. 57
		✓ 12 - 14	pg 13		6-30	59 - 60	N/F
	6-30	15 - 18	pg 17		7-3	43 - 66	61 & 62
turn-in	7-1	19 - 22	pg 21 & 22	turn-in	7-7	71 - 72	73
					7-8	74 - 78	78
						82 - 81	81

Keys
to Reading
and
Study Skills

Second Edition

Harriet Krantz
Joan Kimmelman
Queensborough Community College
of the City University of New York

Holt, Rinehart and Winston
New York   Chicago   San Francisco   Philadelphia
Montreal   Toronto   London   Sydney
Tokyo   Mexico City   Rio de Janeiro   Madrid

Acquisitions Editor: Charlyce Jones Owen
Developmental Editor: Charlotte Smith
Senior Project Editor: Lester A. Sheinis
Production Manager: Nancy Myers
Design Supervisor: Robert Kopelman

To Dorothy, Solomon, Andrea, Gerald, Elyse, and Bruce—with love

Library of Congress Cataloging in Publication Data

Krantz, Harriet.
    Keys to reading and study skills.

    Includes index.
    1. Study, Method of.   2. Reading comprehension.
3. Universities and colleges—Examinations—Study guides.
I. Kimmelman, Joan.   II. Title.
LB2395.K68   1985   378′.1702812   84-15651

ISBN 0-03-071093-6

CBS COLLEGE PUBLISHING
Holt, Rinehart and Winston
The Dryden Press
Saunders College Publishing

Acknowledgments begin on page 297.

Preface

To the Instructor

The second edition of *Keys to Reading and Study Skills* maintains the direction and focus of the first edition; it is a skills text providing an introduction to, and practice with, basic reading and study techniques in college text passages. We are encouraged by the acceptance of *Keys* in classes throughout the country. Therefore, in preparing the second edition, we continued to emphasize the transfer of reading and study skills to college material, a feature praised by those using *Keys*. We varied the passages, clarified the instructional narrative, and expanded or added sections and chapters in accordance with critical evaluations of the text. In addition, we developed journal writing questions that help students to reinforce and to review skills. (See the Unit introductions in the Teacher's Edition.)

Since students in reading and study skills classes often are enrolled in subject courses, they must read, comprehend, and recall important information in their subject texts. Mastery of this information is a major requirement for successful completion of college courses. Often, however, students in reading classes learn skills in isolation; that is, they practice those skills in easy passages that are unrelated to college courses. Many students succeed with materials presented in reading classes but see little or no relation between reading skills and their subject course work. *Keys* provides an opportunity for students to master basic reading techniques with materials taken from subject texts and to relate those techniques to current course work.

Many reading texts give lengthy descriptions of each skill and offer extended practice in short, easy paragraphs, with no progression to difficult material comparable to students' actual subject work. As a result, you must search through a variety of resources in order to provide subject-related exercises. It is through these exercises that students begin to transfer reading skills to their subject courses. Without such transfer, students can only begin to master the basic reading skills. It is difficult to presume that such mastery will take place once the student completes a reading course. *Keys* provides the opportunity for such transfer in a wide range of short and lengthy text exercises.

Keys provides enough practice passages for class and independent use. You may assign extra selections to those students who need further practice. Skills introduced in one section are reinforced in later sections, thus allowing students further practice. For example, note-taking skills are an integral part of the sections describing the major patterns of text organization. These patterns form the basis for anticipating and answering test questions. Each section builds upon previous skills. Thus, the student builds an integrated foundation for mastering subject material, rather than learning or mastering skills in isolation.

To the Student

Keys to Reading and Study Skills provides you with an introduction to, and practice with, basic reading skills. These skills are presented in a logical sequence—from literal and general through inferential and critical reading. After presentation of the skill concept, exercises ranging from easy sentences or paragraphs to short and longer passages are presented. Each exercise, whether sentence, paragraph, or full selection, focuses on the particular skill to be developed. (For example, every selection in the chapter on the sequence-of-events pattern of organization is sequentially ordered.) Thus, you have the opportunity to master each skill in short passages and then to transfer that skill to longer text selections.

When using *Keys*, you can develop a systematic approach to mastering text material. You can begin the transfer process immediately when you apply newly learned skills to the subject exercises and to your current course work. Because each skill is presented and reinforced in the context of actual text selections, you will have the opportunity to apply skills to many subject texts.

Specific Features of Each Section: For the Student and the Instructor

Section One, "Using Context Clues to Determine Word Meanings," offers a basic and realistic approach to understanding new vocabulary by using a variety of context clues to derive word meanings. Difficult words are presented in this section. To use easy and possibly known words defeats the basic skill of using context clues: applying the skill. Thus, in each exercise the focus is on the skill—marking the clue or clues to word meanings—and not on the memorization of that meaning. A new chapter incorporates all types of context clues in a variety of text passages.

Section Two, "Previewing Chapters," is reorganized to present previewing skills in a holistic manner; that is, it presents parts of a business chapter and a health chapter to familiarize you with the types of understandings you can gain by reading different portions of a chapter. These serve as a guide as you preview chapters in your own texts.

Section Three, "Locating Information: Topics, Main Ideas, and Details," presents a sequential development of the skills involved in understanding what the important facts in a passage are—topics, then main ideas, and, finally, details. Mastery of each skill goes beyond the mere identification of a fact to sensing the importance of each fact and its relation to other facts.

Section Four, "Organizing Information in Written Notes," draws on your understanding of important facts—main ideas and details—and presents methods for putting these ideas on paper for future recall. The emphasis is on creating a realistic and logical system of notes that will enable you to study more effectively.

Section Five, "Using Patterns of Organization," reintroduces you to phrases you have probably seen before: simple listing, sequence of events, cause-effect, and comparison-contrast. Rather than learning and practicing in isolation the skills of using these patterns, you must apply your understanding of them to taking notes. In addition, you must use the basic patterns of organization to anticipate and answer test questions based on the selections. A new chapter features mixed patterns drawn from text selections. There is also a quiz at the end of the chapter that helps you to focus on the patterns and key ideas.

Section Six, "Taking Tests," focuses on objective tests and essay tests. In the chapter on objective tests, you will learn and apply techniques for answering a variety of test items, including those that often pose special problems, such as double-negative questions. In the chapter on essay tests, you will use your understanding of the basic patterns of organization as you identify and practice specific essay test questions required by most instructors.

Section Seven, "Drawing Inferences," begins visually in order to help you understand what an inference is. Then, beginning with short paragraphs, you will have practice both in making an inference and in identifying the facts on which it is based. Throughout this section, as the passages become longer and more difficult, the basic skill of providing evidence for an inference is reinforced. You will draw together many types of inferences—assumptions, predictions, generalizations, and conclusions—as the basis for analyzing longer passages using a chart form of notes. Proof is required for each inference as you follow a list of guided questions in the analysis of full selections.

Section Eight, "Reading Critically," also presents a visually based introduction to the skill. Beginning with advertisements, you are guided to an understanding of the author's purpose, mood, tone, and viewpoint. Moving to written material, you will practice each of these skills. Understanding the author's purpose becomes the basis for understanding mood, and so on. Each chapter up through "Distinguishing Between a Fact and an Opinion" uses guided questions and incorporates the previously developed skill. When analyzing the full selections (in the last chapter), you will be applying all previously developed critical reading skills.

Summarizing the New Features of *Keys*

We were encouraged by the enthusiastic acceptance of *Keys;* we carefully considered the comments of our students, our colleagues, and reviewers across the country as we revised and refined the text:

Suggested answers are written in a special Teacher's Edition of *Keys;* these answers correspond exactly to the exercises as they appear in the text.

A new chapter incorporates mixed context clues in a variety of text passages.

The previewing section is reorganized and now presents the main parts of a business chapter and a health chapter to help students focus on the key ideas in the chapter.

A new chapter incorporates mixed patterns of writing in text passages and includes a sample essay quiz on the selected passages.

New paragraphs and longer selections replace or are added to the sections that focus on taking notes, recognizing authors' patterns of writing, drawing inferences, and reading critically.

A more flexible system of marking texts and of taking written notes is incorporated in the note-taking section.

Acknowledgments

The preparation of a text requires the talents, support, and expert knowledge of many people. We wish to thank our editors at Holt, Rinehart and Winston: Charlotte Smith, for her professional and personal concern throughout the revision; Lester Sheinis, for his expert guidance and gentle encouragement through the stages of production; Bob Kopelman, whose design of the text displays an understanding of teachers and students. The following instructors across the United States offered many helpful recommendations that guided us in refining the second edition: Patricia Byrne, Camden County College; Suzette Cohen, Cleveland State University; Laurita Guillory, Southern University; Amy Kurata, University of Hawaii Kapiolani Community College;

Walter Pleasnick, DeKalb Community College; Meralee Silverman, Westchester Community College; and Norma Spalding, San Jose State University.

We are grateful for the assistance of two special friends and colleagues: Rosalind Sackoff and Sandra Seltzer. We appreciate the detailed critical evaluation offered graciously by James Shepherd. To our colleagues in the Department of Basic Educational Skills at Queensborough Community College who offered encouragement in our endeavors, we express our thanks.

We are grateful to our families and friends for their continued support and understanding. Finally, we wish to express heartfelt thanks to our students at Queensborough Community College for their willingness and enthusiasm in working through and helping to evaluate the worth of the text exercises. Their sincere efforts and thoughtful evaluations were invaluable in the reshaping of *Keys*.

Harriet Krantz
Joan Kimmelman

Contents

Keys
to Reading
and
Study Skills

Using Context Clues to Determine Word Meanings

Introduction 1

You often encounter new and difficult vocabulary in your reading—not only in textbooks, but also in newspapers and magazines. Skipping over such words may save time, but skipping words may limit your comprehension of what you are reading. This may not greatly affect your understanding when you are reading a newspaper or magazine, but when you are reading text-books, you must have a thorough understanding of the material. In other words, in a textbook you are responsible for knowing both general words and subject words.

General vocabulary words are the "everyday" words used by an author. These words are assumed to be a part of your vocabulary; therefore, as difficult as they may be, the author usually does not define or explain them. Subject vocabulary words, on the other hand, are usually defined when first used in the text. These terms will be presented later in this section after a discussion of general vocabulary words.

There are many ways of acquiring general vocabulary: using the diction-ary; using prefixes, suffixes, and roots; learning word lists; using context clues. However, using the context in which words appear in order to derive their meanings is perhaps the most practical <u>initial</u> approach to understanding new vocabulary. The term "initial" is stressed here because you cannot always de-rive word meanings from context clues.

Using context clues will often provide a general meaning rather than a complete or exact definition. It is important to understand that you may not always have enough information in the sentence or paragraph to derive the meaning of a word. Very often, you will turn to the dictionary. If you know Greek or Latin prefixes, roots, and suffixes, you can use them to understand new words. This skill, nonetheless, offers several practical advantages to the reader.

Advantages of Using Context Clues

1. You can use context clues in a variety of readings, such as texts, newspaper stories, and novels.
2. You use the skill only when you come across a new term.
3. A word defined one way in one context may have a very different meaning in another context. Therefore, you do not need to mem-orize a meaning that may be incorrect in another context.
4. When you read general vocabulary, you need not get a precise definition; a general meaning of a word usually enables you to go on with the reading.
5. You will be able to understand the precise meaning of subject vocabulary words, on which you will probably be tested.
6. You do not have to memorize prepared lists of words.
7. You do not have to remember "someone else's words"; you ap-ply the skill only to terms you must know.

In this chapter, you will practice a systematic and practical approach to learning new vocabulary, the skill of using context clues to derive new word meanings.

Define the following terms. Do not use a dictionary to help.

1. martinet: *a very strict military disciplinarian / Any very strict disciplinarian OR stickler for rigid regulation*

2. chagrin: *grief, sorrow, vexation / a feeling of embarrassment*

3. capitulate: *to draw up in heads or chapters / to give up or give in, stop resisting (yield)*

4. cursory: *hastily, often superficially, done, performed rapidly with little attention to detail*

5. excoriate: *to strip, scratch, or rub off the skin of / to denounce harshly*

6. debacle: *a breaking up of ice in a river / overwhelming defeat or rout, failure*

You probably had difficulty defining all these words. Now read this paragraph and answer the questions.

The underlined martinet, long known for his strict and dictatorial ways, was chagrined to learn of his mighty army's defeat at the hands of a much weakened *enemy* foe. His troops were forced to capitulate when the enemy seized control of their staff headquarters and claimed victory. After a cursory glance at the treaty, he threw the pen aside and hastily stormed out of the room. Outside, he excoriated his men for their dismal failure and shrieked that he would never let them forget the debacle, or disaster, they had barely survived.

gloomy   utter such a cry

Questions

1. Define the following words:

   martinet: *Military disciplinarian*

   chagrin: *a feeling of embarrassment*

   capitulate: *to give up*

   cursory: *hastily*

   excoriate: *to denounce harshly, blame*

   debacle: *overwhelming defeat*

2. How did you arrive at the meanings for these words? *from the story & dictionary*

The underlined words in the paragraph are difficult words. Yet each can be defined by using specific words or clues that appear in the sentences of the paragraph. You may have thought you "guessed" the correct meanings of the words. More likely you derived the meanings from one or more of the context clues in the paragraph.

Context clues are specific words or phrases in a sentence, paragraph, or passage that provide information you can use to understand new and difficult vocabulary in that sentence, paragraph, or passage. The five basic types of context clues are:

Using the Sense of the Sentence
Using Synonyms
Using Examples
Using Antonyms
Using Stated Definitions of Subject Terms

Your ability to understand and apply these vocabulary skills will strengthen your reading comprehension. Now you will have an opportunity to learn each of these skills, and you will also have an opportunity to apply each type of context clue to new and very difficult words.

Using Sense-of-the-Sentence Clues

2

You can understand the meaning of a new word if you consider the general sense of the sentence or paragraph in which it is located.

Examples   *shape form*

1. It was easy to mold the <u>malleable</u> metal.

   QUESTION: What kind of metal could one mold easily?
   ANSWER: Metal that can be bent
   <u>Malleable</u> means bendable or pliable.

2. The boarded-up house had a <u>fusty</u> smell.

   QUESTION: What kind of smell would an old boarded-up house have?
   ANSWER: Stale or airless
   <u>Fusty</u> means stale or bad-smelling.

> Very often, the **general sense of the sentence or paragraph** will provide clues to the general, if not exact, meanings of difficult words. You must consider the entire sentence and raise questions about it, focusing on the new word.

Practice: Each of the following sentences provides general clues to the meaning of the underlined word. Circle the clues and define the word. The first is done for you.

Meaning

1. Why don't you leave immediately? Your presence can only <u>foment</u> trouble.

   foment: *stir up*

2. His health was <u>vitiated</u> by years of heavy drinking.

   vitiated: *badly damaged impure*

3. During the cutback in oil production, the United States had a <u>paucity</u> of gasoline for cars.

   paucity: *small amount*

4. If you have only a <u>tenuous</u> grasp of Lesson One, how can you move to Lesson Two?

   tenuous: *under stand a little slight*

5. The chef was often complimented on his <u>culinary</u> talents by the restaurant's customers.

   culinary: *of the kitchen cooking*

6. <u>Rudimentary</u> knowledge of physics is necessary before a student can advance.

   rudimentary: *elementary*

7. We <u>perused</u> so many documents while making the data search that we both developed eyestrain.

   perused: *read carefully*

5

8. The young puppy held onto the bone tenaciously, fearing the young boy would take it away.

   tenaciously: *holding firmly*

9. How dare you offer me this pittance when the law guarantees at least a minimum hourly wage!

   pittance: *barely sufficient allowance of money*

10. The approaching clouds will quickly obviate the need for sunglasses.

    obviate: *render unnecessary*

Practice: Use the sense of each sentence to determine the meaning of the underlined word. Circle the portion of the sentence that helped you find the meaning. Write the meaning in the space at the right.

Meaning

1. The light emanating from the third-floor office window means that Marty has stayed late to complete his work.

   emanating: *flow out*

2. Flood waters rushed into the town and reached a height of four feet; houses were soon inundated by the rising waters.

   inundated: *overwhelmed*

3. The noise of the crowd abated when the band started the national anthem.

   abated: *cheered*

4. We approached the deserted castle with great trepidation after everyone had warned us that ghosts and spooks haunted the grounds.

   ghosts reappear frequently

   trepidation: *caution*

5. The pyramid's apex is 250 feet from the ground.

   apex: *the tip*

6. For a long time I earned a salary that was not commensurate with my high skills, extensive experience, and general worth.

   commensurate: *equal direction - size*

7. The heat, humidity, and blazing sun left us enervated after only one mile of jogging.

   enervated: *weakened*

8. At the vertex of her athletic career, she won two Olympic gold medals.

   vertex: *the crown*

9. Since the entire class misunderstood the point of the lesson, many students asked the instructor to elucidate the basic ideas.

   elucidate: *to make clear*

10. Realizing that the plane was too heavy for a safe take-off, the pilot quickly jettisoned some fuel over the water.

    jettisoned: *(throw) goods overboard to lighten a ship, plane et.*

Practice: Determine the meaning of each new word and circle the clues that helped you arrive at that meaning. Write the meaning in the space.

Meaning

1. It's not surprising that Marie is not popular. Her personality is so insipid that no one can find a single thing interesting about her.

   insipid: *not interesting*

2. We watched in horror as the fire razed what had once been our lovely church.

   razed: *continented demolish*

3. After the animal was attacked, the smell of the carrion, lying for six days in the desert sun, was enough to make anyone sick.

   carrion: *decaying of dead body*

4. No one dared enter the high-security area of the atomic plant, for the virulent atomic rods were located there.

   virulent: *deadly*

5. Smoking is proscribed by law in elevators and other public areas.

   proscribed: *forbid the practice*

6. Penniless and homeless, the old man felt he was at the <u>nadir</u> of his hopes as the brutal winter set in.

nadir: *time of greatest depression*

7. Only <u>lax</u> management could have allowed a once profitable company like Wood Tool to slip into utter disrepair and bankruptcy.

lax: *not strict*

8. You've told so many lies that you'll have a difficult time <u>extricating</u> yourself from the situation.

extricating: *to set free*

9. The locks on the space capsule created a <u>hermetic</u> seal equal to that of an undersea diver's helmet.

hermetic: *keep air + gas from getting in*

10. Your <u>astute</u> handling of the difficult situation gave both representatives a feeling that each had gotten the best deal.

astute: *shrewd, skillful, subtle*

Practice: Determine the meaning of each new word and circle the clues that helped you arrive at that meaning. Write the meaning in the space.

Meaning

1. The ballet dancers' <u>lithe</u> figures floated by as they spun, leaped, and gracefully landed onstage.

lithe: *flexible, limber*

2. To everyone, Bob was all smiles and a wonderful guy. Behind that <u>facade</u>, he was just as mean and tricky as the others.

facade: *false appearance*

3. After a two-week <u>hiatus</u>, the employees returned to work fully rested.

hiatus: *break*

4. The actor's brilliant performance drew <u>accolades</u> from the press.

accolades: *awards/honor*

5. You needn't pay for all the cab rides. Let me help <u>defray</u> your expenses by adding an extra $10.

defray: *pay*

6. After getting such attentive service throughout the meal, we were definitely <u>remiss</u> in not leaving a larger tip.

remiss: *thoughtless*

7. The kidnapper was <u>incarcerated</u> for six years after he was found guilty.

incarcerated: *imprison*

8. A <u>myriad</u> of fans surrounded the airport arrival building, trying to get a glimpse of the famous rock star.

myriad: *a great no.*

9. I find your salary offer so <u>lucrative</u> that I will even consider relocating to another city in order to work with you.

lucrative: *producing wealth or profit*

10. What caused the rash on her arm was a mystery. Red spots had appeared and quickly spread from elbow to wrist. Diane decided to see a doctor, who fortunately was able to prescribe an <u>unguent</u> to relieve the itching and redness.

unguent: *ointment*

Practice: Determine the meaning of each new word and write that meaning in the space.

Meaning

1. Without looking, the motorist proceeded through the yield sign into a busy intersection and ran right into the rear of a slow-moving van. Luckily, no one was injured. The driver at fault felt it <u>incumbent</u> on him to pay all damages and willingly offered to do so.

incumbent: *obligatory*

2. "The witnesses you've lined up won't do," said the defense attorney. "In order to build a good defense, I'll need more than a drunken bar friend, a truant, and a girl friend. You've got to locate more <u>credible</u> witnesses."

credible: *capable of being believed*

one who is absent without leave

3. Not only did he knock over a table, spill a glass of water all over himself, and refuse to pay the check, but he also <u>harassed</u> the other customers to the point where a bouncer had to be called.

4. Parking a car in a small space cannot in any way be compared with the <u>consummate</u> skill involved in guiding an ocean liner into its dock.

5. The performer responded to the <u>plaudits</u> of the crowd by singing three additional songs.

harassed: *badger*

consummate: *complete*

plaudits: *applause*

Using Synonym Clues | 3

You can understand the meaning of a new word when you are aware that its synonym may appear in the sentence or paragraph. A synonym can be signaled by any of the following:

Examples

1. By commas:

   She was cognizant, or aware, of the approaching storm.
   Cognizant means aware.

2. By parentheses:

   The conflagration (huge fire) raged through an entire city block.
   Conflagration means a huge fire.

3. By restatement:

   Calm

   Why should I assuage his feelings? I see no reason to soothe him.
   Assuage means to soothe.

4. By dashes:

   Are you averse—opposed—to the court decision?
   Averse means opposed.

Synonyms are words or phrases having the same or nearly the same meaning. When synonyms appear in the same sentence or paragraph, they give you a clue to the meaning of the unknown word. Synonyms are often signaled by commas, parentheses, or dashes. Most often, they appear as restatements of the new words.

Practice: Each of the following sentences contains a synonym clue for the underlined word. Circle the synonym clue and define the word. The first one is done for you.

Meaning

1. How can you extol, or praise, such sloppy work?

   extol: *praise, glorify*

2. After the two-week respite, we did not allow ourselves another break until Christmas.

   respite: *delay*

3. The actress arrived with her entourage—the group of assistants who always travel with her.

   entourage: *personal attendants*

4. The court decision is of paramount (foremost) importance to all future cases.

   paramount: *cheif in importance*

5. My mentor is the best adviser in the entire department.

   mentor: *loyal adviser*

6. You have shown amazing abstinence in staying away from fattening foods.

   abstinence: *refraining from*

7. The hill's gentle acclivity, or upward slope, made the climb easy.

8. The liquid's volatile nature turned the cargo hold into a potentially explosive area.

9. Don't cleave to your family so strongly. Sticking close to home will certainly limit your ability to make new friends.

10. I spotted a horde—or mass—of birds flying south across the inlet.

Practice: Each sentence contains a synonym for the underlined word. Circle the clue to the meaning and define the word in the space at the right.

acclivity: *upward slope*

volatile: *vapor*

cleave: *stick - cling*

horde: *large group, school, flock*

Meaning

1. When you have reached the acme (height) of your athletic abilities, you will be able to enter the marathon.

2. His manner of admonishing us—by sharply criticizing—was extremely embarrassing.

3. Most specially minted gold coins have an intrinsic, or basic, value, far exceeding their face value.

4. The club members' warmth and friendliness created a comforting ambience (atmosphere) which I accepted eagerly.

5. My friend John plans to become a nurse. I am not yet sure about a future career and have not chosen a vocation.

6. Catching crooks with pilfered items is indeed difficult; thieves do not often hold onto the stolen goods.

7. The jury foreman stated, "Two of our jury members are totally intractable. They refuse to change their votes no matter what evidence is presented."

8. For years, tourists have hunted for the cache where a famous pirate used to hide his treasures. Recently someone uncovered Bluebeard's hiding place.

9. The cobra moved sinuously, twisting and turning through the rocky field.

10. Ambassador Adams, the tiny country's liaison to the United Nations, is its connection to world politics.

acme: *highest point*

admonishing: *to caution*

intrinsic: *given part essential part*

ambience: *which surrounds*

vocation: *particular occupation*

pilfered: *tiny stolen things*

intractable: *hard to work with*

cache: *hiding*

sinuously: *indirect devious*

liaison: *similar connection*

Practice: Each of the following contains a synonym for the underlined word. Define the new words.

Meaning

1. Pecuniary matters are best handled by a money manager.

2. The administration's inflexible position on a wage increase means that the position of the union will remain just as intransigent.

3. The acerbity of their remarks did little to reduce the feelings of harshness between them.

4. During an intense questioning by the police, Frank recanted his entire statement about the crime. Not only did he take back his plea of innocence, but he also changed his mind about naming the other gang members.

pecuniary: *pertaining to money matters*

intransigent: *inflexible*

acerbity: *harshness*

recanted: *withdraw take back*

5. Because there is a <u>paucity</u> of oranges, limes, and lemons, we must adjust to the <u>shortage</u> of fresh juice in the markets.

6. The <u>incessant</u> ringing of the telephone so enraged my father that he had it disconnected last week. Now he enjoys a quiet evening at home without the phone's <u>constant</u> interruptions.

7. Governments often investigate the <u>clandestine</u> activities of <u>secret</u> organizations.

8. During the <u>incipient</u> stage of a disease, the initial symptoms are often hidden.

9. (Everyday chores) bore most people, but these <u>mundane</u> activities are perfect for me.

10. Your testimony will be considered <u>germane</u> to this case only if the evidence you offer is directly <u>related</u> to the crime.

Practice: Each paragraph contains a synonym for the underlined words. Circle the clue to the meaning and define the word.

1. How can you <u>feign</u> disinterest in the final game of the series? You've watched the Yankees' games all year, kept track of each player's batting average, read each player's fielding average, read each pitcher's statistics, and sat glued to your set whenever they played. You can't fool me by <u>pretending</u> not to care who wins this last game!

2. The whole idea of swimming in the river is <u>repugnant</u> to me. When you first suggested it, I agreed with you. It seemed like a good idea. Then I considered what the river held: swift currents, strange fish, weeds, and waste deposits. I soon became <u>disgusted</u> at the thought of jumping into that mess.

3. Bob's notes contained mostly <u>picayune</u> facts. In class, he wrote continuously and never missed a word his professor said. Bob never lifted his head during the entire lecture. Afterward, he proudly displayed four pages of neatly written notes. As I read through them, I remarked on his ability to list every <u>little</u> fact without showing an understanding of the key ideas discussed.

4. Cynthia could not <u>confirm</u> Amos's version of the accident. At the time of the <u>mishap</u>, she was asleep in the back seat of the car. Amos claimed that the other vehicle ran through a red light and smashed into his right front fender. As there were no other witnesses, Amos had hoped that Cynthia would be able to <u>corroborate</u> his claims to the insurance company.

5. Sam really wanted a new set of trains. He stared at the bright red <u>caboose</u>, the shiny new coal tender, and the streamlined passenger cars when they first appeared on the toy shelf of the local store. Because he had limited funds, Sam's only hope of getting the trains was to keep <u>pestering</u> his mother. Sam figured he could wear down his mother's resistance by <u>badgering</u> her day and night. This was his only chance for getting the trains.

---

paucity: *insufficiency*

incessant: *continuing*

clandestine: *confidential*

✗incipient: *beginning to exist*

mundane: *common*

germane: *closely related*

Meaning

feign: *pretend*

repugnant: *distasteful*

picayune: *of little value*

corroborate: *confirm*

badgering: *harass persistenly ANNOY*

unfortunate occurrence

a car on a freight train

Using Example Clues 4

Using examples is another way to derive word meanings. Read this sentence and define the underlined word:

Examples

1. The jungle was filled with the sounds of lions, tigers, monkeys, and its many other <u>denizens</u>.
   <u>Denizens</u> means _____.

In this example, <u>denizens</u> means the inhabitants of the jungle. Each animal— lion, tiger, and monkey—is an example of a jungle denizen. These examples should not be confused with synonyms. Synonyms have the same meanings; examples illustrate the term or phrase being defined. You must study the examples and use them as guides to the meaning of the new word.

There are many words and punctuation marks that signal examples in sentences. Consider these:

2. The queen's <u>coterie</u> consisted of ladies-in-waiting, servants, and handmaidens.

3. There are many types of fictional <u>genres</u> : novels, essays, poetry, and plays are some.

4. The <u>environs</u> of the village included the nearby lake, the gently sloping hills, and the grassy plains.

5. There are several characteristics of a <u>loquacious</u> person. He or she makes a point over and over, repeats phrases, never pauses, and usually doesn't know when to stop talking.

> **Examples** illustrate the term being defined and are guides to the meaning of the new word. When a sentence contains examples, there are usually key words and phrases that signal those examples: "many types," "several characteristics," "include," "such as," colons(:), and "consists of" are typical signals.

Practice: Each sentence contains one or more examples of the underlined word. Circle the examples and define the word at the right. The first one is done for you.

Meaning

1. Do you participate in one of the more popular <u>avocations</u>, such as jogging, tennis, or stamp collecting ?

   avocations: *hobbies*

2. The ship's breakup left behind wooden beams, a wide oil slick, and splintered metal. The Coast Guard had a difficult time clearing away the <u>flotsam</u>.

   flotsam: *wreckage*

3. Mimes and jesters were often members of early European courts that favored humorous entertainment provided by <u>harlequins</u>.

   harlequins: *comic characters clown.*

12

4. Coming into view was a huge <u>flotilla</u>. Even the fiercest enemy would flee from so many cruisers and battleships.

5. When you arrange the <u>condiment</u> shelf, put the salt and pepper next to the paprika.

a quarrelsome person   *can be worthless parts*

6. <u>Hoodlums</u>, <u>muggers</u>, <u>thieves</u>, and similar <u>dregs</u> of society prey on weak victims.   *người thất thời*   *Robber*

7. Your travel plans <u>dovetail</u> with mine. Not only are we leaving on the same day, but also we are taking the same flight from International Airport.   *fit exactly*

8. When we examine <u>congenital</u> diseases such as color blindness and hemophilia, we become involved in the genetic branch of science.

man e dong

9. The <u>apathetic</u> student doesn't hand assignments in on time, takes few or no class notes, may or may not buy a text, and spends little time preparing for tests.

wonder at

10. Even the most diet-conscious people <u>marvel</u> when a <u>sumptuous</u> meal is placed on the table. They can't help marvel at rich desserts, fine wines, steaming roasts, creamy vegetables, and exotic fruits of the most tempting kinds.

flotilla: *group of squadron*

condiment: *spice*

dregs: *small remnant*

dovetail: *Carpentry*

congenital: *from birth* *existing at birth*

apathetic: *showing little interest*

sumptuous: *expensive & ... splendid or superb*

from a distant country

Practice: Each exercise contains examples of the underlined word. Circle the examples and define the word.

combining of discordant sounds

Meaning

1. The <u>cacophonous</u> city sounds include construction-site blasting, horns honking, peddlers yelling, and people shouting in the streets.

cacophonous: *harsh*

2. Josie's temperature has been in a state of <u>flux</u>. Last night it was 99 degrees, and this morning it registered 98.2 degrees. By noon, it was back up to 100.1 degrees.

flux: *continuous change*

exciting play, story

3. In the latest spy <u>thriller</u>, the hero wears a wig to conceal his true hair color, covers his face with a mustache and a beard, and wears shoe lifts to make him appear taller. He must remain <u>incognito</u> while trailing the suspected international spy.

incognito: *Identity concealed*

talkative

4. Mrs. Stanton's <u>loquaciousness</u> almost doomed the project. In her presentation, she told too many personal stories, repeated ideas too often, and went into far greater detail than was necessary.

loquaciousness: *talk to much*

5. Newspapers all over the city have headlined "<u>Nepotism</u>," following the politician's disclosures of the secretarial position he gave to his wife and the staff positions he assigned to his nephew and two cousins.

nepotism: *favoritism. The practice of favoring one's relatives when one has power esp. by giving them good jobs*

Practice: Circle the clues to the underlined word in each paragraph. Then define the word.

Meaning

Related

1. Studies have shown that most workers are pleased with the <u>ancillary</u> aspects of their work, such as work conditions, bonuses, health benefits, and vacation allotments.

ancillary: *providing help, support* *maid servants*

2. Each year, college statisticians survey the incoming freshman class to determine the range of financial backgrounds. This year's report showed great <u>heterogeneity</u> in that respect. The freshmen came

heterogeneity: *dissimilar parts*

from lower-class, middle-class, and upper-middle-class financial backgrounds. No single group was in the majority.

3. Great domed patios, surrounded by treelined avenues, dominated the palace grounds. Inside, gold statues, inlaid mosaic floors, and handcrafted rugs filled each room. Dominating each lounge area was a huge signed masterpiece. It is no wonder that today visitors continue to admire the opulence of the king's private estate.

opulence: *decorated with small things to form a picture or design* *wealth, riches*

4. Sensing that the battle was turning against his forces, the soldier dug in for a final stand. Never noticing those fleeing from the scene, he carefully took up his position and calmly awaited the final onslaught. His jaw hardened into pure defiance as he decided to make every effort to hold his position. The young soldier's stoic efforts were later praised by everyone who had known him.

opposing challenging great energy

stoic: *maintains indifferent to pain or pleasure chin story*

5. Pity the poor students who wait for the last night to study for finals. They must cram an entire semester's work into one evening. And so they must stay awake all night. By morning, the average "crammer" has bags under bloodshot eyes and usually looks drawn. Such a haggard condition makes test-taking an almost impossible task.

violent attack

study intensely

haggard: *Exhausted*

Practice: Each paragraph contains examples that help explain the underlined word. Circle the clues to the meaning of the word and write the definition.

Meaning

1. Because of his gregarious nature, Mark was rarely alone. Giving parties, taking friends to dinner, joining clubs, and meeting new people were often part of Mark's everyday life.

gregarious: *Sociable*

2. Having a shopping center one block away, a park around the corner, and a medical facility on the grounds appealed to the elderly residents who depended on the proximity of such services.

proximity: *Vicinity*

3. How do you explain the reports about your brusque behavior toward customers? People say you are nasty, give abrupt answers, and refuse to assist them in any way.

what going - co'lac

brusque: *abrupt, blunt*

4. The meat was not seasoned, the salad was not crisp, and the vegetables were overcooked. What could be less appealing than such an insipid meal?

insipid: *without sufficient taste*

Using Antonym Clues 5

A sentence may contain an antonym for an unknown word. Recognizing an antonym can help you to understand the meaning of the new word. Consider the following example.

Example

Return the money of your own <u>volition</u> rather than be forced to hand it over.

<u>Volition</u> is the antonym of "be forced" to do something.
<u>Volition</u> means not being forced to do something or doing something of your own free will.

Antonyms are words or phrases that have opposite or nearly opposite meanings. Remember that context clues such as antonyms may not give you exact meanings, but they will give a good understanding of the new word. When a sentence contains antonyms, there are usually key words that signal opposite or near-opposite meanings: "rather than," "but," "on the other hand," "not," "while," and "however" are typical signals.

Practice: Each of the following sentences contains an antonym for the underlined word. Circle the antonym clue and define the word. The first is done for you.

Meaning *weak & soft*

1. The model's figure was <u>flaccid,</u> (not firm.)
   flaccid: *flabby*
2. Some people relax in a <u>supine</u> position whereas others relax standing up.
   supine: *lying on back*
3. Urban dwellers often escape to <u>bucolic</u> places.
   bucolic: *farming/country*
4. <u>Itinerant</u> salespeople often want the greater security of desk-bound office jobs.
   itinerant: *traveling*
5. Storming out of the room only <u>exacerbates</u> the situation rather than eases it. *make more bitter*
   exacerbates: *aggravate*
6. I prefer the plant with <u>variegated</u> leaves, not the solid-colored one.
   variegated: *colored*
7. Rioters <u>pillaged</u> the stores but left the homes undamaged. *Rob*
   pillaged: *striped*
8. Immigrants often <u>assimilate</u> into a local society rather than keep their native customs.
   assimilate: *absorb/adapt*
9. Narrow-minded people should develop more <u>catholic</u> views about politics. *universal extent*
   catholic: *wide-ranging*
10. Their <u>assiduous</u> planning made it impossible for them to make the usual careless errors.
    assiduous: *diligent*

15

Practice: Determine the meaning of each underlined word by looking for its antonym in the sentence. Circle the clue that helped you with the meaning.

Meaning

1. Concerned residents of the apartment complex faced a plethora of problems but few solutions.

plethora: *Super abundance*

2. The social sciences have always been my forte whereas foreign languages remain my weakness.

forte: *strong point*

3. Relaxed regulations replaced the once stringent dormitory rules.

stringent: *forceful*

4. It is common for teenagers to deprecate their parents' values while praising their peers' ideas.

deprecate: *protest against*

5. In her youth, the old crone had been admired for her beauty and grace.

crone: *ugly*

6. Which is worse: someone with a voracious appetite or someone who eats little or no food?

voracious: *large*

7. The virus was so debilitating that it took months for her to regain her strength and general health.

debilitating: *to make weak*

8. The incipient stage of a disease can be treated more easily than the later stages when complications usually arise.

incipient: *beginning*

9. Cacti are indigenous to California but alien to Maine.

indigenous: *particular region*

10. The reformed alcoholic came out of the depths of despair and reached the zenith of his efforts when he was able to attend a cocktail party without needing a drink.

zenith: *point*

Practice: Circle the antonym in each sentence that helped you arrive at the meaning of the new word. Write the meaning in the space.

Meaning

1. Henry's sneaky climb to the executive level of company management surprised those of us who thought him to be ingenuous in his dealings with others.

stealthy (secretly & deceitfully)

ingenuous: *naive, inexperienced*

2. Your reticence in accepting the date amazes me; yesterday you were eager for him to call.

reticence: *silence*

3. Would you consider this particular cult a pseudoreligion, or do you believe it has its roots in established moral and ethical codes?

pseudoreligion: *false religion*

4. When you take lecture notes, stick to the key ideas and related details. Amusing stories are merely superfluous.

superfluous: *excessive*

5. How can you write a paper citing only abridged works? Take the extra time to read the original full-length works, which include all key ideas.

abridged: *shorter*

6. You can't possibly vote for a senator about whom you know so little. At least wait until you have been apprised of his voting record.

apprised: *informed*

7. The "Indy 500" car race is basically a straightaway race whereas the course of the Grand Prix of Monaco contains miles of tortuous country roads.

tortuous: *full of twist*

prefix pseudo : false, sham

8. The judge set sentence at five years with no possibility of parole or reduction of sentence. This action drew cries of outrage from the defendant's lawyers, who wanted an <u>indeterminate</u> sentence imposed.

9. Your version of the <u>alleged</u> robbery will be taken into consideration when the jury determines the proved events of the crime.

10. It is best to seek professional counseling rather than to rely on <u>lay</u> opinions.

indeterminate: *undecided*

alleged: *described*

lay: *laity — opha ordinary trong nghe*

Practice: Determine the meaning of the underlined word in each sentence by using its antonym. Circle the clue that helped you.

Meaning

1. The subject of representational artwork is clear and easy to recognize whereas the subject of surrealistic artwork is frequently <u>enigmatic</u>.

enigmatic: *puzzling*

2. Most of the protestors were <u>vociferous</u>, but a few picketed quietly.

vociferous: *crying out. noisly*

3. The arrival of the police at the riot site greatly increased rather than <u>mitigated</u> the tension. LESSEN

mitigated: *soothed*

4. Why should we pay for these tickets when everyone else is getting them <u>gratis</u>?

gratis: *free*

5. How can people still blame that poor fellow when he was completely <u>exonerated</u> by the judge?

exonerated: *cleared*

6. When I compare the <u>cogent</u> argument you presented with John's weak and rambling defense, I must side with you.

cogent: *convincing*

7. A responsive audience encourages me to try harder whereas an <u>apathetic</u> group turns me off.

apathetic: *uninterested*

8. Traditionally, California is in the <u>vanguard</u> of social legislation while the Eastern states are at the rear.

vanguard: *forefront*

9. Because I was not at the game, I can give only a <u>vicarious</u> rather than a firsthand account of the action.

vicarious: *imagined*

10. Dan was rarely sad; rather, he usually was described as <u>ebullient</u>.

ebullient: *excited*

Practice: Determine the meaning of each underlined word by using its antonym. Circle the clue that helped you.

Meaning

1. I finally had time to read the widely popular <u>unexpurgated</u> version of the book, and it left me wide-eyed; it was so much more descriptive than the edited version.

unexpurgated: *dirty tuc tuc*

2. Perhaps your friends would visit more often if you were to praise rather than to <u>castigate</u> their actions.

castigate: *criticize*

3. After being in many classes where the instructor almost put me to sleep, I was encouraged to read more by Dr. Brown's <u>scintillating</u> lecture. *gui tich & shine*

scintillating: *act of scintillating*

4. <u>Generic</u> compounds can be substituted for expensive name-brand drugs.

generic: *pertaining to /*

5. Bob always changes his mind whereas his brother is always intransigent. *gui rieu lập truóng*

6. The captain's bellicose actions threatened the outcome of the peace negotiations.

7. Many elderly people can't move around quickly; they are no longer as spry as in their youth.

8. Some rock stars enjoy ephemeral fame whereas others remain popular for years.

9. After entering the old mine, we hunted for a few specks of gold. *small spots* After an hour we were still empty-handed, and so we decided to egress from the dark hole in the mountain.

10. Many people who are normally energetic become lethargic as the weather turns hot and humid.

---

stubborn
uncompromising

intransigent: irreconcilable

bellicose: warlike

✓**spry:** active

✓**ephemeral:** very short

✓**egress:** exit

lethargic: sluggish

Defining Subject Terminology

6

For each of the context clues discussed previously (sense of the sentence, synonyms, examples, antonyms), a general meaning of new vocabulary was sufficient for comprehension.

Examples

1. The office <u>staff</u> contributed money for their secretary's wedding gift. <u>Staff</u> means the working members of the office.

2. The old man leaned on his hickory <u>staff</u>, the cane he used daily. <u>Staff</u> means a rod or pole used for support.

3. The convict survived on only water and bread, the <u>staff</u> of life. <u>Staff</u> means a basic support of life.

4. Will we need to <u>staff</u> the booth or will we leave it vacant? <u>Staff</u> means to fill a position.

You can determine the general meaning of "staff" by using the context clues in each of the sentences above.

There are, however, textbook terms that <u>do</u> require precise definitions. These words make up the course "terminology." Unlike general vocabulary, subject vocabulary terms require specific and complete definitions. Instructors <u>will probably</u> test your understanding of these terms.

Example

The musical <u>staff</u> is the group of five lines with four spaces between them on which musical notes are written.

Question

Define <u>staff</u>: _to fill a position_

In this context, <u>staff</u> has a very special meaning. It is neither office personnel nor a walking cane; it is not the process by which one fills positions of employment, nor is it bread. <u>Staff</u> has a technical and special meaning in music and is clearly defined in the sentence: "a group of five lines with four spaces between them on which musical notes are written."

Subject vocabulary terms are words and phrases that have special meaning in a particular subject or discipline. Subject definitions must be complete and precise.

19

The difficulty is knowing how much to include in a complete and precise definition. Too often the term is defined vaguely. Here is an inaccurate definition of <u>staff</u> from the example:

Inaccurate Definition

A musical staff means a group of five lines.

Questions

Is this a group of five lines? ~~✗✗~~ _____

Is it a musical staff? _____

Here are two steps to follow in deriving a complete and precise technical definition.

1. First, identify the category in which the subject word belongs.

The musical staff is | *lines* |
                          (category)

2. Next, add the specific characteristics that give special meaning to the term.

_____*five*_____
special characteristic #1

The musical staff is | *lines* | — *four spaces between them* ___
                       (category)   special characteristic #2

on which musical notes are written
special characteristic #3

Practice: Each of the following sentences provides a definition for the underlined word or phrase. In the space at the right, define the underlined word by listing the category and any special characteristics needed for a complete definition. The first one is done for you.

Meaning

1. <u>Kinematics</u> is the branch of mechanics that deals with pure motion.

Branch of	*deals with pure motion*
mechanics	characteristic
category	

2. The moon rocks have proved to be <u>anhydrous</u>; that is, they contain no trace of water.

moon rock	*No trace of water*
proved	characteristic
category	

3. <u>Viruses</u> are disease-causing organisms visible only through an electron microscope.

disease causing	characteristic
organism	*visible through electron*
category	characteristic *microscope*

4. Burt is being fitted for a <u>prosthesis</u> (artificial limb) to replace the leg he lost.

| *artificial* | *being fitted* |
| *limb* | *replaced leg* |

5. <u>Memory</u> is the ability to store and to recall information.

| *ability to* | *recall information* |
| *store* | |

6. <u>Myofibrils</u> are thin threads in the cytoplasm of muscle cells.

7. A <u>short-term institution</u> refers to a correctional facility holding prisoners no longer than one year.

8. A <u>bark</u> is one kind of sailing vessel having three or more masts. *Cột buồm*

9. The most familiar type of mental retardation is <u>Down's syndrome</u>, also called mongolism because the facial features have an oriental appearance.

(Freedman, 215)

10. The most basic elements of a language are <u>phonemes</u>—the elementary sounds made by a speaker.

(Freedman, 135)

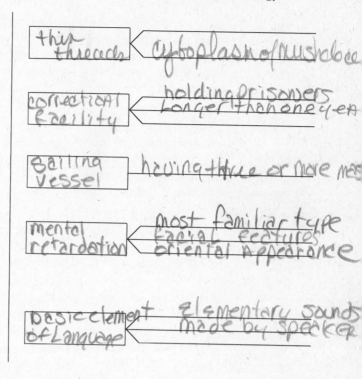

this threads ← cytoplasm of muscle cell

correction facility ← holding prisoners longer than one year

sailing vessel — having three or more mast

mental retardation ← most familiar type / facial features / oriental appearance

basic element of language — elementary sounds made by speaker

Practice: Each of the following paragraphs provides a definition for the underlined word or phrase. In the space at the right, define the underlined term.

Meaning

1. Students should read carefully the stated <u>prerequisites</u> and <u>corequisites</u> listed with each course description. A prerequisite to a course is a requirement that must have been completed prior to enrollment in that course. A corequisite to a course is a requirement to be taken at the same time as that course. *vì chúng - chú ý mình là hòa ca*

prerequisites: *A requirement that must have been completed prior to enrollment*

corequisites: *a requirement to be taken at the same time as that cours*

2. Anthropologists use the term <u>ethnocentrism</u> to describe the universal human tendency to interpret and evaluate foreign beliefs and practices in terms of the values of one's own cultural tradition. Because <u>kinship</u> is not particularly important in contemporary American society, American students often ethnocentrically refuse to believe that it is important in other societies. *present*

quan hệ họ hàng - kindred / family relationship

ethnocentrism: *tendency to interpret & evaluate foreign beliefs & practices in term of the values of one's own cultural tradition*

(Kottak, 73)

3. <u>Mutation</u> refers to a change in the makeup of an individual, a change that occurs in the genetic material and is passed on to successive generations. The term mutation has often been applied at two levels of biological organization: the chromosome and the gene. *Chromosomal mutations* are those changes that are large enough to be seen with the light microscope. . . . Today there is a trend not to regard events leading to aneuploidy, euploidy, and chromosomal aberrations as mutations. Rather, the term mutation is reserved for changes at the level of the gene. A *gene mutation* is a change in a relatively small amount of genetic material.

kế hi thế không, lâm ca

mutation: *a change in the makeup of a individual that occurs in the genetic material and is passed on to successive generation*

(Johnson, DeLanney, Cole, and Brooks, 379)

4. <u>Injunctions</u>—court orders prohibiting some practice—are sometimes obtained by management to prevent excessive <u>picketing</u> or

injunctions: *Court orders prohibiting some practice*

the act of preventing someone from entering a firm during the workers' strike

certain unfair union practices. Prior to the passage of the Norris–La Guardia Act, injunctions were frequently used to prohibit all types of strikes. Since then, their use has been limited to restraint of violence, restriction of picketing, and prevention of damage to company property.

(Boone and Kurtz, 185)

5. Nevertheless, when one turns from the <u>substantive law</u>—in which the forbidden acts and their punishments are described—to the <u>procedural law</u>, which describes how the community will deal with violators, one cannot help being struck by the fact that an equally important objective is the protection of the offender.

(Korn and McCorkle, 90)

6. Of the eleven descendants who are members of Harry's descent group, who live in his village, and who enjoy access to his estate, only four are full <u>agnates</u>, Harry's descendants through male links only.

(Kottak, 88)

7. <u>Weather</u> refers to the condition of atmospheric elements at a given time and for a specific area. That area could be as large as the New York Metropolitan Area or a spot as small and specific as a weather observation station. The study of the changing conditions of the atmosphere is known as <u>meteorology</u>.

A description of the climate of an area comes from many observations of its weather over a period of years. <u>Climate</u> describes an area's average weather, but it also includes those common deviations from the norm or average that are likely to occur, as well as extreme situations, which can be very significant. Thus we could describe the climate of the southeastern United States in terms of average temperatures and precipitation through a year, but we would also have to include mention of the likelihood of hurricanes during certain periods of the year. <u>Climatology</u> is the study of the varieties of climates found on our planet and their distribution over its surface.

(Gabler, Sager, Brazier, and Pourciau, 100)

8. A <u>market</u> consists of people, whether they are consumers, company purchasing agents, or purchasing specialists for a government (local, state, or federal).

But people alone do not make a market. Many people may desire the new $125,000 colonial house on Valley Drive, but not everyone can afford it. A market requires not only people but also purchasing power and the authority to buy.

(Boone and Kurtz, 223)

9. Children of siblings of the same sex are <u>parallel cousins</u>. Children of siblings of the opposite sex are <u>cross cousins</u>. Thus your mother's sister's children are your parallel cousins—the children of two sisters. Your father's brother's children are also your parallel cousins—the children of two brothers. Your father's sister's children are your cross cousins—the children of two sibings of the opposite sex. For the same reason, your mother's brother's children are also your cross cousins.

(Kottak, 97)

10. <u>Harmony</u> pertains to the movement and relationship of intervals

---

substantive law: *describes the forbidden acts & their punishments*

procedural law: *how community will deal with violators*

agnates: *fatherhood relationships*

weather: *this heat*

meteorology:

climate: *khi hau*

climatology:

market:

parallel cousins:

cross cousins:

harmony:

and chords. In a larger sense, <u>harmony denotes the over-all orga-nization of tones in a musical work in such a way as to achieve order and unity.</u>

(Machlis, 15, 17)

Practice: Define the following subject terms.

Meaning

1. Space is not empty at all. It is filled with particles consisting of pure gravitational energy—which John A. Wheeler calls "geons." Geons, massed together, make up the solid structure of the curved walls of space-time, and it is in this solid, spongelike structure that holes exist.

(Berry, 98)

geons: *particles consisting of pure gravitional energy*

2. There is a relationship between frequency (the number of vibra-tions per second) and the "highness" or "lowness" of sound. This sense of high and low is called <u>register</u>; the higher the frequency, the higher the register.

(Schwartz, 12)

register: *frequency.*

3. Materials that have very few free electrons, high stability and den-sity, and low mobility are called <u>insulators</u>, since a very high elec-tromotive force is required to produce any sizable current flow through such materials.

(Boylestad, 34–35)

insulators: *Materials that have very few free electrons, high stability & density, and low mobility*

4. In order to analyze and describe any new language, an inventory of all of its sounds and an accurate way of writing them down are needed. Some sounds of other languages may be very much like the sounds of English, others may be sounds that we have never consciously produced; but since we all have the same vocal equip-ment, there is no reason why we should not be able, with practice, to reproduce all the sounds that anyone else makes. Once this is accomplished, the sound patterns of language can be studied to discover the abstract rules which tell us which combinations of sounds are permissible and which are not. This study is known as <u>phonology</u>.

aim is how

(Haviland, 98)

phonology: *The study of the sounds*

5. <u>Conductors</u> are those materials that permit a generous flow of elec-trons with very little electromotive force applied.

(Boylestad, 34)

conductors:

6. The <u>umbilical cord</u>, connecting the child to the placenta, contains blood vessels that carry oxygen, water, and nutrients to the infant and carry waste products away. The mother's and infant's blood do not mix. *Umbilical cord* (um-BILL-lick-ul). A flexible tube or hol-low cord connecting the unborn child to the placenta.

(Rathus, 57)

umbilical cord: *that connecting the child to the placenta*

7. By its very nature, <u>philosophy</u> is a do-it-yourself enterprise. There is a common misunderstanding that philosophy—like chemistry or history—has a content to offer, a content which a teacher is to teach and a student is to learn. This is not the case. There are no facts, no theories, certainly no final truths which go by the name of "philosophy" and which one is supposed to accept and believe.

philosophy: *The study of the nature and meaning of existence, reality, knowledge, goodness etc.*

Rather, philosophy is a skill—more akin to mathematics and music; it is something that one *learns to do.*

Philosophy, that is, is a *method.* It is *learning how* to ask and re-ask questions until meaningful answers begin to appear. It is *learning how* to relate materials. It is *learning where* to go for the most dependable, up-to-date information that might shed light on some problem. It is *learning how* to double check fact-claims in order to verify or falsify them. It is *learning how* to reject fallacious fact-claims—to reject them no matter how prestigious the authority who holds them or how deeply one would personally like to believe them.

(Christian, xvi)

8. Some corporations are referred to as <u>conglomerates</u>. A conglomerate is simply a company made up of a number of previously independent companies (or subsidiaries) in different industries. An example would be Heublein, Inc., a company that is mainly involved in wines and liquors yet has Kentucky Fried Chicken as a subsidiary. Typically, conglomerate headquarters provides general guidance for the operation of the subsidiary units, while top executives in the individual companies provide specific management direction.

(Mauser and Schwartz, 72)

9. <u>Horticulture</u> refers to nonmechanized systems of plant cultivation which make intensive use of neither land nor human labor. Characteristic cultivating tools of horticulturists are hoes or digging sticks.

(Kottak, 27)

10. A term that is frequently used synonymously with fever is <u>pyrexia</u>. <u>Hyperpyrexia</u> and <u>hyperthermia</u> are used interchangeably to designate an abnormally high fever, that is, 40.6°C. (105°F.) or over. Habitual <u>hyperthermia</u> refers to a condition in which the average daily temperature is slightly above normal limits. <u>Hypothermia</u> is an abnormally low body temperature.

(Du Gas, 305)

conglomerates: *a company made up of a number of previously independent companies or subsidiaries*

horticulture: *nonmechanical systems of plant cultivation*

pyrexia:
hyperpyrexia: *abnormally high fever 40.6°C*
hyperthermia:

habitual hyperthermia: *a daily temperature which is slightly above normal limits.*

hypothermia: *Abnormally low body temperature*

Applying Mixed Context Clues

7

You have seen that you can use the sentence or the paragraph in which a word is located to help you understand its meaning. Moreover, you can focus on a specific clue to help you.

Examples   *form   easily made into a new shape – changed influenced*

1. It was easy to <u>mold</u> the <u>malleable</u> metal. (general sense)   *comfort or calm.*

2. Why should I <u>assuage</u> his feelings? I see no reason to <u>soothe</u> him. (synonym)

3. The queen's <u>coterie</u> consisted of ladies-in-waiting, servants, and handmaidens. (example)

4. City dwellers often escape to more <u>bucolic</u> surroundings. (antonym)   *country*

5. The musical <u>staff</u> is a group of five lines with four spaces between them on which musical notes are written. (stated definition)

Practice: Use the context (the sentence or paragraph in which the word is located) to determine the meaning of each underlined word. Write the meaning in the space.

severe & repeated

1. <u>Migraine</u> headaches are commonly referred to, but in actuality do not occur that often. They classically start with an "<u>aura</u>," such as seeing spots before your eyes or seeing colors.

2. As private property replaced <u>communal</u> land, conflict among brothers increased and was extended to neighbors and more distant relatives. Hostility was openly expressed in adult life rather than being <u>repressed</u>.

   Đỡ rất chân đất

   (Kottak, 244)

3. <u>Protective coloration</u> is common. Mice, lizards, and arthropods that live on the sand are often light-colored, and such light-colored species, if removed from their home territories, will immediately return to them. Snails that live on mottled backgrounds are often banded. Grass snakes are grass-colored, as are many of the insects that live among the grasses.

   (Curtis, 871)

4. One of Sherlock Holmes's defects—if, indeed, one may call it a defect—was that he was exceedingly <u>loath</u> to communicate his full plans to any other person until the instant of their fulfilment. Partly it came no doubt from his own masterful nature, which loved to dominate and surprise those who were around him. Partly also from his professional caution, which urged him never to take any chances. The result, however, was very trying for those who were acting as his agents and assistants. I had often suffered under it, but never more so than during that long drive in the darkness. The great

Meaning

aura: *symtom, effect.*

communal: *used by a community*

repressed: *hold back control, restrain*

protective coloration:

loath: *be Reluctant*

a difficult or painful experience

ordeal was in front of us; at last we were about to make our final effort, and yet Holmes had said nothing, and I could only underline{surmise} what his course of action would be.

(Doyle, 202)

surmise: *To suppose as a reasonable guess*

5. Outside the tavern the night was lighted by a rocking yellow moon that held a white star in its horn. In the gloomy castle on the hill a lantern underline{gleamed} and darkened, came and went, as if the gaunt Duke stalked from room to room, stabbing bats and spiders, killing mice. "underline{Dazzle} the Duke with jewels," the underline{minstrel} said aloud. "There's something in it somewhere, but what it is and where, I cannot think." He wondered if the Duke would order him to cause a fall of purple snow, or make a table out of sawdust, or merely underline{slit} him from his underline{guggle} to his underline{zatch}, and say to Saralinda, "There he lies, your latest fool, nameless minstrel. I'll have my underline{varlets} feed him to the geese."

(Thurber, 26)

shining light

guggle:

zatch:

varlets: *The knight's servant.*

cut, open

tiếng ưng uc   *musician*

Practice: Define each of the following underlined terms.

Meaning

1. If you recognize the input, another part of your brain then takes over and "memorizes" the most underline{salient} or important parts of the stimulus for a few seconds while the rest of your brain decides what to do with the incoming message.

(McConnell, 425)

salient: *noticeable, important*

2. One of the factors related to drug price is the manner in which prescription drugs are sold. When a drug is purchased under a brand name, its price is many times higher than if the same drug were bought by its generic name. The underline{generic name} refers to the chemical ingredient in the drug. The underline{brand name} refers to the name given to a drug by a particular company. Thus, several brand-name drugs of different companies can all contain the same generic drug.

(Sinacore and Sinacore, 305)

generic name: *chemical ingredient in the drug*

brand name: *name given to a drug by a particular company*

3. Another important feature of private enterprise is the right to start one's own business. *An individual who starts a business* is called an underline{entrepreneur}. While licenses may be required for certain businesses, there are relatively few obstacles in the way of a person who wishes to become an entrepreneur.

(Mauser and Schwartz, 13)

entrepreneur: *business man*

4. A distinction is usually made in contemporary law between underline{criminal} and underline{civil}. Conduct believed to be against the interests of the society or state is sanctioned under underline{criminal law}; conduct against the interests of private individuals is punishable under underline{civil law}. This distinction is not as neat as it sounds. For example, consider the act of assault which is directed against a specific individual but which is also a threat to the public interest, underline{inasmuch} as individuals want to feel that they are generally safe from assault. Assault therefore involves both a criminal and a civil violation of law (Quinney and Wildeman, 1977).

because

(Hess, 470)

criminal law: *social law*

civil law: *individual law*

5. Energy is defined as the power to do work. All forms of energy are interconvertible, that is, they may be changed from one form to another. An example would be the heat and light which are generated by an electric lamp—both are forms of electrical energy. Energy is neither created nor destroyed during any chemical or physical process; it is merely changed in form. This fact is one of the most basic tenets of science and is called the law of conservation of energy. Acceptance of this law is not only fundamental to understanding science; it is vital as well to such everyday activities as losing or gaining weight. Every dieter has to face up to the fact that food energy taken in must either be expended as heat or work, or it will inevitably end up stored as fat.

(Carpenter and Calloway, 69)

6. The branch of cultural anthropology that studies human languages is called linguistics. Linguistics may deal with the description of a language (the way it forms a sentence or conjugates a verb) or with the history of languages (the way languages develop and influence each other with the passage of time). Both approaches yield valuable information, not only about the ways in which people communicate but about the ways in which they understand the external world as well. The colloquial language of most North Americans, for example, includes a number of slang words, such as "dough," "greenback," "dust," "loot," and "bread," to identify what a Papuan would recognize only as "money." Such situations help identify things that are considered of special importance to a culture. Through the study of linguistics, the anthropologist is better able to understand how people perceive themselves and the world around them.

(Haviland, 13)

7. The oldest and most persistent typology of governmental forms rests on this key variable of location of real power. In the fifth century B.C. the Greek historian Herodotus classified all governments as either monarchies (government by single persons), aristocracies (government by elites), or democracies (government by all). A century later Aristotle made his famous revision of this typology, distinguishing between three forms in each of which a different segment of the community rules in the interests of all (monarchy, aristocracy, and polity) and three in each of which a different segment of the community rules in its own selfish interests (tyranny, oligarchy, and democracy).

(Ranney, 200)

8. Exactly what is poverty? How many poor are there in the U.S. and who are they? While one may have an intuitive notion of poverty, arriving at an objective measure of poverty is futile. How many poor there are depends on the definition chosen. For poverty is to some degree a subjective evaluation.

(Scott and Nigro, 404)

9. Richter knew that many insects and other lower animals show the same sort of "circling" behavior if you cut off one of their "feelers" or antennae. An ant that has lost its left antenna will tend to circle to the left, and a lobster deprived of its right "feeler" will circle to the right. Richter wondered if there might not be some connection

Râu mép, quai nón [handwritten]

or correlation beween the length of a rat's whiskers and the direction in which it swam in the tub. Perhaps rats always turned their heads toward the side where their whiskers were the shortest.

(McConnell, 310)

correlation:

10. The government employs many accountants in the Department of Commerce whose job it is to classify all transactions that take place in the economy over the year. They measure the value of all consumer and capital goods that are produced as well as the value of all services provided, like haircuts and television repairs, down to the last possible dollar. Every item in the economy is put into its precisely defined slot. They distinguish between consumer nondurable and durable goods, and capital goods. Consumer nondurable goods are those lasting for less than a year, for example perishable goods like food, and nonfood items such as socks, nylons, or pencils. Commodities lasting a year or more are called either consumer durables or capital goods. Consumer durables are items like cars, washing machines, and home furniture. Capital goods are most things that firms use as inputs in production such as buildings and equipment. However, a car owned by a firm is classified as a capital good, not as a consumer good. These are arbitrary classifications. For this discussion we shall treat all commodities as assets.

(Scott and Nigro, 137)

consumer nondurable:

durables:

Practice: Define each of the underlined terms.

Meaning

1. In a sense, then, Piaget and Freud offer complementary rather than conflicting theories of the intra-psychic development of young people, for Piaget emphasizes *conscious mental operations,* while Freud emphasized *unconscious processes and motives.*

(McConnell, 528)

complementary:

2. Many legislative chambers have adjoining lobbies in which legislators and their guests can meet and talk informally. From this practice has emerged the term "lobbying," which refers to direct efforts by representatives of pressure groups to persuade public officials to act as the groups wish. Legislators are still the main targets of lobbying, but executives, administrators, and even judges are also frequently and regularly approached.

   Having gained access to one or more decision-making points, the lobbyist can employ various techniques of persuasion. He can make a formal presentation of his group's position, marshaling facts, figures, and arguments to show it in the most favorable light. He can threaten the legislator or executive with dire consequences at the next election, and he can reinforce his threat by stimulating a flood of telegrams, postcards, and letters from the official's constituents. He can offer to trade his group's support of some pet project of the legislator or executive for the latter's support of his own group's proposal. This practice is a variety of "logrolling." *Thông đồng* [handwritten]

(Ranney, 156–157)

lobbying:

dire: *great, terrible, a causing great fear for the future* [handwritten]

logrolling: *mutual help* [handwritten]

result [handwritten]

3. Psychology stands at that scientific crossroads where genetics, biochemistry, physiology, sociology, and anthropology meet to form that unique organism we call the individual human being. Although

some people tend to emphasize one or two of the three major viewpoints, most psychologists tend to take a <u>holistic</u> approach toward understanding and solving human problems. That is, we know full well that your bodily processes influence how you think and feel, that what goes on inside your psyche or mind can change the way in which your bodily processes operate, and that both your mind and your body are strongly influenced by your social environment.

tắt máy tiếng nổ

(McConnell, 14)

4. . . . the car thundered across the top of the lawn, buried its nose in a large bush, choked, <u>stalled</u>, and stopped. Its driver got out and gazed at it. While he was doing this it <u>backfired</u> suddenly—a tremendous <u>report</u>, a backfire to end all backfires. He frowned, took a hammer from the back seat, opened the <u>bonnet</u> and hit something inside. Then he closed the bonnet again and resumed his seat. The engine started and the car went into reverse. . . .

nhiều máy

(Crispin, 26)

5.   The attitudes of people toward alcohol are as varied as the nature of its uses. Some view any use of alcohol as being highly <u>immoral</u>, whereas others see nothing wrong with its use in moderation. <u>Inebriation</u> is alternately viewed as something humorous, disgusting, or as a sign of illness (alcoholism). Our attitudes with regard to alcohol and its use become rather personal in nature and are dependent on our experiences, what others close to us think, and what we know about it.

Scientists classify drugs according to the effect they have on the body. Three of these classifications are (1) <u>sedative</u>—this type of drug has a quieting effect, relieving tension, (2) <u>analgesic</u>—analgesics relieve pain without producing sleep (aspirin), (3) <u>anesthetic</u>—this type of drug will bring about the loss of sensitivity to pain.

(Sinacore and Sinacore, 343)

6. Many factors make it difficult to evaluate the effectiveness of psychotherapy scientifically. Science deals with objective events, things that can readily be measured. But by its very nature, <u>intra-psychic</u> therapy concerns itself wth changes that occur inside a person's mind—changes that can seldom be seen or <u>scrutinized</u> under a microscope. The success rates of various forms of treatment, then, must always be considered in terms of *what changes therapists hope to achieve.*

(McConnell, 657)

---

holistic:

report: explosion

bonnet: hood

immoral:

inebriation: drunk

sedative: quieting effect, relieving tension

analgesic: relieve pain without producing sleep

anesthetic: bring about the loss of sensitivity or pain

intra-psychic: the changes that occur inside a person's mind

scrutinized: examine, look closely

Previewing Chapters

Introduction

8

What happens when you decide to buy a pair of jeans? Which of the following lists describes the steps you might follow? Which group of activities takes longer? Which is more helpful?

List A

1. Go to the clothing store.
2. Take a pair of jeans into the dressing room.
3. Try on the jeans.

List B

1. Go to the clothing store.
2. Locate the jeans department.
3. Look for the correct size.
4. Check the style, color, and price.
5. Take several pairs of jeans into the dressing room.
6. Try on the jeans.

You probably follow the activities in List B and recognize that they take longer to complete than the activities in List A. Taking extra time to "look over" the size, style, color, and price of the jeans <u>before</u> you go into the dressing room helps you to narrow the choices. The extra time, therefore, is time well spent. You can feel confident about finding something to suit you.

Similarly, you can make better use of your time as you read your textbooks. You can find out a great deal about what you will read in a chapter if you "look over" portions <u>before</u> you read it thoroughly. Just as you don't randomly take any pair of jeans into the dressing room, you also shouldn't open a book and begin to read immediately. In both instances, you have little or no idea of where you are headed.

Looking over a chapter before reading it thoroughly is called previewing or surveying the chapter. This is an important skill that provides you with a sense of the key ideas <u>before</u> you read the chapter thoroughly. When you preview, look at specific parts of the chapter: the introduction, the major subtitles, the summary, the review questions, any boldfaced or italicized words, and any visuals. In addition, consider what you know about the subject.

Previewing is a study technique in which you look at selected parts of a text chapter to gain a sense of the important ideas and the scope of material. Previewing provides you with an understanding of

1. your familiarity with the subject.
2. the range of material the author covers.
3. the key ideas the author develops.
4. the way the author organizes important ideas.
5. the important terms and concepts the author defines.

Previewing a Business Chapter

Here you have an opportunity to preview portions of a business chapter. Read the introduction, subtitles, visuals, summary, and review questions. Each is followed by a brief series of questions designed to help you focus on the key ideas. These questions are typical of questions you can consider as you preview similar portions of your text chapters.

The Introduction

In an **introduction** to a chapter, the author usually notes the general and specific topics and to what extent each will be developed in the chapter. You should take advantage of the introduction to help you understand the range and depth of ideas the author will present.

Practice: Preview the following chapter introduction by reading it and highlighting or underlining the ideas the author will focus on in the chapter. Then answer the questions that follow.

1 Fashion and Fashion Apparel

The word *fashion* is a good example of a word with various meanings; it can be an encompassing term as well as a specific reference. For our purpose, we choose the definition that puts it into truest perspective: that which is *accepted* by a substantial group of *people* at a given *time* and *place.*

The reader can properly respond to this definition by saying that fashion is no more than the current culture. What people believe in, what they practice, what they accept adds up to the culture of the time, the fashion of the age. Culture and fashion can indeed be synonymous, but what consumers accept is influenced both by the availability of technically feasible products and by the broad influences in the environment that affect consumer attitude about those products. The broad influences on consumer selection are technology, economic conditions, social values, current cultural attitudes, and political climate—conditions that marketers do not create. The marketer must nevertheless employ strategies that respond to these conditions by offering products with the features consumers want.

(Packard, 2)

substantial : important, of some size or value?

1. How does the author define fashion? *accepted by a substantial group of people*

2. The two factors that affect what consumers accept are: *time* and *place*

3. How many conditions affect consumer selection of products? *five*

4. Are culture and fashion synonymous? *yes*

5. What is your definition of fashion? *a style of feeling one wears, creativity of the mike. Ones way of expression or culture*

The Subtitles

Textbook authors divide chapter subjects into important subtopics and label them with boldfaced subtitles. By looking at the subtitles, you get a sense of the chapter organization, sequence of ideas, and major subject divisions. When you turn each subtitle into a question, you are setting a purpose for your reading, and you are assessing your familiarity with the topics. You can create questions for each subtitle based on what you think might be included in the chapter. You can use phrases such as: who is (are)—what—when—where—which—why—how. Creating questions about subtitles will provide a purpose for later reading and will serve as a guide to determining how much time and effort you will need for the chapter.

Practice: Read the following subtitles from the fashion chapter and think of a question for each. As you do, consider what you know about the topic and what you think the author will discuss in the chapter. Then answer the questions that follow.

1 FASHION AND FASHION APPAREL *clothes*

Influences on Fashion Acceptance   3
    Technology   3
    Economics   3
    Social values   4

(Packard, xi–xii)

1. How many influences on fashion will the author discuss? _____ *five* _____
2. What appears to motivate people to accept fashion apparel? _____ *Social Position* _____

3. Circle any words in the subtitles that appear difficult and that you will need to define as you read.

The Visuals and Special Terms

When previewing, you can find additional aids in understanding the chapter. New **technical vocabulary** terms usually appear in **bold-face** or *italicized* print. Previewing the chapter enables you to judge the number of new terms you will want to note in reading the chapter itself.

Looking at the chapter **illustrations** can provide you with an additional sense of the nature of the chapter and its level of difficulty. **Photos, charts, diagrams, maps,** and **cartoons** visually depict, explain, and clarify portions of the chapter. They aid you in visualizing difficult text material.

60

(Brown Brothers)

86

(Georges Tirfoin/Sygma)

Practice: Consider these pictures in the fashion chapter. Answer the questions that follow.

1. What is the probable span of years between these photographs? _____ 60^s _____

2. How do these pictures reflect cultural acceptance of fashion styles? _understanding_ the body, Not to be ashame _____

_____

Practice: The following terms are boldfaced or italicized in the chapter. Read them and check those you are familiar with.

_____ consumer obsolescence   ✗ fashion
_____ cyclical nature of fashion   ✗ high style
✗ elements of change   _____ pop-art
✗ factory   _____ section work

Name two places in the fashion text where you can find the meaning of these

Influences on fashion. Acceptance
...ion Apparel Climate

The Summary

Authors often summarize the major ideas, topic relationships, and theme developments in a list or in paragraphs at the end of a chapter. Reading the **summary** provides another opportunity to determine what key ideas the author emphasizes. The author may emphasize additional points not mentioned in either the questions or the introduction. This is another opportunity for you to understand what the author is signaling as important. When you know the ideas the author has termed important, you can use those understandings as you read. You can identify key ideas quickly because the author has signaled their importance in the summary.

Practice: Highlight or underline the most important ideas summarized by the author. Then answer the questions that follow.

SUMMARY

The word *fashion* has a multiplicity of meanings; in its broadest sense it is synonymous with culture. Its definition includes four conditions: people, acceptance, time, and place. Therefore, fashion apparel, for our purpose, is clothing accepted by a substantial group of people at a given time and place.

When a fashion came into being can be determined only after the fact; prediction of what will become fashion is the difficult responsibility of all fashion marketers. Simply put, fashion is a resultant state—the product of acceptance. Hence, styles created by designers, featured by producers, and offered by retailers are not fashions until they are accepted by ultimate consumers. The length of acceptance is the basis for categorizing a fashion. A short-lived one is a fad, the longest can be an artifact of culture, one that is handed down from generation to generation (denim jeans).

The general environmental factors that influence acceptance of a style are economics, social values, cultural aspects, technology, and political forces. Specific reasons for apparel acceptance are numerous and subjective, and include sociological and psychological values. An oversimplification of consumer purchase behavior, an encompassing motivation, is a search for a state of betterment. Included as specific reasons for acceptance are events and personalities who motivate emulation.

Interesting aspects of fashion marketing are investigating environmental factors of past eras to ascertain why certain fashions came to the fore, and then estimating the probable future degree of importance of present market offerings. Since fashion apparel is cyclical in nature, what was accepted in the past will return to prominence in an updated version. When and to what degree of importance are the questions.

Ready-to-wear had its beginning in Europe when four events occurred in the nineteenth century:

- The development of machinery to mass produce fabrics
- The invention of the sewing machine
- The creation of paper patterns
- The invention of a factory system based on the division of labor

United States manufacturers soon adopted these European developments. Ready markets for factory-made clothing included three groups—sailors, government (uniforms for Civil War soldiers), and plantation owners, who had to provide clothing for slaves. Fifty-five years later, about 1920, modern ready-to-wear was established for the production of women's clothing, when availability of skilled immigrant labor, the development of rayon, and more liberalized attitudes about women's role in society created a favorable environment. The importance of the American fashion industry is based on mass production for mass acceptance.

(Packard, 29)

1. What four factors must be included in a definition of fashion?

   People   *acceptants*
   time   *place*

2. Name the four groups who contribute to making an item fashionable:

   designers   *producers*
   retailers   *consumers*

3. What general and specific factors influence fashion acceptance?

   Sociogical   *psychological*

4. Does the author present a cyclical explanation of fashions? *yes*

5. What four events does the author emphasize in the history of the ready-to-wear industry?

   the development of machinery to mass product fabrics
   The invention of the sewing machines
   the creation of paper patterns
   the invention of a factory system based on the division of labor

6. What distinguishes a fad from an artifact of culture? *something made by man* *Short lives - distingui of*
   a short lived interest   *longest - artifact of culture*

7. Why is it important to study past fashions? *Interesting aspects of fashion*
   Marketing are investigating environmental factors of pass eras to ascertian why certian fashion came to the fore

8. On what is the importance of the American fashion industry based? _____

_____ *European development* _____

9. Who were the first customers of factory-made clothing? _*Sailors*_____ ,
_*government*_____ , and _*plantation owners*_____

10. What three factors created a favorable environment for ready-to-wear in the 1920s?

_*Skilled immigrant labor*_____

_*development rayon*_____

_*liberalized attitudes*_____

The Review Questions

> Authors frequently include **review questions** at the end of a chap-
> ter. By including review questions, the author is saying, "If you have
> understood this chapter, you should be able to answer these ques-
> tions, which I feel are important." Pay attention to what the author
> is saying. Review questions focus on the key facts and idea relation-
> ships in the chapter.

Practice: Highlight or underline the key idea in each question.

QUESTIONS FOR DISCUSSION

1. Explain how each of the following is an influence on fashion:

   Social values
   Cultural values   } *they all contribute*
   Technology
   Economics
   Political climate

2. Explain the need for fashion in products other than apparel. *Product, material to make apparel*
3. Discuss at least five motivations that influence people in their apparel
   purchases. *technology, Economics, Social values, Culture, Political*
4. Identify three fashions that were the result of specific events. *provide clothing for slaves climate*
5. Do subcultural values play a part in fashion acceptance? Illustrate with
   two fashions. *Yes,*
6. List the events that led to the establishment of modern ready-to-wear.
   A) development of machinery
   B) Invention of sewing machine
   C) creation of paper pattern

7. Discuss why the development of modern ready-to-wear started with men's apparel. *Society*

8. Manufacturing and retailing of ready-to-wear in America started in Massachusetts. Why?

9. Discuss the development and significance of a factory system in the production of ready-to-wear. *for mass acceptance , mass production*

10. What is the relationship of the industrial revolution to ready-to-wear?
provide clothing for slaves (Packard, 28–30) *, sailors & soldiers*

Previewing a Health Chapter 10

Use the following portions of a health chapter to reinforce your previewing skills: introduction, subtitles, visuals, special terms, and review questions. (Notice that this chapter does not include a summary.) The questions that follow each section are designed to help you recognize the important ideas in the chapter. These questions are typical of the types of questions you can consider as you preview portions of your text chapters.

The Introduction

Practice: Read the following introduction and highlight or underline the important ideas the author will discuss. Then answer the questions.

9 Communicable Diseases

Since its earliest days, humanity has always been plagued with the trauma of disease. With the discovery of the microbe, significant progress was made in counteracting those diseases caused by germs. In spite of the success against communicable diseases that has been achieved, we have failed to eradicate a single disease. Every communicable disease ever known still exists today in some part of the world. However, progress cannot be solely measured by the ability to eradicate disease; there are other means of measuring success.

A comparison of long-term death rates from selected communicable diseases illustrates the dramatic downward trend in the number of deaths from these diseases. Similarly, a decreasing incidence of a particular illness suggests that a measure of control has been achieved.

(Sinacore and Sinacore, 211)

1. How have we made progress in the fight against disease? _We have been making a lot of progress in fighting against disease. However_ and _we have failed to eradicate a single disease_

2. What communicable disease have we eradicated? _None_

The Subtitles

Practice: Read the following subtitles from a health chapter and think of a question for each. As you do, consider what you know about the topic and what you think the author will discuss in the chapter. If you cannot answer questions 5, 6, and 7, continue to preview the health chapter to locate the answers.

CHAPTER 9: COMMUNICABLE DISEASES

Communicable Diseases
    Terminology of Communicable Diseases
    Organisms That Cause Disease
    ✓Spreading Diseases

Resistance and Immunity to Disease
    Disease Immunity
    Types of Immunity
    ✓Vaccines
    Interferon

Some Communicable Disease Problems
    Influenza and Pneumonia
    ✓Sexually Transmitted Diseases (STDs)
      ✓Gonorrhea
      ✓Syphilis
      Other STDs
    Controlling STDs

(Sinacore and Sinacore, 211–235)

1. What does STD mean? *Diseases caused by the sexual intercourses*

2. Name two ways diseases might be counteracted: _____

  and _____

3. What term in the section on Immunity will you need to define? _____

4. Are influenza and pneumonia transmitted by sexual contact? *No*

5. Define a vaccine: *a poisonous substance (containing weak virus) used to protect people against diseases*

6. Define interferon: *a protein substance formed by the body when interacting with viruses*

7. What causes gonorrhea? *Bacterium*

8. Are STDs uncontrollable? *yes they are controllable*

The Visual Aids

Practice: Look at the graphs and their captions to understand how much information they supply. Answer the questions about them.

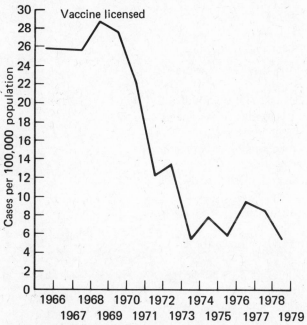

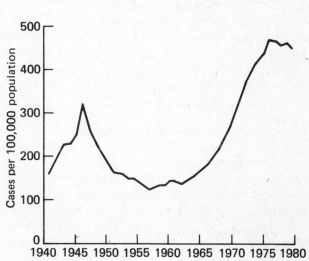

Figure 10–1. Rubella (German measles)—reported case rates by year in the United States, 1966–1979. Reported rubella incidence in 1979 was less than 20 percent of that reported in 1969, the year of vaccine licensure. [Annual Summary 1979, Center for Disease Control, Morbidity and Mortality Weekly Report, Vol. 28, No. 54 (September 1980), p. 70.]   *(Sinacore and Sinacore, 218)*

Figure 10–2. Gonorrhea—reported civilian case rates by year in the United States, 1941–1979. [Annual Summary 1979, Center for Disease Control, Morbidity and Mortality Weekly Report, Vol. 28, No. 54 (September 1980), p. 33.]   *(Sinacore and Sinacore, 224)*

1. Which two decades saw the most dramatic increases in the number of reported cases of gonorrhea?

_____15_____ and ___18_____

2. Did licensing the rubella vaccine eradicate the disease? _____No_____

3. In 1970, which disease affected more people per 100,000? _____Rubella_____

4. Has the incidence of rubella consistently decreased since the vaccine was licensed? __Yes___

5. How can these charts help you to understand the text? _____

_____

_____

_____

_____

The Special Terms

Practice: Read the glossary terms and check those that you are familiar with. Then answer the questions that follow.

GLOSSARY

Active immunity. Long-lasting resistance to infection acquired through the production of antibodies by the body either in response to a disease invasion or through injection of a vaccine.

Acupuncture. The oriental science concerned with the alleviation of pain and the treatment of disease by inserting fine needles into the body at designated points called loci.

Antibodies. Proteins in the blood that are generated from reactions to foreign substances, such as antigens.

Antigen. A foreign protein substance which, when introduced in the body, will stimulate the production of antibodies.

Chancre. A usually painless and open sore that appears at the site of a syphilitic infection.

Gonococcus. The bacterium (*Neisseria gonorrhoeae)* that causes gonorrhea.

Immunity. Protection from specific communicable diseases.

Interferon. A protein subtance formed by the body when interacting with viruses. This substance has the ability to protect other cells from viral infections.

Paresis. Severe mental disturbance that often occurs in the final stages of untreated syphilis.

Passive immunity. Short-term resistance to infection acquired by the administration of preformed antibodies.

Reye's syndrome. A serious complication of influenza or other virus-caused infection.

Spirochete. The corkscrew-shaped organism *(Treponema pallidum)* that causes syphilis.

Vaccine. A preparation of weakened or dead disease organisms or their toxin products that is given to a person or an animal to cause immunity.

Vectors. Insects or animals that serve to transmit disease.

(Sinacore and Sinacore, 236)

1. When you read about "spirochete," "paresis," and "chancre," what topic are you reading about?

_____

2. How are "antibodies" and "antigens" related? _____

_____

3. How are "active" and "passive immunity" different? _____

_____

4. How are "active" and "passive immunity" similar? _____

_____

The Review Questions

Practice: Read each review question carefully and highlight or underline the word or phrase that is the key idea within each question. Then answer the four questions that follow. (You will need to look back at other parts of the chapter you have just previewed.)

REVIEW QUESTIONS

1. Describe the progress that has been made in the control of communicable diseases.
2. How can you distinguish between control of a disease and its eradication? What kind of effort would be necessary to eradicate a disease?
3. Define (1) morbidity, (2) mortality, (3) incidence, (4) prevalence, (5) vectors, (6) immunity, (7) antigen, (8) antibody.
4. Distinguish between an active and a passive immunity.
5. What have been some of the difficulties in the development of preventive measures for influenza?
6. How may interferon revolutionize the incidence and treatment of diseases caused by viruses?
7. What is known about the cause and transmission of mononucleosis? Why is kissing disease probably a misnomer for this condition?
8. How do infectious and serum hepatitis differ?
9. What have been some of the inhibiting factors in dealing effectively with the problem of infectious hepatitis?
10. Why is the detection of gonorrhea particularly difficult in women? What can be the detrimental effects of this disease?
11. What are the implications of the increased resistance of gonorrheal infection to penicillin therapy?
12. Why is syphilis a difficult disease to detect and effectively treat? Why is it often referred to as the great imitator?
13. What can be the effects of advanced cases of syphilis?
14. Genital herpes is a STD that is rapidly increasing in incidence. Why is this disease of particular concern?
15. What are some of the suggestions that have been made by public health leaders to bring our expanding STD problem under control?

(Sinacore and Sinacore, 235)

1. The portion of the chapter in which you can find answers to questions 1 and 2 is the _____

2. The answer to question 3 is located in _____

3. The answer to question 4 can be found in _____

4. Questions 5 through 15 can be answered once you read _____

Applying Previewing Skills   11

As you preview a chapter in one of your texts, highlight or underline the ideas the author will focus on. The following questions relate to each portion of the chapter you are previewing.

Chapter Title: _____

Introduction

1. What general topics will the author discuss?

_____   _____

_____   _____

_____   _____

_____

2. Place a check next to the topics you are familiar with.

Subtitles

1. What broad subjects does the author focus on in the chapter?

_____

_____

_____

_____

2. Which subtitled subjects are you familiar with? Check them.

Visuals and Special Terms

1. What types of visuals appear in the chapter (charts, pictures, and so on)?

_____   _____

_____   _____

2. Are there many subject terms, dates, or numbers boldfaced or italicized in the chapter? _____
_____

Summary

1. What key ideas does the author emphasize?

_____   _____

_____   _____

_____   _____

_____   _____

2. What key terms does the author emphasize?

_____   _____

_____   _____

_____   _____

_____   _____

Review Questions

1. What key ideas will you need to understand as you read the chapter?

_____   _____

_____   _____

_____   _____

_____   _____

_____   _____

_____   _____

_____   _____

Locating Information: Topics, Main Ideas, and Details

Introduction

College textbooks are more difficult to read than the ones you studied in high school. However, you will find that they are easier to understand if you use a systematic approach when you read them.

1. Locate the topics discussed in them.
2. Locate the main ideas about topics.
3. Locate the details that support the main ideas.

These are skills you will learn as you study the following chapters.

As successful college students read their textbooks, most of them mark important information to study by highlighting or underlining it. Therefore, as you learn to read textbooks with better understanding, you will also learn how to underline or highlight important information in them to study for your tests.

Identifying the Topic   13

Good comprehension begins with an understanding of the topic or subject. It is essential to read a paragraph in its entirety before deciding what the general subject is. Reading only the opening sentence or phrase is often misleading. Consider these examples, in each of which the first fact is the same. Are the topics of each list the same?

Example

TOPIC _Body Organs_

Skin
Heart
Liver
Lungs

TOPIC _Parts of the Face_

Skin
Eyes
Mouth
Nose

The **topic**, usually expressed in a few words, is the general subject of a group of items or of ideas. It is necessary to consider all the items in a list or all the ideas in a paragraph, to see what they have in common, and to decide what the topic is.

Practice: Read each list. One item in each list is the topic (or subject) that includes the other items. Circle the topic.

1. Deans
   Presidents
   Bursars
   Registrars
   (College officials)

2. Disciplines
   Social sciences
   Humanities
   Sciences
   (Technologies)

3. Test tube
   (Apparatus)
   Burner
   Culture dish
   Scalpel

4. Summaries
   Questions
   Introductions
   (Parts of a chapter)
   Subtitles

5. Synonyms
   (Context clues)
   Antonyms
   Examples
   Definitions

6. Massachusetts
   (New England)
   Vermont
   Maine
   New Hampshire

7. Football games
   Basketball games
   (Contact sports)
   Wrestling matches
   Judo matches

8. (Course requirements)
   Text readings
   Lectures
   Related readings
   Term papers

9. Maps
   Charts
   (Visual aids)
   Diagrams
   Graphs

Practice: Read each list. Decide what the topic of each list is, and, in a few words, write that topic on the line.

1. **TOPIC** _Math-Geometry_

$E = mc^2$
Rate $\times$ Time = Distance
$C = 5/9 (F - 32)$

2. **TOPIC** _Workers Upset_

Strike
Picket
Boycott

3. **TOPIC** _Computer Languages_

FORTRAN
COBOL
BASIC

4. **TOPIC** _College Posictons_

Instructor
Lecturer
Assistant professor
Associate professor

5. **TOPIC** _Organizations_

AFL-CIO
NATO
UN
NOW

6. **TOPIC** _Body Parts_

Kidney
Pancreas
Heart
Lungs

7. **TOPIC** _Instruments_

Strings
Woodwinds
Brass
Percussion

8. **TOPIC** _Myths_

Mermaid
Unicorn
Leprechaun
Elf

9. **TOPIC** _Angles_

Straight
Obtuse
Acute
Right

10. **TOPIC** _the Mine_

Id
Ego
Superego

11. **TOPIC** _foreign Money_

Franc
Lira
Peso

12. **TOPIC** _Groups_

Mamas and Papas
Stones
Beatles

13. **TOPIC** _Authors_

Arthur Conan Doyle
Agatha Christie
Mickey Spillane

14. **TOPIC** _Italian foods_

Spaghetti
Ravioli
Macaroni

15. **TOPIC** _Shapes_

Circle
Square
Triangle

Practice: Read each group of related sentences. Decide what the topic is and write the topic (or subject) on the line. The first one is done for you.

1. **TOPIC** _Reformatory Sentences_

The reformatory sentence is a rehabilitative one.
Sentences last from one day to three years.
Inmates' ages range from sixteen to twenty-one years.
The median amount of time served is two to four months.
An observer can easily see that reformatories have special characteristics.

2. **TOPIC** _Committing Parking Violations_

Any person committing parking violations will be fined or disciplined.
Any person whose vehicle has a fraudulent or counterfeit parking decal will be fined $25.
Any person found in possession of a parking decal reported lost or stolen will be fined $50.
Any person whose vehicle bears an unauthorized parking decal will be fined $15.

3. TOPIC *Basic tax Preparation Course*

A comprehensive analysis of basic income tax principles as they affect
individuals, partnerships, and corporations will be offered.

There will be many topics covered in the basic tax preparation course.

There will be application of tax concepts of gross income, adjusted gross
income, taxable income, exemptions, deductions, and credits as interpreted under the Internal Revenue Code, regulations, and court decisions.

There will be laboratory practice in the preparation of tax returns and
forms.

4. TOPIC *Transfer Programs*

Students who plan to continue their liberal arts or preprofessional education beyond the associate degree usually enter one of the transfer
programs.

Transfer programs are equivalent to the first two years of study in a four-
year college.

Transfer programs have special characteristics.

Students who complete one of the transfer programs may enter a four-
year college at the junior class level.

Practice: Read each paragraph, decide what the topic is, and write it on
the line.

1. TOPIC *Correctional Institution Administration*

Most correctional institution administrations list vocational rehabilitation as a main objective of inmate programs. There are, however, numerous weaknesses in such programs. One such weakness is an emphasis on mass treatment through offerings of skilled trades to large groups.
Most programs rely on meager or out-of-date equipment and generally
offer training in obsolete trades. Programs' standards are often below
those of "outside" industry. Finally, there seems to be little relation between instruction and practical application.

2. TOPIC *Trademarks*

Trademarks run the gamut from highly abstract designs to human
figures. They can be simply a typographical design of the brand name or
an illustration completely unrelated to the brand name. They can make
use of color, photographs, or drawings. They can be modern or traditional, abstract or pictorial, masculine or feminine, simple or complex,
animate or inanimate. The possibilities are endless.

(Mandell, 193)

3. TOPIC *Internal Respiration*

Internal respiration takes place throughout the body. It is the exchange of gases between the blood and the cells, with oxygen diffusing
from the blood into the cells and carbon dioxide diffusing from the cells
into the blood. The cells are separated from the capillaries by a film of
lymph, and the gases pass through this fluid.

(Johnson, DeLanney, Cole, and Brooks, 143)

4. TOPIC _Many Terms_

Many terms are used to express tempo, or rate of speed, in musical scores. These terms are usually given in Italian, and express tempos of deliberate slowness through very fast speeds. Examples of these tempos are adagio, or very slow; moderato, or moderate; allegro, or fast; and presto, very fast.

5. TOPIC _People Change_

People change. From moment to moment we aren't the same. We wake up in the morning in a jovial mood and turn grumpy before lunch. We find ourselves fascinated in a conversational topic one moment, then suddenly lose interest. One moment's anger often gives way to forgiveness the next. Health turns to illness and back to health. Alertness becomes fatigue, hunger becomes satiation, and confusion becomes clarity.

(Adler and Rodman, 37)

Determining the Main Idea

14

Understanding the main idea of a paragraph is the foundation for good comprehension. The main idea of a paragraph is directly related to both the topic and the details in the paragraph.

Here is a main idea sentence highlighted in a paragraph.

Example

There are many types of context clues that help us understand the meanings of new words. One type of clue is the synonym. There is also the antonym clue. In addition, one can look for a definition or for an example clue. Finally, an important context clue is the sense-of-the-sentence clue.

The following display shows how the main idea of this paragraph is related to its topic and to its details.

Topic	Main Idea Sentence	Details
Context Clues	There are many types of context clues that help us understand the meanings of new words.	Synonyms Antonyms Examples Definitions Sense of the sentence

The **main idea** of a paragraph is a general statement the author makes about the topic. It is also the general statement the author makes about the details in the paragraph.

When you decide which sentence in a paragraph states the main idea, mark it for future recall by highlighting it, circling it, or enclosing it in brackets. The main idea sentence is highlighted in the example. Following are examples of the sentence circled and enclosed in brackets.

There are many types of context clues that help us understand the meanings of new words.

[There are many types of context clues that help us understand the meanings of new words.]

Exercises in this chapter and other chapters require you to mark main idea sentences. Decide whether you will highlight them, circle them, or enclose them in brackets.

Practice: Here are sentence lists for which you wrote topics when you studied Chapter 13. One sentence in each list is a main idea sentence—a sentence that makes a general statement about the topic and details. Mark the main idea sentence in each list by highlighting it, circling it, or enclosing it in brackets.

1. TOPIC ____*Reformatory Sentences*____

The reformatory sentence is a rehabilitative one.
Sentences last from one day to three years.
Inmates' ages range from sixteen to twenty-one years.
The median amount of time served is two to four months.
An observer can easily see that reformatories have special characteristics.

2. TOPIC ____*Parking Violations*____

Any person committing parking violations will be fined or disciplined.
Any person whose vehicle has a fraudulent or counterfeit parking decal will be fined $25.
Any person found in possession of a parking decal reported lost or stolen will be fined $50.
Any person whose vehicle bears an unauthorized parking decal will be fined $15.

3. TOPIC ____*Basic Tax Preparation Course*____

A comprehensive analysis of basic income tax principles as they affect individuals, partnerships, and corporations will be offered.
There will be many topics covered in the basic tax preparation course.
There will be application of tax concepts of gross income, adjusted gross income, taxable income, exemptions, deductions, and credits as interpreted under the Internal Revenue Code, regulations, and court decisions.
There will be laboratory practice in the preparation of tax returns and forms.

4. TOPIC ____*Transfer Programs*____

Students who plan to continue their liberal arts or preprofessional education beyond the associate degree usually enter one of the transfer programs.
Transfer programs are equivalent to the first two years of study in a four-year college.
Transfer programs have special characteristics.
Students who complete one of the transfer programs may enter a four-year college at the junior class level.

Practice: Here are paragraphs for which you wrote topics. Read each paragraph and decide which sentence is the main idea. Mark that sentence.

1.   Most correctional institution administrations list vocational rehabilitation as a main objective of inmate programs. There are, however, numerous weaknesses in such programs. One such weakness is an emphasis on mass treatment through offerings of skilled trades to large groups. Most programs rely on meager or out-of-date equipment and generally offer training in obsolete trades. Programs' standards are often below those of "outside" industry. Finally, there seems to be little relation between instruction and practical application.

2.   Trademarks run the gamut from highly abstract designs to human figures. They can be simply a typographical design of the brand name or an illustration completely unrelated to the brand name. They can make use of color, photographs, or drawings. They can be modern or traditional, abstract or pictorial, masculine or feminine, simple or complex, animate or inanimate. The possibilities are endless.

(Mandell, 193)

3.   Internal respiration takes place throughout the body. It is the exchange of gases between the blood and the cells, with oxygen diffusing from the blood into the cells and carbon dioxide diffusing from the cells into the blood. The cells are separated from the capillaries by a film of *lymph,* and the gases pass through this fluid.

(Johnson, DeLanney, Cole, and Brooks, 143)

4.   Many terms are used to express tempo, or rate of speed, in musical scores. These terms are usually given in Italian, and express tempos of deliberate slowness through very fast speeds. Examples of these tempos are adagio, or very slow; moderato, or moderate; allegro, or fast; and presto, very fast.

5.   People change. From moment to moment we aren't the same. We wake up in the morning in a jovial mood and turn grumpy before lunch. We find ourselves fascinated in a conversational topic one moment, then suddenly lose interest. One moment's anger often gives way to forgiveness the next. Health turns to illness and back to health. Alertness becomes fatigue, hunger becomes satiation, and confusion becomes clarity.

(Adler and Rodman, 31)

Locating the Main Idea in Varied Parts of Paragraphs

15

The main idea is a statement the author makes about the paragraph topic. It is also the general statement that relates to the details in the paragraph.

Practice: Here is a paragraph for which you previously identified the topic and the main idea sentence. That sentence is marked in paragraph 1. Read paragraphs 2, 3, and 4, and mark the main idea sentence in each. If it is not stated, write the main idea in the margin.

1. The reformatory sentence is a rehabilitative one. Sentences last from one day to three years. Inmates' ages range from sixteen to twenty-one years. The median amount of time served is two to four months. An observer can easily see that reformatories have several special characteristics.

2. An observer can easily see that reformatories have several special characteristics. The reformatory sentence is a rehabilitative one. Sentences last from one day to three years. Inmates' ages range from sixteen to twenty-one years. The median amount of time served is two to four months.

3. The reformatory sentence is a rehabilitative one. Sentences last from one day to three years. An observer can easily see that reformatories have several special characteristics. Inmates' ages range from sixteen to twenty-one years. The median amount of time served is two to four months.

4. The reformatory sentence is a rehabilitative one. Sentences last from one day to three years. Inmates' ages range from sixteen to twenty-one years. The median amount of time served is two to four months.

When the main idea is located in the last sentence, as in paragraph 1, it sums up the details in that paragraph. When the main idea is located in the first sentence, as in paragraph 2, it introduces the details in the paragraph. A main idea stated in the middle of the paragraph, as in paragraph 3, serves as a bridge between the beginning and closing details. Sometimes the main idea is not stated in the paragraph, as in 4, yet you must pull together the details and topic and state the main idea in your own words.

Location of the Main Idea	Purpose of the Main Idea
first sentence ———————➔	introduces details
middle sentence ——————➔	is a transition between beginning and ending details
last sentence ———————➔	sums up details
unstated ————————➔	covers the details, must be stated by the student

Practice: Read the following ten paragraphs and mark the main idea sentence in each. If the main idea is not stated, write it in your own words next to the paragraph.

1.   Gorillas, the largest of living primates, are among the shyest and the gentlest, according to recent field studies. Gorillas have almost completely abandoned trees, with the exception of some of the smaller animals that sleep in nests in the lower branches. The larger gorillas sleep on the ground, and all feed on ground plants. They live in groups ranging from eight to 24 individuals, with about twice as many females as males, and a number of juveniles and infants. Each gorilla troop has a large, mature (silver-backed) male as a leader.

(Curtis, 951, 955)

2.   Music is used for many purposes today, and not all of them involve entertainment. It is used in advertising to attract attention to promote products. Huge amounts of money are spent to create clever thirty-second "hits," which subliminally pressure consumers to make purchases. Music is also used as a pacifier; the music piped into elevators, supermarkets, airplanes, and shopping centers is designed to be ignored. It serves its purpose best when it is least obvious. This music encourages listeners to relax, slow down, and buy. Business firms provide background music for their workers, to blot out distracting noises and increase efficiency. Farmers supply the same "canned" music to their livestock to increase milk and egg production.

(Hickok, 430)

3.   The search for a diet that promises to help one lose weight and still eat unlimited amounts of food continues. Each year a new diet emerges that promises a quick and easy way to lose weight. Diet books remain on the best seller list for months, each promising that its approach is a breakthrough in weight-loss management. Other books will tell one that it is OK to go on an eating binge and will provide the reader with the number of minutes needed to walk, jog, swim, or bicycle to work off the binge. There is no question that Americans are obsessed with dieting and, in some instances, will pay handsomely to lose weight. Something has to be said about the multimillion-dollar weight-loss business.

(Sinacore and Sinacore, 194)

4.   Most smokers have filled their daily activities with cues that continue to say "time to light up." And when smokers feel the urge to light up, they can think of a thousand reasons to do so, no matter how strong their resolve to quit. Smokers may not know their real reasons for smoking, but their reasons may include calming their nerves, relieving boredom, keeping their hands occupied, or satisfying basic oral needs. Like the alcoholic and the heroin addict, smokers who stop have withdrawal symptoms. Unlike them, smokers have no Alcoholics Anonymous or Synanon to turn to for help. Giving up smoking can be extremely difficult.

(Insel and Roth, 236)

5.   Special committees are small groups appointed to accomplish a single defined task or objective. They continue to function only until that job is done and their report is made to the parent organization. When the PTA plans a special program, including entertainment, refreshments, and displays of new educational materials, it might well create a special committee to plan and execute the details of the program. This group would then meet on call of its chairman, decide which of the members should be in charge of each aspect of the program, arrange for whatever assistance was needed to make the physical arrangements, serve the refreshments, etc., see that everything went according to plan, and file a report at the regular meeting following the program. At this point, their report would be received "with thanks," and the committee discharged. Traditionally oriented organizations refer to the special committee as an *"ad hoc"* committee, using the Latin phrase meaning literally "for this." When "this" is done, the committee has no further responsibility.

(Ewbank, 29)

6.   (The best way for a dramatist to hold the attention of an audience) is to develop an atmosphere of constantly increasing suspense. The writer creates suspense, in the first place, by arousing his audience's curiosity about the way things are going to turn out. This may involve a suspense question about the eventual result of the action, or if the nature of the outcome is fairly obvious—that the young lovers will live happily ever after, for example—the suspense question asks how this happy conclusion is to be reached in view of all the apparent obstacles. The writer develops suspense, in the second place, by creating characters who engage the interest and sympathy of the viewers. As these viewers begin to worry about whether these characters will find a way out of the troubles enveloping them, the feeling of suspense initiated by curiosity begins to mount. The playwright accentuates this process by multiplying both uncertainty and anxiety until the tension reaches a fever pitch at the climax of the play. Suspense, then, is composed of two ingredients: curiosity and concern.

(Willis, 98)

7.   People do not marry without some idea of what marriage will be like. As children they observe their own parents and as adults they observe others in marriage. People have expectations about marriage and the roles they and their spouses will play. The early weeks and months of marriage often fulfill some of these expectations, but they are, at times, replaced by discouragement, anxiety, and conflict. One of the serious problems people who enter marriage share is the way they perceive their roles.

(Lefton, 528)

8.   (Show business has a universal appeal, and the store demonstration is a kind of showmanship in business.) Claims may be made in advertisements, but "seeing is believing." Demonstrations also add a certain glamour to the store. Therefore, many manufacturers have demonstrators who travel from store to store. Hoover, for example, shows its cleaning equipment in operation on the salesfloor. People watching it can ask questions that can be answered by an expert and may be able to try the product themselves. The key to good live demonstrations is effective demonstrators with both an expert knowledge of the product and also a flair for the dramatic. In lieu of live demonstrators, some manufacturers use tape machines and slide projectors or movies to demonstrate their products. There are also mechanical displays capable of demonstrating the product in action. One, for example, dipped a running watch in a tank of water and then hit it with a hammer to show that it was waterproof and shockproof.

(Mandell, 592)

9. (Alcohol affects the *cardiovascular system* in numerous ways.) Alcoholics may have heart abnormalities as a direct result of alcohol. This condition is in addition to the effects of malnutrition and vitamin deficiency, both common in alcoholics. Blood pressure does not change much after moderate intake of alcohol, but the pulse rate may go up. Alcohol causes blood vessels near the skin to dilate, and drinkers often feel warm, their skin flushes, and they sweat more. Flushing and sweating contribute to loss of heat from the body, and the internal body temperature falls. High doses of alcohol may affect the body's ability to regulate temperature, causing it to drop sharply, especially if the surrounding temperature is low. Drinking alcoholic beverages to keep warm in cold weather thus does not work and it can even be dangerous.

become wider

(Insel and Roth, 262)

10. (Large ensembles usually require the leadership of a conductor.) Placed in front of the orchestra or chorus, usually on a podium, the conductor directs the ensemble and is responsible for all aspects of the performance. The craft of conducting is a complex one, and conducting techniques and styles are highly individual and vary widely. In general, the conductor's right hand indicates the tempo and basic metrical structure of the music. With his left hand, the conductor cues the entrances of instruments, the shadings of dynamics, and indicates other nuances relating to the expressive character of the music.

make a signal meaning

(Hickok, 49–50)

Practice: Read the following five paragraphs and mark the main idea sentence in each. If the main idea is not stated, write it in the space next to the paragraph.

1. (Committee task assignments,) in all but a very limited number of instances, will fall into either one of two broad patterns. First, a committee may be appointed to investigate a problem and to develop from that investigation a policy or plan to be reported to the parent organization with a recommendation for action. Second, a committee may be appointed to investigate the acceptability of one or more proposed courses of action that the parent organization has neither the time nor the immediately available resources to consider as a body, and to report a recommendation to the parent organization for action.

(Ewbank, 32)

2. LSD is one of the most powerful psychoactive drugs there is. A dose of 100 micrograms, an amount so small that it can hardly be perceived, will produce noticeable effects in most people. These effects are of three kinds. There are *somatic changes,* which include slight dizziness, weakness, nausea, and dilation of pupils. There are *perceptual changes,* among them disorders of vision, an improved sense of hearing, an altered sense of time, and a phenomenon known as *synesthesia.* With synesthesia, the sensory modes are blended, and people hear colors and see sounds. *Psychic changes* also accompany psychedelic use. These include rapid changes of mood, feelings of *depersonalization,* distortions in how people see their bodies, and alterations in the relationship between self and external reality.

The effects of powerful LSD – a psychoactive drug. body

(Insel and Roth, 285)

3. (The advertiser has several sources for mailing lists.) One of these is his own resources. He may have lists of present or past customers called *house lists,* or he may prepare lists from such sources as birth or marriage announcements in the newspapers, telephone or city directories, and salesmen's reports. If he does not wish to prepare his own lists, he can turn to commercial list houses. These firms specialize in preparing mailing lists, which may be highly specialized by such classifications as occupation, hobby, income, geographic location, ownership (of homes, brands of automobiles, and so forth), age, or family size. Many firms that have built their own lists, such as magazine publishers, rent these lists to interested direct mail advertisers. Such lists may be highly correlated with the advertiser's prospects—for example, a photographic equipment manufacturer who uses the subscription list of a photography magazine. Finally, there are mailing list brokers. Although they themselves do not own any lists, they act as agents in obtaining for advertisers the use of others' lists. For the advertiser, the broker's major value is his knowledge of what lists are available; for the list owner, he provides a source of business. Standard Rate and Data Service now publishes semiannually a catalog called *Direct Mail List Rates and Data*. This catalog lists some five thousand direct mail lists available and includes sources, cost per thousand, and other specifications.

(Mandell, 399)

4.   Voluntary exchanges take place in what we call a market. Markets are institutions that aid in the process of exchange by allowing communication between potential buyers and potential sellers of goods and services. This is the underlying function of all markets, no matter how primitive or sophisticated they might be. For example, in the formally structured New York and American Stock Exchanges, stockbrokers can immediately put potential buyers and potential sellers in touch with each other. The New York and American Stock Exchanges are highly centralized in terms of this function. At the other extreme are very decentralized, informal markets for such services as tutoring, babysitting, occasional home repair, and gardening. You can probably think of many other decentralized, informal markets that you often use.

(Miller, 10)

5.   One of the youngest and most vital of the world's mythologies is the classic Western, which was developed by the motion-picture industry on a foundation laid down by the dime novels and wild-West shows of the late nineteenth century. The idealized stories it tells have little relation to life as it really existed in the old West. The leading character is a transcendent figure, like the Lone Ranger, who, representing the forces of good, rides into town to meet and vanquish the forces of evil before disappearing into the mists on the trail, to be seen no more. The motives of the villain whose machinations make his exploits necessary are often as cloudy as those of the hero, but one thing is clear; he is all bad and the hero is all good. Contrasts of white and black are characteristic of the classic Western; the grayness that distinguishes ordinary humanity is alien to the form. Other stock characters of the classic Western are the derelict professional—the lawyer, doctor, or minister—who betrays the creed of his profession except perhaps for one glorious, soul-restoring moment; the effete easterner who, disdaining the use of violence, is often humiliated or killed; the anemic good girl who is generally the school marm; and the bad girl who works in the saloon. The climactic moment of the Western is the final confrontation between the hero and the villain, which often takes place on a street deserted by the rest of the townspeople, who cower in fear behind doors and windows.

(Willis, 210)

Identifying Details

16

No matter what position the main idea occupies in the paragraph (beginning, middle, end, or outside—unstated), it is supported by the important details in that paragraph. It is necessary to determine which details are important and relate to the main idea.

However, not all details in a paragraph are necessarily important. Some details may be repetitive or unrelated and are therefore not needed. An effective method of determining which details are important and related to the main idea is to turn the main idea into a question that begins with who, what, when, why, or how. The important details will answer that question. The main idea sentence is highlighted in the following paragraph.

Example

Each year, thousands of students drop out of high school for a variety of reasons. Educational surveys uncover many contributing causes. Some students see (1) little relationship between class work and vocational goals. (2) Economic pressures at home may force the teenager to seek full- or part-time employment. In addition, (3) family responsibilities may demand much of the student's time. The (4) daily school routine presents an unchanging and often boring schedule. Associated with this problem is the (5) inability of school personnel to develop new programs and methods designed to meet the needs of potential dropouts. In addition to these factors, the (6) student's problems and needs may lead him to drop out.

The six details that are numbered and underlined in this paragraph are answers to a question that begins with why.

Why do thousands of students drop out of high school?

Study the details in the paragraph to understand how they explain why thousands of students drop out of high school.

The main idea sentence in a paragraph is explained, illustrated, or generally supported by the details in the paragraph.

When you mark details, underline them as illustrated earlier. Or, if you highlight main ideas, you may highlight details by using a color other than the one you use to highlight main ideas.

Practice: Each of the following five exercises contains a main idea sentence and a list of detail sentences. Turn the main idea into a question using one of these terms: who, what, when, why, or how. Decide which details answer (support or illustrate) the main idea question. Check the important details that relate to the main idea sentence and mark the portion of the detail that answers the question. The first one is done for you.

1. The medical examiner's job covers a wide range of medical knowledge and skills.

What knowledge and skills are needed by a medical examiner?

  ✓   The medical examiner searches for bacterial and viral causes of death.
  ✓   He must have a thorough knowledge of all body physiology.
  ✓   Organic and inorganic chemistry are the basic tools of the medical examiner.
         The medical examiner works for the state.

2. Rationalization is a defense mechanism theorized by Freud.

What is   To find reasons for

         It involves making excuses to justify one's behavior.
         Rationalization robs ego of strength.
         Freud lived in the nineteenth century.
         Continued rationalization implies an inability to deal with the real world.

3. One can make a good impression during a job interview.

How can

         The applicant should act confidently.
         The applicant should know as much as possible about the company.
         The applicant should look at the interviewer and maintain eye contact.
         The applicant should always make a good impression on the second interview.

4. Exercising provides many benefits for the average person.

What

         Many people report weight loss resulting from exercise.
         People find they have increased stamina.   strength
         Overexertion can be one danger for the mature adult.
         People report reduced strain and tension after starting exercise programs.

5. The trained biologist devotes time and energy to a variety of work experiences.

How

         Biologists earn degrees from American and overseas universities.
         Many biologists teach or are members of scientific boards.
         The biologist may teach or be actively engaged in the design of research experiments.
         Many trained biologists work in major laboratories and conduct high-level experiments.

Practice: The main idea sentence is highlighted in the following paragraphs. Think of the main idea sentence as a question and mark the details that answer the question. The first one is done for you.

1. No matter how often one goes through the experience, registering for college classes can be frustrating and exhausting. Students wait in long lines at almost every stage of the registration process. Courses often "close," and courses must be fit into existing or completely reworked schedules. Thousands of people jam the registration area, and soon the room temperature soars. Registration takes place before classes begin. Often students, cannot locate advisers and can easily make inappropriate program changes. At some schools, students register by mail.

2. Small farmers and agricultural laborers have been steadily displaced over the last few decades by mechanized agriculture, and they can no longer earn a decent living on the land. Automation in many industries has displaced unskilled workers, but these workers lack the training that would enable them to compete for jobs in industries using advanced technologies. Many workers are trapped in the less-skilled service industries—as shoe shiners, domestic cleaners, dishwashers, or car-park attendants. The poor, if they are able to find employment at all, are concentrated in those jobs that offer only low wages and little security.

quite good

(Worth, 252)

3. Containerization refers to the practice of packing goods in a container at the point of origin, where a seal is placed on it that is not broken until it reaches its ultimate destination. Light-weight aluminum containers . . . can be cheaply transferred from truck to train, from ship to plane at lower handling costs. Packages of many sizes and shapes can be packed together; because containers are sealed, shipments never get divided; and losses from pilferage and weather exposure are eliminated. Growth in use of containers and adaptations of the method can be expected in the future. Thus, containerization has many advantages.

s leading

(Mauser and Schwartz, 330)

4. Not all college freshmen are prepared or willing to give up their dependent status. They may feel that their family has abandoned them. At the same time, the parents may not be tolerant of the new values and ideas that the student brings home. The student who lives with parents and commutes to school is in a particularly difficult position as he or she may have to function at two conflicting levels in two quite different environments. College freshmen face many problems.

(Jones, Shainberg, and Byer, 43)

Practice: Read the following business text passage and mark the main idea sentence and its related details in each paragraph.

Survey information can be collected in several ways, some of which are described below:

The *mail questionnaire is a set of questions sent to a selected group of people.* This technique is often used when information from a wide area is needed. If a large number of people return questionnaires, it is a low-cost way to collect information. The chief disadvantage is that often only a small percentage of people return the questionnaires. Also, the people who respond may not be typical.

In *personal interviews, trained interviewers ask questions of selected people.* While interviews generally are held in homes, offices, or stores, researchers occasionally interview people at athletic events, on streets, in buses, outside theaters, and so on. The personal-interview technique usually results in a high percentage of interviews in relation to people approached, thus overcoming a disadvantage of the mail questionnaire. On the negative side, personal interviews are expensive. The "human element" is also present, which can cause bias in the answers given by the respondent.

The telephone is used extensively for collecting information, especially about radio and television listening habits. One organization specializes in calling a certain number of people daily and asking, "Is your radio or television set turned on? If so, to what program are you listening?" Telephone interviewing is the quickest way to obtain data, and the cost per interview is low. Interviews, however, must be brief, and questions ordinarily cannot be of a personal nature because of the reluctance of people to talk about personal matters to strangers.

A fourth method for securing information is the *panel,* or *consumer-jury, interview, in which the people who form the panel are selected carefully to represent a group typical of those to whom the business wants its product to appeal.* Panels range in size from a dozen people to a hundred or more. Members of the panel may be questioned about anything from their shoe-buying habits to their favorite household pets. They may or may not be compensated for their cooperation. The main advantage of the panel is that information on many topics is readily available. However, the method has its limitations. Its members may answer questions as "experts" rather than as ordinary shoppers. Moreover, panels are hard to maintain. People drop out, fail to cooperate, or otherwise make it difficult to keep the group a representative one.

(Mauser and Schwartz, 448–449)

Organizing Information in Written Notes

Deciding on a correct main idea and supporting details is essential to comprehension. Once you have determined the important facts, you can note them for future recall. Consider this paragraph.

Example

Each year, thousands of students drop out of high school for a variety of reasons. Educational surveys uncover many contributing causes. Some students see little relationship between class work and vocational goals. Economic pressures at home may force the teenager to seek full- or part-time employment. In addition, family responsibilities may demand much of the student's time. The daily school routine presents an unchanging and often boring schedule. Associated with this problem is the inability of school personnel to develop new programs and methods designed to meet the needs of potential dropouts. In addition to these factors, the student's problems and needs may lead him to drop out.

Following are four sets of notes for the information in this paragraph. Use checks to indicate which two of the sets of notes contain correct information and are well organized for studying and learning the information in the paragraph.

_____ **Set 1**

Thousands of students leave high school. Why? Little relationship between class and vocational goals. Economic pressures force teens to work. Family responsibilities demand time. Daily school routine is boring. No new programs to meet needs of potential dropouts. Student's problems.

_____ **Set 2**

A. Reasons why high school students drop out
   1. little relation between class and vocational goals
   2. economic pressures force teens to work
   3. family responsibilities demand time
   4. daily school routine is boring
   5. no new programs to meet needs of potential dropouts
   6. student's problems

_____ **Set 3**

A. Thousands drop out of high school for many reasons
   1. why?
   2. educational surveys
   3. little relationship
   4. economy forces teens to work
   5. family responsibility
   6. associated with problems of poor school personnel
   7. student's own problems

_____ **Set 4**

Reasons for thousands of high school dropouts	little relation between class and vocational goals economic pressures force teens to work family responsibilities demand time daily school routine is boring no new programs to meet needs of potential dropouts student's problems

You should have checked Set 2 and Set 4. Set 1 contains the correct information, but only Set 2 and Set 4 contain the correct information and are well organized for studying and learning the ideas in the paragraph. In Set 2 and Set 4, the main idea is concisely expressed and stands out clearly; the details are neatly listed so that they can be learned efficiently.

Taking **written notes** from a text requires that you read and understand the important ideas, condense those ideas in your own words, and summarize the ideas in a well-organized way that will help you to study.

Use the format illustrated in Set 2 or Set 4 to make notes of the information you want to learn for quizzes, tests, and examinations.

Taking Notes on a Paragraph

Chapter 17 introduced two popular methods for taking notes—outlines and split-page notes. The methods are similar in several ways: they both give prominence to main ideas and they both list supporting details in well-organized ways. Consider the two formats:

Example

Outline

A. Main idea
   1. detail
   2. detail
   3. detail

Split-Page Notes

Main idea	detail
	detail
	detail

In **outlines**, main ideas are written at the margin and labeled, using capital letters; details are indented and labeled, using numbers. In **split-page notes**, main ideas and details are separated by a vertical line that divides the page.

In addition to their similar formats, both outlines and split-page notes provide the opportunity to restate important ideas from the text passage in a concise manner. Exercises in this chapter and other chapters require you to take written notes from text passages. Your notes should reflect the important ideas clearly, concisely, and accurately.

Practice: In the following paragraphs, the main idea sentence and its supporting details are marked. Condense and organize the important ideas in an outline **or** in split-page notes. The first one is done for you.

Notes

1. *main Idea* Taking good photographs is a highly complex skill. A good picture must be composed properly in terms of space, shape, and color. Correct light exposure needs careful planning. The film must be developed accurately under exact conditions. *Sentence details*

A. Taking good photos a complex skill
   1. need space, shape, and color composition
   2. correct light exposure
   3. film developed under exact conditions

or

Taking good photos complex skill	• need space, shape, color composition
	• correct light exposure
	• develop film under exact conditions

2. There are several good reasons why hospitals are so expensive. First, regardless of how many beds are filled, there are many fixed costs that a hospital must pay: emergency rooms with expensive equipment that sits idle most of the time but that must be ready twenty-four hours a day; operating rooms; salaries for administration, nurses, and supporting staff; heating, cooling, lighting, and custodial costs; and so on. Second, a hospital is a workshop for doctors, who need and expect up-to-date, sophisticated equipment to be available. Third, hospital patients count on first-rate care; the average patient is attended by three to five highly qualified staff members.

(Grawunder, Pruitt, and Steinman, 358)

A There are several good reasons hospitals are expensive
1. Need cost, emergency rooms, expensive equip., salaries and custodial costs.
2. up-to-date, sophisticated equipment
3. Patients first-rate-care

3. The main purpose of taxation is to provide funds for government operations and public services. Taxation is also used to influence the economy. For example, to stimulate private investment in energy development or some other needed but risky venture, the government may give tax breaks to encourage people to invest. Adjustments in income tax rates are sometimes made to stimulate consumer spending and capital investment by business. Tariffs are levied to restrict the amount of foreign goods sold in the country, thereby protecting domestic businesses from foreign competition.

(Mauser and Schwartz, 563)

A Main Purpose of taxation
1. Provide funds, government oper., Public Serv.
2. Stimulate economy & consumer spending

Practice: Read each paragraph and mark the important ideas. Then use those ideas as you take written notes on the paragraph.

Notes

1. In mature life, sex differentiation continues, while the process of role definition becomes ever more complicated. The woman finds that she may have to become an economic provider as well as mother and housekeeper and that she must do this without robbing her husband of his masculine ego feelings. She must be an informed citizen, an intelligent conversationalist, and an active community worker, yet not neglect her primary duties in the kitchen and nursery. She must be a seductive siren, skillful, patient, and responsive, but she must also be a chaste creature, modest and demure, feeling the stir of passion only toward her husband! She must be a skillful—but not *too* skillful—

trinh tiết
attractive
SIREN : Thần nữ
quiet & serious

A Mature Life
1. economic provider & mother
2. Informed citizen, intelligent conversationalist & community worker
3. modest, demure,
4. Skillful

sportswoman, yet remain a feminine clinging vine. She must be a household purchasing agent, a business manager, and a financial consultant when necessary; at all other times she must be completely ignorant of money matters. Her total role as wife and mother thus includes many different roles, some of them inconsistent with one another. It is little wonder women often find it difficult to play this complex and paradoxical role.

(Horton and Hunt, 107)

2. *Personality* is one's total behavior tendency system. Our *heredity* gives us a set of needs and potentialities which other factors may channel and develop; our *physical environment* is relatively unimportant in personality development; our *culture* provides certain fairly uniform experiences for all members of our society; our *group experience* develops personality similarities within groups and differences between groups; the *unique experience* of each person shapes his individuality.

(Horton and Hunt, 101)

3. The disk jockey is concerned about the music policy of his station, but he is even more concerned about its operating policy. Generally speaking, the disk jockey may (1) work combo (combine engineering with announcing) or (2) work with engineering help. If he has engineering help, he is not, in a literal sense, a disc jockey, since he does not play the discs; to emphasize his emancipation from turntables, cartridge machines, and consoles, this announcer usually calls himself a "personality" or "talent." But whether he is a "jock" or a "personality," the popular music announcer is subject to variable policies governing his work: (1) he may not be allowed to ad-lib or otherwise reflect his own personality on the air, or he may be expected to project his individuality and build a personal following; (2) he may be allowed to select his own music, he may have to follow a scripted "playlist," he may have a playlist but be allowed to arrange the sequence of records, or he may be expected to choose his own favorites from a larger master list; (3) when he is not on the air, he may or may not have other duties of varying kinds.

(Hyde, 199)

Notes

5 business manager + financial consultant

6 complex + paradoxical role

2.A Personality
1 Developed, Physical environment,
2 Culture
3 Experience
A - Heredity
4. Unique experience

A. Disk Jockey's concerns are music policy + operating policy.
1. combine engineering with announcing
2 work with engineering help.
3. may not project his individuality + build a personal following
4. may not select his own music
5 not on air, may or may not have other duties

clothings   serious, sober, sedate

4.   Styling of men's apparel from the days of the industrial revolution to the 1950s could be characterized as staid and slow to change. The average man owned a small wardrobe assortment that contained a limited number of tailored suits, one of which was reserved for important-occasion wear. The average man hated to shop and gave the chore little forethought; in fact, he tended to buy for replacement rather than newness. Suit styling was practically timeless since the sporadic changes were slight modifications of details. A suit or coat showed little style variation from season to season, year to year, and style predictability was precise. It was a placid, classic business that permitted longevity for well-run firms.

happening irregular

calm, peaceful

(Packard, 132)

5.   Hunting is universally a male occupation. There seem to be several reasons for this, and some of them appear to be rooted in the biological differences between men and women. In the absence of modern contraceptive devices and formulas which can be bottle fed to infants, women in their prime are apt to be either pregnant or nursing mothers. In either case, their ability to travel long distances on foot, something that is essential to successful hunting, is significantly restricted. In addition to wide-ranging mobility, the successful hunter must also be able to mobilize rapidly high bursts of energy. Although some women can certainly run faster than some men, it is a fact that in general men can run faster than women, even if the latter are not pregnant or encumbered with infants to be nursed. Finally, there is a higher risk attached to hunting than to the tasks that usually occupy women in hunting and gathering societies. To place women at risk is to place their offspring, actual and potential, at risk as well.

(Haviland, 177)

A Men's Apparel
1) Limited, Tailored suits, Important-occasion wear
2) Suit styling, season to season, year to year

A Hunting Universally Male Occupation
1) Several reasons, Biological differences between men women
2) pregnant - nursing
3) on distance travel on foot is restricted
4) higher risk in hunting

Taking Notes on Several Paragraphs

19

In Chapter 18 you made outlines or split-page notes for single paragraphs, but in this chapter you will make notes for passages that are more than one paragraph long. The textbook passages in this chapter all contain more than one main idea. As a result, your notes will include more than one main idea.

Example

Outline

A. Main idea
   1. detail
   2. detail
B. Main idea
   1. detail
   2. detail
   3. detail
   4. detail

Split-Page Notes

Main idea	detail
	detail
Main idea	detail
	detail
	detail
	detail

Do the exercises by marking the main ideas and details in the passages and by then making clear and concise outlines or split-page notes for them.

Practice: Read the following passage and mark the important main ideas and supporting details. Then complete the written notes.

Orchestras, bands or large choral ensembles are directed by a *conductor* who coordinates tempo, gives cues for entrances, and controls the total balance of all the sounding forces. In these and other ways the conductor shapes various aspects of performance. Although synchronizing the group's beat is essential to the conductor's craft, there is much more to conducting than just beating time. A conductor may work with the players on phrasing and articulation, or subtle nuances of balance, or technical problems: the bowing or fingering of a tricky passage. *a slight difference in color, sound etc.* Most important, perhaps, the conductor is the only person on stage who really knows what everyone is doing, and who is directly concerned with the total effect. The conductor is responsible for the study of the complete *score* (see the next chapter), whereas the orchestral players are reading from *parts*. Only the conductor, standing on a podium at the direct center of the action,

Notes

A. Musical conductor's jobs
   1. directs orchestra, band, choral ensemble
   2. coordinates tempo
   3. cues entrances
   4. controls balance of sounds
   5. synchronizes beat
   6. works with players on phrasing, articulation, balance
B. Conductor's concern for total effect
   1. *synchronizing the groups beat*
   2. *work with players phrasing + articulation*
   3. *subtle nuances of balance*
   4. *technical problems (bowing fingers)*
C. *Conductor has complete control of*
   1. *responsible for complete score*
   2. *standing podium, direct center of action*

74

ruling with power

can grasp the total balance of the sound made by many individual players. Furthermore, one person has to make the ultimate decisions about tempo (how fast is "allegro con brio?") and phrasing; otherwise, every player in the orchestra might be making a different decision, with some rather unfocused results. *too tao , dictatorial*

For all these reasons, conducting is a somewhat autocratic profession. Certain conductors are indeed tyrannical, while others work wonders with genial prodding or a protective parental image. Some enjoy being "one of the guys," and others prefer to keep their distance. They must all possess a dazzling assortment of musical skills, a sure sense of their musical wishes, and the ability to transmit those wishes to 100 other musicians (half of whom probably wish that they were conducting instead). They must shape these 100 "voices" into a single musical personality. Much like their closest counterparts in other areas of group performance—theatrical directors and athletic coaches—conductors have demanding jobs and extraordinary responsibilities. To use one last analogy, they are masterly "performers" on that most difficult of Western "instruments," the orchestra.

(Schwartz, 98–99)

3. making decisions about tempo (allegro con brio)
4. phrasing
5. must posses assortment of musical skills
6. shape all voices into single musical personality
7. demanding jobs
8. extraordinary responsibilities
9. a master proformer
10. instrumenting the orchestra

genial prodding : cheerful push
dazzling : sang chói, lộn chói mắt
assortment : mixed things

Notes

• Musical conductor's 6 jobs	• directs orchestra, band, choral ensemble • coordinates tempo • cues entrances • controls balance of sounds • synchronizes beat • works with players on phrasing, articulation, balance
• Conductor's concern for total effect	• synchronizing the groups beat • work with players phrasing + articulation • subtle nuances of balance • technical problems control (finger + bowing)
• conductor has complete control	• responsible for complete score • standing podium, direct center of action • making decision about tempo. • phrasing • must posses assortment of musical skills • shape all voices into single musical personality • a demanding job • extraordinary responsibilities • a master performer • instrumenting the orchestra

Practice: Take notes on the following groups of paragraphs. Note that the main idea sentences are highlighted for you.

Notes

1.   Television has three primary ways of handling weather information in regularly scheduled newscasts. In the first, most often used on small or low-budget stations, the anchor man delivers the report. Larger stations retain a professional meteorologist who not only reports the weather but explains the causes of meteorological phenomena, subtly and continually educating his audience. Many meteorologists engage in television reporting as only one part of their professional careers. Third, a professional announcer, though not a trained meteorologist, may become a specialist in weather reporting. There are several ways of staging weather programs for television, all involving a map. The simplest kind of map is the outline variety used in geography classes. Rubbing it with charcoal dust or spraying it lightly and evenly with dull black paint reduces glare. A felt-tipped pen may then be used to emphasize the borders. The map is pinned to a wall and weather information is marked in with a felt-tipped pen during the telecast. A similar but somewhat less effective method is tracing an outline of the area being discussed on a blackboard and chalking in information. Opaque or blackboard maps have at least two important disadvantages: the weather reporter usually blocks at least part of the map from the television audience, and he must write awkwardly because he is crowded as far to one side of the map as possible. Some weather reporters get around these disadvantages by preparing their maps before the program gets underway and then just pointing to what they are talking about when they are on the air. This way they never need to block the map from the audience or develop writer's cramp.

(Hyde, 186–188)

2.   A professional thief steals for a living. That is his profession, and it has certain characteristics that distinguish it from other professions. One of the most important of those skills is the ability to manipulate people. Within the profession, each act of stealing is carefully planned. Members of the profession move often and may work all over the United States.

Handwritten notes (right column):

A Three primary ways of handling weather information.
1. small or low-budget, the anchor delivers the report.
2. Larger station retain a professional meteorologist.
3. professional announcer, may become a specialist weather reporter.
   to perform for public show

B Several ways in staging weather programs for television involving a map.
1) Out line variety.
2) tracing an out line

A Professional thief
1) has certain characteristics that distinguish from other profession

Control, influence, manage

Handwritten margin notes (top): about to happen — imminent

Handwritten margin notes (left): dislike / moral principles

Professional thieves may have personal hostilities with other professional thieves, but even so, they would always warn them of impending danger from police authorities. Professional thieves also avoid doing things that might put other professional thieves in danger. They give each other assistance when needed and often share their "earnings" with members who are in prison. They will advise each other of bad and good places to work. They have well-developed codes of ethics that are more binding than those of legitimate commercial firms.

Thieves work together in a mob. They discipline each other in various ways, one of which is exclusion. If a thief "squawks" (informs) on another, the other thieves will spread the word and no mob will admit the thief. He therefore loses his chance to work, since professional thieves do not work alone.

If a mob arrives at a place to work and finds another mob already at work, it will leave for two reasons: security and professional courtesy. Another maxim of the profession is "don't grift on the way out," which means that professional thieves get rid of what they steal before they steal more items. An amateur, on the other hand, might steal several items from various stores. But a professional will take his one score (successful theft, referring to the value of the item stolen), plant it, and then return to steal more.

(Reid, 271)

Handwritten notes (right column):
2) have personal hostilities with other professional thieves.
3) have well-developed codes of ethics
4) work together as a mob.
lawful & correct — reasonable or acceptable
a group of criminals — gang
rule
gambling

Practice: Take notes on the following groups of paragraphs.

Notes

1.   The first level of management in the union, generally referred to as the shop steward or committeeman, is elected by the members. The executive board, the executive officers, the top-ranking management men of the union, and the various levels of supervision within the union are all elected by the membership. Thus there is not the natural reticence toward communication upward through the union that there is in the management organization. The shop steward was elected to his job in the union by the men under him. Thus the men feel free to transmit their gripes and grievances to their shop steward. At the same time the shop steward feels he must please the workers who elected him so he handles the grievances. He is under pressure to pass the griev-

Handwritten notes (right column):
A) first level of Management In the union.
A)

Notes

ances up higher in the union organization or
to carry it to management's representative to
get satisfaction. If low-level management
men cannot or will not give satisfaction, the
union organization can easily carry the griev-
ance to a higher level in its own organization
and then to a high-level management representative. Thus workers can communicate
with the high-level management men if it is
essential. In the management organization,
workers do not want to gripe repeatedly to   *complain*
their foreman for fear of reprisals. *punishing*

A second major function of the union
for workers is to provide a power structure
that allows worker's representation to be
somewhat equivalent to management's representation. When the feelings of workers are
brought up through the union communication system, they can then be taken to higher
levels of management by a person representing a large group of individuals who can materially affect the company concerned. An individual worker can gripe to his foreman on
the job, but the individual worker always
knows that the factory can keep on operating
without him. When a top union representative talks to top levels of management, he
represents a large number of workers and
can greatly affect the industry.

In addition to providing a communication system and the power structure for
workers, at least three other personal needs
are fulfilled by unions. (1) The worker is
made to feel he is important. Instead of a
worker, he is a member and a really first-
class citizen. He is vital to the organization,
and the organization treats him and makes
him feel this way. (2) The worker is made to
feel that he belongs to a very powerful
group. The power of the group is not only
within the employing company, but is recognized throughout the United States, especially in terms of social and political power.
Unions are well known for their power to influence legislation and legislators toward activities of value to workmen. (3) The union
frequently provides members with facilities
for meetings, athletic activities, and group
get-togethers of a social nature. These needs
are often not filled in the worker's society by
his community nor by his employer.

(Brown, Berrien, Russell, and Wells, 368–369)

hold lightly

2. ⟨b⟩ Politicians are frequently difficult to interview. Most believe that they must consistently cling to the positions which won them election. They all must seek office at frequent intervals, and a careless statement on any of a thousand issues could alienate an important bloc of voters. Further, an elected official may have two opinions on certain issues: one representing the will of his constituents, the other his personal conviction. By the demands of his profession he must watch his tongue, so he discovers effective ways of turning aside questions he does not wish to answer. Seldom does a politician reveal a changed or newly acquired position in an interview; such newsmaking events are generally confined to news conferences which consist largely of carefully worded written statements.

⟨4⟩ The purpose of interviewing politicians is not to catch them out in inconsistencies but to clarify issues and stands. Some interviewers carefully research all past statements made by an official, look into current and anticipated political issues, and then try to "corner" their guest. Sometimes this means pursuing him with apparently contradictory statements in the hope that he will admit an inconsistency; at other times it develops into an attempt to force the guest into an extreme, controversial, or careless statement. Politicians know this game well and can easily escape unscathed from such combat. When interviewing a politician well known as a white supremacist, there is little point in trying to get him to admit that he is a racist. He can easily fill a half-hour with bland, unsensational ambiguities. The relentless pursuit of a headline-making statement is not only fruitless and purposeless, but boring as well. Let this be your guide: when interviewing a politician who holds extreme but covert positions, try to help him express clearly the beliefs he is willing to state publicly; do not waste your time trying to force, goad, or trick him into making statements that common sense tells you he will not make.

(Hyde, 232–233)

Politicians are frequently difficult to interview.

cause to stop being friendly

belief — opinion

to enclose within limit.
to limit

The purpose of interviewing politician

not harmed
to seem what too strong
usual
unclearness
ever harsh or pressing
hidden, secret
urge

Taking Notes on a Chapter

20

Authors usually divide chapters into major topics and label each with a subtitle. Each subtitle labels and is the subject of the group of paragraphs that follow it. Because each subtitle represents a new group of paragraphs, this distinction must be clearly shown in written notes.

> Authors divide chapter subjects into major topics, and they label those topics with boldfaced **subtitles**. In an outline, subtitles are labeled with Roman numerals, and they are written at the left margin. In split-page notes, subtitles are written at the left margin, and they are underlined.

Compare the following skeleton outline and split-page notes for a short textbook chapter.

Example

Chapter Title: _____   Date: _____

I. First Subtitle

  A. Main idea of first paragraph
    1.
    2. } details
    3.

  B. Main idea of second paragraph
    1.
    2.
    3. } details
    4.

  C. Main idea of third paragraph
    1. } details
    2.

II. Second Subtitle

  A. Main idea of first paragraph
    1.
    2.
    3. } details
    4.
    5.

  B. Main idea of second paragraph
    1.
    2. } details
    3.

Chapter Title:	Date:
First Subtitle	
Main idea of first paragraph	detail detail detail
Main idea	detail detail detail detail
Main idea	detail detail
Second Subtitle	
Main idea of first paragraph	detail detail detail detail detail
Main idea	detail detail detail

Chapter notes are usually much longer than these examples because most chapters have more than two subtitles.

Remember that the purpose of taking notes is to condense and organize important information. You may omit some textbook paragraphs because they add little to your understanding, and you can sometimes combine the details in two paragraphs under one main idea in your notes. Within the structure of note-taking methods, there is a degree of flexibility.

Practice: Take notes on the following subtitled parts of chapters.

Notes

Factors In Data Selection

Factors in Date Selection

Three factors appear to be related to the selection of dating partners: prestige considerations, physical attractiveness, and personality characteristics. *Prestige considerations* are based on our understanding that when we obtain things valued by our peers, we gain status in their eyes. Similarly, when we date someone who has characteristics valued by our peers, we gain prestige. If going out with the captain of the football team or the head cheerleader is valued by our friends, we might seek to date these people so as to improve our status with our friends. Dating a pre-med student may be more prestigious than dating a forestry major and, if so, would improve our status with our peers. Because prestige considerations relate to the values of a specific reference group—for example, our friends—they are not objective; that is, prestige considerations may vary according to sex, age, and region of the country. What is valued by your reference group? How does that affect your dating decisions?

The second factor related to the selection of dating partners is *physical attractiveness*. Facial attractiveness, physique, grooming, and dress all enter into the physical attractiveness equation. Although researchers have found physical attractiveness to be more important to males than it is to females, it is a factor in dating for both sexes. Of course, there is no concrete ideal against which all dates are measured. Some men and women find a tall date attractive, whereas others do not. Some men and women like plump dates, whereas others do not. Beauty *is* in the eye of the holder.

The last factor related to dating is the consideration of *personality characteristics*. Although figures support the importance of physical attractiveness in choosing a date, the influence of personality characteristics is also evident. Men and women do not seem to differ significantly in their ranking of personality characteristic, although

Notes

men tend to consider intelligence and companionship more important than women do, and women value thoughtfulness, consideration, and honesty more than men do.

(Dintiman and Greenberg, 347)

General Functions of the Blood

There are three general functions of blood and lymph: transportation, regulation, protection.

Transportation results in the movement (1) of *nutrients;* (2) of *oxygen* for cell respiration; (3) of *wastes* such as carbon dioxide to the lungs and urea to the kidneys and skin; (4) of *hormones* (see Chapter 10; the fact that blood carries secretin and cholecystokinin from the site of action in the pancreas and gall bladder, respectively, was mentioned in Chapter 7 and is representative of the blood's role in carrying hormones); (5) of *enzymes* in an active or inactive state, with the latter being represented by prothrombin (see the discussion of clotting in Chapter 12).

There is *regulation* (a) of *metabolism* and other body functions by the interaction of transported hormones with their targets and by the quantity of hormones (see Chapter 9); (b) of *temperature* by changes in the bore of blood vessels under nervous, endocrine, and environmental control; (c) of the *internal environment* in terms of salt balance, osmotic state, water concentration, and acidic or basic state of tissues.

Protection to the organism is provided (a) from loss of blood through clotting; (b) from invasion through the action of phagocytic cells; (c) from foreign substances or pathogenic organisms by developing immunity (Chapter 12).

(Johnson, DeLanney, Cole, and Brooks, 161)

Stressors Related to College Life

For most people, college life is an experience that is both enjoyable and fondly remembered, but it can also be very stressful. Many of the stressors affecting college students are health-related. The close living quarters shared by students residing in dormitories or apartments foster the rapid spread of communicable diseases. Influenza epidemics and bouts of mononucleosis are frequent visitors to college campuses. Other stressors, such as lack of sleep, examinations, and inadequate nutrition, also contribute to the spread of such diseases.

The psychological stressors associated with college life have to do with changes and decisions, which are normal and part of the maturing process. Students living away from home for the first time may find it difficult to make their own decisions, independent of the family. Who will do the laundry? Who will make the bed? Who will shop for food and cook? And will there be enough time left over for studying? Separation from people whom one has seen every day of one's life can be a strain as well, and for some students, homesickness is an intense stressor.

Of course, there are substitutes for the people one misses. Friends of the same and the opposite sex often replace the absent family members. The process of making friends in itself can be stressful, however, especially for people who fear they will fail at this task.

Of course, not all college students are young people. The older college student, who may be working while going to school, or returning to school after the children have left home or after retirement, encounters stressors as well. One of the major stressors of adults returning to school is the fear of failure. However, older students do have more experience to draw upon than younger students do, and this can help them understand and apply the information learned in school. College campuses are changing today, and the older student population is increasing. In an effort to help older students manage the stressors they will encounter, many colleges offer counseling for career changes, methods of study, fear of failure, and test taking. In effect, these are stress education activities.

(Dintiman and Greenberg, 72)

Psychologists

Experimental psychologists mostly work in scientific laboratories. They perform experiments to help develop a basic understanding of human nature. There are many different types of experimentalists. Some study such processes as perception, learning, or motivation in human and animal subjects. Others, such as the biological psychologists, investigate such things as the effects of drugs and surgery on performance. Developmental psychologists look at how people grow and mature from infancy to old age. Social psychologists study the behavior of people in groups and organizations. Educational psychologists are primarily interested in how humans

Notes

learn in schools and other educational settings. Most experimentalists teach at colleges and universities. Others work in government and industrial laboratories.

More than half of the psychologists in the US work in what are called "applied settings." *Clinical psychologists,* for example, try to help people like Joe solve their problems. Most clinical psychologists work in clinics or hospitals, or treat patients in their own offices. *Counseling psychologists* usually offer expert advice on personal or educational problems. Some counseling psychologists are in private practice; others work in schools or clinics. *Industrial psychologists* tend to work for business or government organizations. For the most part, they deal with personnel problems and management decision making.

Experimental psychologists may observe behavior either in the laboratory or in real-life settings. They also develop tests and take surveys. Applied psychologists may also develop knowledge in a variety of ways. But chiefly they conduct interviews, give tests, and apply information gathered from experiments and surveys. Clinical and counseling psychologists usually deal with one person at a time, although occasionally they work with groups. Industrial psychologists tend to focus on work groups and organizations.

(McConnell, 17)

Practice: Take notes on the following portion of a psychology chapter.

Notes

Chapter: Sigmund Freud

Libido

While Freud was mapping out the *regions* of the mind, he tried as well to determine the psychological processes that energized, focused, moved, and even blocked the spotlight of consciousness.

Freud decided the body continually creates *psychic energy* much as a dynamo continually produces electrical power. Freud called this psychic energy *libido* and believed that it is the motivating force that "powers" *all of your thoughts, feelings, and behaviors.* A build-up of libidinal energy creates a painful drive state that forces you to become aware of some unsatisfied need. You then tend to focus on activities that will allow you to release the pent-up energy and hence reduce the drive. Thus *expending* libidinal energy is associated with sensory pleasure, while *repressing* libidinal energy almost always leads to painful tension and anxiety.

Id, Ego, and Super-ego

An infant is *conscious*, but it doesn't "know" enough to keep itself alive. How then does it survive its first years on earth?

The Id

According to Freud, you were born with a collection of basic instincts or biological drives that are the *source* of your libidinal energy. Freud called this set of instinctual drives the *id,* from the Latin word for "it." These drives are mediated by the lower centers of your brain, such as the limbic system and the hypothalamus. As such, the id is buried at the deepest level of your unconscious mind, far removed from conscious reality. Freud described the id as a "cauldron of seething excitement" which has no inner structure or organization, which operates in illogical ways, and which seeks only the pleasures that come from discharging its pent-up energies.

The id keeps an infant alive because it obeys the *pleasure principle,* which demands the *immediate* gratification of all the infant's needs. Since most of these needs are related to bodily functions—such as hunger, elimination, aggression, and sensual stimulation—the newborn child survives because it is *biologically programmed* to release its libidinal energy in life-sustaining ways.

The Ego

The id helps the infant survive because it is selfish and impulsive. But, as the infant matures, the "real world" begins to make demands on the child—and punishes it severely if the child doesn't respond in socially appropriate ways. As the infant is forced to delay gratification of some of its instinctual needs, it gradually becomes aware that there is a difference between its own desires and those of other people. And, once the child begins to distinguish between itself and the outer world, its *ego* or *conscious self* comes into being.

According to R. M. Goldenson, the *ego* is a group of mental functions or processes that enable you to perceive, reason, make judgments, store memories, and solve various problems. Your id was present at birth. Your ego developed slowly as you learned to master your impulses, delay immediate gratification of your needs, and get along with others.

Your ego is the part of your personality that is in communication with the external world. For the most part, then, your ego operates at a conscious (or preconscious) level, but it includes some unconscious processes as well. Thus like your id, your ego is subject to the demands of the pleasure principle. But as you mature, your conscious self is more influenced by what Freud called the *reality principle*—the practical demands of daily living. On occasion, however, your ego may be torn between the opposing forces of pleasure-seeking and reality. It often resolves this conflict by trying to satisfy your instinctual desires (id) in socially approved ways.

The Superego

There is more to your personality, however, than id and ego, than pleasure principle and reality principle. For, as you grow, the people around you demand that you adopt society's "rules and regulations." To do so, you must build up a *conscience* that keeps you from violating the rules, and an *ego-ideal* that you must strive to attain. Freud called this part of your personality structure the *superego* and regarded it as a part of your ego that splits off and begins to act on its own.

Your superego develops slowly (and unconsciously) during the first five years of your life as you increasingly imitate the thoughts and actions of others—primarily those of your parents. During adolescence and young adulthood your superego matures even more as you come into contact with adults (other than your parents) whom you admire and whose values you take on in part or in whole. For the most part, this socialization process occurs at an *unconscious* level, as your superego gains the power to criticize and supervise both your id and your ego. Your superego is thus your "unconscious voice" that helps you discriminate social rights from wrongs without your being aware of why you do so.

(McConnell, 484–486)

Practice: Take notes on the following portion of a psychology chapter.

Notes

Chapter: Objective Tests

Objective tests have several purposes. One is to *measure present traits, skills, and knowledge.* Another is to *predict future performance.* A few objective tests attempt to serve both purposes simultaneously.

Achievement Tests

An achievement test is a psychological scale that measures how much you have learned about a given topic. The test does *not* indicate either *why* you learned as much as you did, nor how much you *could have learned* under different circumstances. People with high IQ's will do poorly on achievement tests if they haven't learned much about the topic, or if they once knew the material but now have forgotten it. People with lower IQ's will do well if they have studied the subject thoroughly. Thus achievement tests tell us little or nothing about your motivation or your IQ. They simply measure present knowledge.

Academic achievement tests are useful within school systems, but they don't necessarily give us much information about how well people will do after they have left the academic world. For instance, early in 1981 many city officials in Sacramento, California took a sixth grade math achievement test. The mayor missed 20 out of 25 questions, and the best score made by any of the officials was 80 percent correct. However, dozens of sixth grade students got perfect scores. Presumably the city officials once knew the material, but had simply forgotten it over the years.

Aptitude Tests

In its purest form, an aptitude test attempts to determine whether you possess enough of a certain trait—or certain personality factors—in order to succeed in some job or other situation. Some are fairly simple tests that measure such skills as mechanical or clerical aptitude. Other tests, such as those given to prospective airline pilots, measure a broader range of abilities. Scores on these simple scales tend to predict future performance fairly well.

Unfortunately, many devices that are called *aptitude* tests are really combinations of *achievement* and *intelligence* tests. The Scholastic Aptitude Test is one such, for it tends to measure how much you have already learned about a given academic subject and thus is an achievement test. The SAT also measures—to some extent—how "test wise" you are, and how good you are at solving the types of problems you are likely to face on examinations while in college. Since the SAT correlates rather well with intelligence test scores, it provides a rough measure of your IQ. And since SAT scores are reasonably good at predicting future grades in college, it would seem to be a *valid* academic screening device.

There are, however, several problems associated with scales such as the SAT. One problem is the cultural bias that seems to be built into the test. People from disadvantaged backgrounds tend to do poorly on the SAT, although they may do well if admitted to college. The second problem has to do with coaching. As we noted earlier, both Bloom and Broder and Whimbey have shown that teaching people *cognitive skills* tends to raise their SAT scores. The fact that disadvantaged individuals benefit more from coaching than do advantaged individuals tends to reinforce the belief that the SAT is a biased instrument.

Finally, there is the thorny issue of what SAT scores and school grades actually mean *outside of college*. Harvard psychologist David McClelland noted in 1973 that both your IQ and your SAT scores predict rather well how you will do in medical school. But they tell us little or nothing about how good a physician you will be. For the skills and traits needed to practice medicine successfully and humanely in real-life settings are quite different from those required to get through medical school.

Similar evidence about the limited usefulness of the scholastic aptitude tests comes from a 1963 study by L.R. Harmon. He investigated the professional contributions of physicists and biologists who had taken advanced degrees. He then compared the actual "life's work" of these scientists with their achievement test scores taken when they were still students. Harmon reports no correlation at all between what the scientists actually accomplished in life and their test scores as students.

Personality Tests: The MMPI

Not all objective tests have to do with achievement or aptitude. Some attempt to measure personality traits. The *Minnesota Multiphasic Personality Inventory,* or MMPI, is perhaps the most widely used personality test in the United States today. The MMPI was created to be as reliable as possible—and research suggests that its reliability is indeed fairly high.

In its original form, the MMPI consisted of some 560 short statements that were given to large numbers of people, some of them mental patients, some of them presumably normal. The statements mostly concern psychiatric problems or unusual thought patterns, such as: (1) Someone is trying to control my mind using radio waves; (2) I never think of unusual sexual situations; and (3) I never have been sick a day of my life. When you take the MMPI, you respond to each statement either by agreeing or disagreeing, or by saying that it is impossible for you to respond at all.

As you might expect, the mental patients used in the original sample reacted to many of the statements in quite different ways than did the normal subjects. Depressed or suicidal patients gave different responses than did patients diagnosed as being schizophrenic or paranoid. The authors of the test were able to pick out different groups of test items that appeared to form "depression" scales, "paranoia" scales, "schizophrenia" scales, and so forth. If an otherwise normal individual takes the test and receives an abnormally high score on the "paranoia" scale, the psychologist interpreting the test might well worry that the person could become paranoid if put under great psychological stress or pressure. By looking at the pattern or *profile* of a subject's scores on the different MMPI scales, a psychologist might also be able to predict what areas of the subject's personality needed strengthening.

(McConnell, 526–527)

Using Patterns of Organization

Introduction 21

Textbook authors usually present material clearly and in an organized manner. Thorough comprehension begins when you preview the chapter. It continues when you sense the way in which authors organize the ideas presented in the chapter. Consider four basic methods of organizing text information:

Four Ways of Organizing Information

Patterns	Facts Are Organized to Emphasize
Simple Listing:	**a description of characteristics**
Sequence of Events:	**a chronological order or the steps in a process**
Cause—Effect:	**the reasons or results of an action or idea**
Comparison— Contrast:	**the similarities or differences between two subjects**

Example

Sample Chapter Titles	Probable Pattern of Organization
1. Four Characteristics of a Good Speech	Simple Listing
2. The Stages of Growth in the Human Embryo	Sequence of Events
3. The Economic Aftermath of World War II	Cause—Effect
4. Monogamy vs. Polygamy	Comparison—Contrast

Learning to preview helps you to anticipate the way an author organizes and presents ideas. You can then apply this understanding to note-taking and test-taking situations and to recognizing that an author may vary the method of organization in a chapter. When you understand the author's way of organizing ideas, you can focus attention on key relationships in the chapter. No longer are facts read, noted, and recalled in isolation. Rather, you begin to read subject material in a different manner. You now sense a relationship between ideas, and can use that understanding to develop better test-taking techniques.

Each of the following chapters focuses on one of the ways or patterns authors use to organize and present subject material. Developing a sense of each pattern will lead to a deeper understanding of text material, more meaningful note-taking techniques, and a proficiency in anticipating and forming test questions similar to those instructors ask.

Understanding a Simple Listing of Facts

22

Sensing a Listing in Paragraphs

When an author describes the characteristics of people, places, events, objects, or ideas, the author is discussing their important features. These are unique qualities that should be noted and remembered.

Example

A verbal interview offers many advantages. First, a spoken exchange gives the interviewer a chance to follow up on ideas that emerge as important. Another advantage of face-to-face interviewing comes from the nonverbal messages that accompany a spoken exchange. Tone of voice, emphasis on certain words, disfluencies such as stammers and stutters, and the other paralinguistic clues we discussed in Chapter 5 add a new dimension to any interaction. For the same reason, in-person interviewing with its accompanying postures, gestures, facial expressions, and so on offers more information.

(Adler and Rodman, 204, 205)

Notes

A. <u>A list of</u> advantages in verbal interviews
   1. interviewer can follow up important ideas
   2. nonverbal clues are evident
   3. postures, gestures, facial expressions offer information

Sensing that this paragraph presents a listing of facts about a verbal interview, you can put that understanding to use by including the phrase "A list of" in your written main idea. The details make up the list of advantages. The restated main idea and details are concise, clear, and useful; they indicate that you will want to remember a list. There is no particular order in which to remember the advantages; just be sure to remember them. Entire chapters won't usually follow an organization of listing, but subtitled sections and paragraphs often do.

When an author organizes information to emphasize a list of characteristics, components, or features of a subject, the author is using a **simple-listing pattern.** What you will want to remember are the parts or features of the subject.

There are many key words that signal the simple-listing pattern:

several	many	first
second	finally	also
in addition	(1)	(2)
key considerations	following components	are made up of

Practice: Read the following paragraphs and mark any word or phrase that signals a listing of ideas. Your written notes should include the phrase <u>a list of</u> in the main idea. The first paragraph has been started for you.

Notes

1.   The earliest and still most common way of classifying criminals is in terms of the legal title identifying the criminal act. Thus, a felon is one accused or convicted of a felony: a murderer, one accused or convicted of a murder. This method suffers from a variety of disadvantages. (1) It creates a false impression of homogeneity by suggesting that individuals committing the same act are similar in other respects. (2) It tells nothing about the person, or about his personal characteristics or circumstances. (3) It creates a false impression of specialization by implying that criminals confine themselves to one particular kind of crime for which they happen to be caught or convicted at a particular time. (4) Finally, though it purports to define the actor in terms of his act, its precision in describing the act itself is frequently questionable.

(Korn and McCorkle, 143)

A. <u>A list of</u> 4 disadvantages of classifying criminals by their crimes
  1. _____
     _____
  2. _____
     _____
  3. _____
     _____
  4. _____
     _____

or

<u>A list of</u> 4 disadvantages of classifying criminals by their crimes	• • • •

2.   A culture cannot survive if it does not satisfy certain basic needs of its members. The extent to which a culture achieves the fulfillment of these needs will determine its ultimate success. "Success" is measured by the values of the culture itself rather than by those of an outsider. A culture must provide for the production and distribution of goods and services considered necessary for life. It must provide for biological continuity through the reproduction of its members. It must enculturate new members so that they can become functioning adults. It must maintain order among its members. It must likewise maintain order between its members and outsiders. Finally, it must motivate its members to survive and engage in those activities necessary for survival.

(Haviland, 43)

3.   There are many ways these disease organisms are transmitted from a source of infection to a susceptible person. Transmission can be accomplished through direct contact with an infected person, as in touching, kissing, or sexual intercourse. Transmission of infectious agents can also take place through indirect contact, that is, through the touching of contaminated articles, such as eating utensils, clothing, food, and so forth. Droplet in-

fection takes place when the agents are carried by small droplets through the air, usually a matter of a few feet. This represents a type of contact infection because of the close proximity of the people involved. Coughing, sneezing, or talking can serve as a means of facilitating droplet infections.

(Sinacore and Sinacore, 215)

4.   Reward or positive reinforcement has at least two functions. First, it gives you pleasure, usually by satisfying some need or reducing some drive or deprivation state. But rewards also have an *informational* aspect to them, for they give you feedback as to how well you are doing, and how close you are coming to a goal. Positive reinforcement, then, *increases the probability* that an organism will *repeat the response* that led to the appearance of the rewarding stimulus.

(McConnell, 355–356)

Practice: Read the following paragraphs and mark any phrases that signal a listing pattern. Include the phrase <u>a list of</u> in your main ideas.

Notes

1.   The ten functions most commonly performed by the purchasing department, as reported by the National Industrial Conference Board, are to issue purchase orders, interview suppliers' sales representatives, negotiate with suppliers, analyze bids and prices, select suppliers, make adjustments with suppliers, maintain records on suppliers, develop new sources of supply, follow up on orders, and maintain a list of suppliers.

(Mauser and Schwartz, 295)

2.   Everything required for good delivery of any speech becomes even more important in a speech to persuade. You must maintain good eye contact throughout to communicate your sincerity; if you fail to look at your audience, they may suspect a lack of honesty on your part. Your movements, gestures, and voice must be firm and strong to indicate confidence in yourself and in your arguments; a speech of this kind puts you in a leadership position, and people will not follow someone who lacks self-confidence or confidence in his or her proposals. You must emphasize your important points with vocal inflections, gestures, and visual aids so your listeners can follow the logical steps in your argument. And you must use dialogue, gestures, and facial expressions throughout your speech, especially in your anecdotes, to convey your own feelings about the problem and to help the audience feel the emotional impact of the problem as well as understand it.

(Shrope, 151–152)

3.   The four subdisciplines of anthropology—sociocultural anthropology, archeological anthropology, biological anthropology, and anthropological linguistics—are united by their common interest in human behavior of the present and past. Sociocultural anthropology examines diversity of the present and very recent past. Archeological anthropology approaches diversity of the past by reconstructing social, economic, religious, and political patterns of prehistoric populations. Biological anthropology examines diversity, in genetic make-up and outward expression, of human populations of the present and past. Anthropological linguistics documents diversity among contemporary languages and studies ways in which speech habits change in different social situations and over time spans of various lengths.

(Kottak, 14)

4.   What functions do prisons perform? Most obviously, they punish criminals for their wrongdoings. Clearly, prisoners do suffer, and most people consider this just. . . . Second, prisons are supposed to protect the public by taking known deviants off the streets. In addition, they are thought to act as a deterrent, discouraging those on the outside from breaking laws and those on the inside from committing crimes after they are released. Finally, there is much talk of prisons rehabilitating offenders through training programs and counseling, so that when they are released they approach life with a new, law-abiding frame of mind. These different goals present each prison warden with a difficult and conflicting mandate.

(Light and Keller, 341)

5.   There are a variety of ways to distribute samples. Direct sampling places the sample in the hands of the consumer through house-to-house distribution, which is very costly, or through the mail. The post office permits addressing mail to "occupant," making costly mailing lists unnecessary. Samples may be distributed to customers by dealers. It is difficult, however, to be certain that the retailer distributes the samples properly, if at all. Samples also may be offered through advertisements or mail containing coupons or "hidden offers" that may be mailed to the manufacturer for the product or redeemed at the retail store. These coupons may offer the product free or at a reduced price. Demonstrators in retail outlets may distribute samples and at the same time show the customer how to use the sample properly. Finally, sampling may be done through sample kits, generally sold, that contain a variety of samples. One manufacturer of pipe tobacco, for example, offered a package containing a number of different blends so that the consumer could choose the one that most appealed to him.

(Mandell, 604)

Anticipating Test Questions

When you understand the simple-listing pattern in a subtitled section of a chapter, you will be better able to organize your notes for a test. Simple lists require you to note and remember a group of ideas that describe a topic. You should be able to define or state in your notes the characteristics of each given topic, that is, the details that support the main idea. When you study simple-listing notes, you can anticipate probable test questions. In the following example, mark the main idea and details. Then notice how those ideas appear in the sample questions.

Example

Good drivers share several characteristics. First, they are usually alert. Next, they do not drive recklessly. They also are aware of their vehicles' power and capabilities. Finally, they observe traffic regulations.

Here are key simple-listing words and phrases used in objective test items, that is, matching questions, fill-ins, multiple choices, and true-false statements.

1. **List** or **state several characteristics** of a good driver.
2. **Give** or **enumerate several characteristics** of a good driver.
3. A good driver does **all** but which of the following:
   a. Drives recklessly
   b. Is alert
   c. Is aware of car's power
   d. Observes traffic rules
4. **One characteristic** of a good driver is that he or she observes traffic _____.
5. T or F: **An example of** good driving is not being alert.

Here are key simple-listing words and phrases used in essay test questions (see Chapter 29 for a discussion of essay tests).

1. **Discuss the ways** in which good drivers cope with weather conditions.
2. **Describe all** the essentials of good driving in bad weather.
3. **Explain how** good drivers manage to drive in bad weather.
4. **Develop fully the essentials of** good driving.

When you sense that the author is presenting a descriptive list of ideas, use the phrase **a list of** in your written main idea. Be sure that the details are a list that describes the main idea.

When studying, use the simple-listing pattern to anticipate a test question by using one of these typical key words in a sample test question:

list	**describe**	**enumerate**	**develop**
give	**state**	**explain**	**discuss**

Practice: Take notes on the following selections and mark any words that signal the simple-listing pattern in each. Then answer the questions that follow each selection. The question following selection one is done for you.

Notes

1. **Classifying Consumer Goods**

A variety of classifications have been suggested for consumer goods, but the system most typically used has three subcategories: convenience goods, shopping goods, and specialty goods. . . .

First, convenience goods are products the consumer seeks to purchase frequently, immediately, and with a minimum of effort. Items stocked in twenty-four-hour convenience stores, vending machines, and local newstands are usually convenience goods. Newspapers, chewing gum, magazines, milk, beer, bread, and cigarettes are all convenience goods.

Next, shopping goods are products purchased only after the consumer has compared competing goods in competing stores on bases such as price, quality, style, and color. A young couple intent on buying a new color television may visit many stores, examine perhaps dozens of television sets, and spend days making the final decision. The couple follows a regular routine from store to store in surveying competing offerings and ultimately selects the most appealing set.

Finally, the specialty goods purchaser is very familiar with the item sought and is willing to make a special effort to obtain it. A specialty good has no reasonable substitute in the mind of the buyer. The nearest Mercedes dealer may be twenty miles away, but the driving enthusiast might go there to obtain what he or she considers one of the world's best-engineered cars.

(Boone and Kurtz, 233)

What essay question would your instructor ask about this selection?

Describe or explain the three categories of consumer goods.

Notes

2.   Religion serves a variety of functions for the individual and for society. People turn to religion to cope with death and to make personal hardships and tragedies easier to bear. They look for the meaning of life and for guides to regulate its conduct. Religion can glorify and celebrate human events and provide transcendent or visionary experiences. To individuals it offers a powerful means of relieving anxiety, but it is not the only force to do so. Over the course of human history scientific mastery has replaced metaphysical explanations with physical ones, raising the problem of whether religion might one day become irrelevant. For society, religion creates and reinforces a sense of community and consensus. It discourages antisocial behavior and offers a means for reintegrating transgressors. It serves to legitimize secular authority.

(Light and Keller, 496)

Write four true-false questions based on this passage.

1. _____

2. _____

3. _____

4. _____

Write a short essay question that would test a student's understanding of the passage.

_____

_____

Notes

3.   The first primates appeared about 70 million years ago, and our own line began to diverge from that of our closest relatives, the great apes (the chimpanzee, gorilla, and orangutan) about 14 million years ago. The higher primates share a number of common characteristics, all of which give us clues to our own evolutionary background. First, they tend to be very sociable: they live in groups with a high degree of affection and interaction among the members. Second, they have high intelligence, with brains that are exceptionally heavy in relation to body weight. This is especially true of human beings, whose brains have evolved to an unparalleled complexity. Third, primates have sensitive hands. In other mammals the hands have become highly specialized: the horse has a hoof, the porpoise a flipper, the bat a wing. Other animals can only paw or nuzzle at objects, but primates can use their hands as instruments for lifting, gripping, and manipulating things. In the higher primates the thumb can be placed opposite the forefinger to give a firm, precision grip. The importance of this single characteristic cannot be overestimated: try writing, sewing, or using any tool efficiently without opposing the thumb to the forefinger! Fourth, primates are extremely vocal; they are among the noisiest of all species and constantly call and chatter to one another. In human beings, this characteristic has developed into the capacity for language. Fifth, primates have a potential for upright posture. Many primate species are capable of walking on their hind legs, although they do so only rarely and for short distances. In human beings, however, bipedal (two-footed) standing and walking have become normal.

(Robertson, 53)

List the words that give you a clue to the paragraph organization.

_____   _____

_____   _____

Write a short essay question that your instructor might ask to test your comprehension of this paragraph.

_____

_____

Answer the question you've made up. (Use separate paper.)

4. Nonverbal Communication Serves Many Functions

Verbal and nonverbal communication are interconnected elements in every act of communication. Nonverbal behaviors can operate in several relationships to verbal messages.

First, nonverbal behaviors can *repeat* what is said verbally. If someone asked you for directions to the nearest drugstore, you could say, "North of here about two blocks," and then repeat your instructions nonverbally by pointing north.

Nonverbal messages may also *substitute* for verbal ones. When you see a familiar friend wearing a certain facial expression, you don't need to ask, "How's it going?" In the same way experience has probably shown you that other kinds of looks, gestures, and other clues say, "I'm angry at you," or, "I feel great," far better than words.

A third way in which verbal and nonverbal messages can relate is called *complementing*. If you saw a teacher talking to a student whose head was bowed slightly, whose voice was low and hesitating, and who shuffled slowly from foot to foot, you might conclude that the student felt inferior to the teacher, possibly embarrassed about something. The nonverbal behaviors you observed provided the context for the verbal behaviors—they conveyed the relationship between the teacher and student. Complementing nonverbal behaviors signal the attitudes the interactants have for one another.

Nonverbal behaviors can also *accent* verbal messages. Just as we can use *italics* in print to underline an idea, we can emphasize some part of a face-to-face message in various ways. Pointing an accusing finger adds emphasis to criticism (as well as probably creating defensiveness in the receiver). Shrugging shoulders accent confusion, and hugs can highlight excitement or affection. As you'll see later in this chapter, the voice plays a big role in accenting verbal messages.

Nonverbal behavior also serves to *regulate* verbal behavior. By lowering your voice at the end of a sentence, "trailing off," you indicate that the other person may speak. You can also convey this information through the use of eye contact and by the way you position your body.

Finally—and often most significantly—nonverbal behavior can often *contradict* the spoken word. People often simultaneously express dif-

Notes

ferent and even contradictory messages in their verbal and nonverbal behaviors. A common example of this sort of "double message" is the experience we've all had of hearing someone with a red face and bulging veins yelling, "Angry? No, *I'm not angry!*"

(Adler and Rodman, 115, 116)

Write two sample essay questions an instructor might ask. Try to use a listing signal word or phrase in each.

1. _____

_____

2. _____

_____

Practice with Longer Selections: Read the following passages carefully. After you take notes on the material, answer the questions.

Selection of Employees

Various methods are used, including tests and guided interviews, to select qualified employees. In large companies the following forms and procedures generally play a part in the selection process.

The Application Form and Résumé

On a job application the applicant is generally asked to give name, age, sex, marital status, address, telephone number, work history, military record, education and training, and general references. Other information, such as membership in organizations, hobbies, and job goals, may also be requested.

The Civil Rights Act of 1964 and its amendments make it illegal for employers to request a personal picture or information on race, creed, religion, national origin, or ancestry on either an application form or in a "help wanted" advertisement. However, an exception is made when such information relates to a <u>bona fide</u> requirement for the job.

For higher-level jobs, applicants also commonly provide employers with a <u>résumé.</u> This is an outline of one's employment history, educational achievements, skills, and other job qualifications. Career <u>aspirations</u>, references, and other information may be included as well.

While the applicant will still have to complete a job application, the résumé provides an opportunity to personalize, to present significant details of one's accomplishments—something that is seldom possible within the confines of a standardized application form.

The completed application form and the résumé serve four purposes. First, the act of filling out an application or organizing a résumé is itself a test of the applicant's suitability, since it reveals something of his ability to follow directions, to express himself, and to give facts neatly and correctly. Second, it is a guide for the interviews that follow. Third, if the applicant is hired, the forms become a part of the person's permanent work record and are used for reference when promotion, transfer, discharge, or similar actions are considered. Last, if there are no immediate job openings for an applicant, the forms may be filed and referred to when appropriate openings do occur.

Testing the Applicant

Tests attempt to measure the applicant's mental and mechanical abilities, skills, personality, or attitudes. Generally, the lower the level of the job, the more reliance is placed on tests and the higher the level the job the less use is made of tests. People applying for executive-level positions are often not tested, since management skills—such as leadership ability and ability to communicate effectively—are difficult to measure in this way. The employer must rely more on the person's record of accomplishments and on the impressions made in the interviews.

Most personnel directors recognize that tests—even those that directly measure a skill—will not precisely predict the applicant's performance if he or she is hired. While tests may measure ability to do something, they do not measure whether someone wants to do something. The fact that a person can add and subtract without making mistakes does not necessarily mean he or she will make a good bookkeeper. Tests are not good at measuring such intangibles as ambition, energy, boredom potential, or ability to work under pressure. Thus, the wise personnel director uses tests only as a rough guide.

Checking References

Personnel departments often check the claims and background of applicants, or ask outside investigators to do the checking. Educational claims are verified and former employers are usually questioned to determine how the applicant performed on his or her previous job and how he or she was regarded by associates. Credit ratings may also be checked, and if the applicant was convicted of a crime, police and court records may be checked. A major falsification on an employment application or résumé is grounds for refusal to consider an applicant or immediate dismissal if the applicant is already on the job. In some cases employers may even prosecute and sue for damages.

Interviewing

During the selection process, applicants are almost always interviewed one or more times by the person for whom they will work if hired. There may also be interviews with other people, such as the next higher person in the department or a peer of the applicant (i.e., a person who holds a position similar to the one in which the applicant is interested).

During interviews, the applicant may be asked to explain or expand on statements made on the application form or résumé. If the employee is expected to meet the public, the interview will reveal what sort of general impression the applicant will make in personal-contact situations. In such cases the interviewer will probably take special note of the applicant's use of language, grooming, posture, and mannerisms. The interview also gives the applicant an opportunity to find out more about the job and working conditions. Interviews with the applicant's potential supervisor are particularly valuable, in that both parties get an idea of whether they would enjoy working with the other person.

The interview is often the most important stage in the hiring process. Unfortunately, it may also be the stage at which discrimination in hiring takes place. Since hiring decisions are always somewhat subjective, it is difficult to determine the particular reasons why one applicant was accepted and another was rejected.

(Mauser and Schwartz, 239, 240, 241, 243)

Notes

Selection of Employees

Notes

Vocabulary: Using the context, define the following words.

1. bona fide: _____

2. résumé: _____

3. aspirations: _____

4. intangibles: _____

5. verified: _____

6. peer: _____

Sample Questions: Answer these questions on separate paper.

1. What are some features of the résumé and the application form?
2. What are the advantages and shortcomings of testing low-level and high-level job applicants? List and describe the characteristics of each.
3. Discuss at least five advantages the interviewer receives from conducting interviews with prospective job applicants.
4. List three advantages the interviewee has during an interview.
5. What kinds of things might an employer be checking on when he or she hires an outside investigative firm?

The Departments Within the Hospital

The Medical Department.   The medical department includes the members of the medical staff who are responsible for the care of the patients. Often this department <u>designates</u> a board whose members keep watch on the quality of medical care given by the physicians attending the patients.

The Nursing Department.   The nursing department includes registered nurses, practical nurses, nurse's aides and often orderlies. These people usually give direct care to the patients under the guidance of the head of the department and according to the policies of the hospital administration. The head of the nursing department is usually the director of nursing; she may have an assistant director as well as supervisors and head nurses to carry out administrative duties.

If a hospital has a school of nursing, it is often included within the department of nursing. However, a school of nursing can <u>affiliate</u> with a hospital and yet be a separate entity financially and administratively.

The Dietary Department.   The dietary department includes dietitians as well as cooks, kitchen maids, tray girls, and dishwashers. The chief responsibility of this department is to supply food to the patients, and sometimes to the staff of the hospital. This responsibility usually includes the preparation of therapeutic diets for many patients.

The Laboratory Department.   The function of the laboratory department is to perform laboratory tests ordered by the physician. These tests include blood serology and chemistry tests, urinalyses, bacteriological tests, and analyses of specimens for pathological diagnosis. The laboratory technician collects some specimens; the nursing staff is responsible for the collection of others.

The X-ray Department.   One of the obvious functions of the x-ray department is to take x-rays of patients as ordered by the physician. In addition to the x-ray technicians who work in the department, many hospitals employ doctors who are specialists in interpreting x-rays and can aid other physicians in their diagnostic work. The use of x-ray equipment, radium, etc., for therapeutic purposes is also an important function of many x-ray departments.

The Maintenance Department.   The number of services provided by the maintenance department varies from hospital to hospital. The department often performs carpentry, plumbing and electrical services, as well as cleaning, heating and possibly laundry services.

The Pharmacy Department.   The pharmacy department provides pharmaceutical supplies that are ordered by the physician for the patients. The pharmacist prepares some of the medications himself, while others are purchased commercially and are dispensed to the nursing units.

The Business Department.   This department is responsible for the financial business of the hospital. It prepares the patient's hospital bills, administers the hospital payroll and is involved in budget preparation and general hospital business.

The Central Supply Department.   The central supply department of the hospital is usually responsible for the cleaning, the sterilizing and often the delivery of equipment used in the institution. It may also be responsible for the purchasing of supplies if the hospital has no purchasing department. In some hospitals the central supply department is included in the nursing department.

The Personnel Department.   This department is responsible for hiring personnel and for job placement within the hospital. Some nursing departments assume the responsibilities for hiring nurses, whereas at other hospitals this task is handled entirely by the personnel department.

The Social Service Department.   Many hospitals have a separate department to provide welfare services for the patients. Among the concerns of the social worker are family finances and nursing home placement. Usually he maintains liaison between the hospital and other welfare agencies in the community.

Other Departments.   Large hospitals may have many other departments. There may be separate departments for electrocardiography, physical therapy, public relations, and hairdressing. The services that hospitals supply vary considerably; however, no matter how many departments there may be, they have a common goal: to help meet the needs of the hospital patient and his family.

(Du Gas, 21–22)

Notes

The Departments Within the Hospital

Vocabulary: Using the context clues in the selection, define the following.

1. designates: _____

2. affiliate: _____

3. therapeutic: _____

4. pathological: _____

5. liaison: _____

Sample Question: Answer the following essay question on separate paper.

You are admitted to your local hospital for a minor operation. Describe the personnel who will serve your needs during your stay in the hospital.

Faulty Listening Behaviors

Although it may not be necessary or desirable to listen effectively all the time, it's sad to realize that most people possess one or more bad habits that keep them from understanding truly important messages. As you read the following list of these poor listening behaviors, see which ones describe you.

1. Pseudolistening.   Pseudolistening is an imitation of the real thing. "Good" pseudolisteners give the appearance of being attentive: They look you in the eye, nod and smile at the right times, and even may answer you occasionally. Behind that appearance of interest, however, something entirely different is going on, for pseudolisteners use a polite <u>facade</u> to mask thoughts that have nothing to do with what the speaker is saying. Often pseudolisteners ignore you because of something on their mind that's more important to them than your remarks. Other times they may simply be bored or think that they've heard what you have to say before, and so they tune out your remarks. Whatever the reasons, the significant fact is that pseudolistening is really counterfeit communication.

2. Stage hogging.   Stage hogs are only interested in expressing their ideas and don't care about what anyone else has to say. These people will allow you to speak from time to time, but only so they can catch their breath, use your remarks as a basis for their own <u>babbling</u>, or to keep you from running away. Stage hogs really aren't conversing when they dominate others with their talk—they're making a speech and at the same time probably making an enemy.

3. Selective listening.   Selective listeners respond only to the parts of a speaker's remarks that interest them, rejecting everything else. All of us are selective listeners from time to time, as for instance when we screen out media commercials and music as we <u>keep an ear cocked</u> for a weather report or an announcement of time. In other cases selective listening occurs in conversations with people who expect a thorough hearing but only get their partner's attention when the subject turns to their favorite topic—perhaps money, sex, a hobby, or some particular person. Unless and until you bring up one of these pet subjects, you might as well talk to a tree.

4. Filling in gaps. People who fill in the gaps like to think that what they remember makes a whole story. Since we remember half or less of what we hear, these people manufacture information so that when they retell what they listened to, they can give the impression they "got it all." Of course, filling in the gaps is as dangerous as selective listening: The message that's left is only a distorted (not merely incomplete) version of the message that could have been received.

5. Assimilation to prior messages. We all have a tendency to interpret current messages in terms of similar messages remembered from the past. This phenomenon is called *assimilation to prior input.* A problem arises for those who go overboard with this and push, pull, chop, squeeze, and in other ways mu- tilate messages they receive to make sure they are consistent with what they heard in the past. This unfortunate situation occurs when the current message is in some way uniquely different from past messages.

6. Insulated listening. Insulated listeners are almost the opposite of their selective-listening cousins. Instead of looking for something, these people avoid it. Whenever a topic arises they'd rather not deal with, insulated listen- ers simply fail to hear it, or rather to acknowledge it. If you remind them about a problem—perhaps an unfinished job, poor grades, or the like—they'll nod or answer you and then promptly forget what you've just said.

7. Defensive listening. Defensive listeners take innocent comments as personal attacks. Teenagers who perceive parental questions about friends and activities as distrustful snooping are defensive listeners, as are insecure bread- winners who explode anytime their mates mention money, or touchy parents who view any questioning by their children as a threat to their authority and parental wisdom. It's fair to assume that many defensive listeners are suffering from shaky public images and avoid admitting this by projecting their own insecurities onto others.

8. Ambushing. Ambushers listen carefully to you, but only because they're collecting information that they'll use to attack what you have to say. The cross-examining prosecution attorney is a good example of an ambusher. Needless to say, using this kind of strategy will justifiably initiate defensive- ness on the other's behalf.

9. Insensitive listening. Insensitive listeners offer the final example of people who don't receive another person's messages clearly. As we've said before, people often don't express their thoughts or feelings openly but instead communicate them through subtle and unconscious choice of words and/or nonverbal clues. Insensitive listeners aren't able to look beyond the words and behavior to understand their hidden meanings. Instead, they take a speaker's remarks at face value.

It's important not to go overboard in labeling listeners as insensitive. Of- ten a seemingly mechanical comment is perfectly appropriate. This most often occurs in situations involving phatic communication, in which a remark derives its meaning totally from context. For instance, the question "How are you?" doesn't call for an answer when you pass an acquaintance on the street. In this context the statement means no more than "I acknowledge your existence, and I want to let you know that I feel friendly toward you." It is not an inquiry about the state of your health. While insensitive listening is depressing, you would be equally discouraged to hear a litany of aches and pains everytime you asked, "How's it going?"

(Adler and Rodman, 94-97)

Notes

Faulty Listening Behaviors

Vocabulary: Use the context of the selection to define each word.

1. facade: _____

2. phatic communication: _____

_____

3. babbling: _____

4. mutilate: _____

5. keep an ear cocked: _____

Sample Question: Locate the definition of poor listening at the right that matches its faulty behavior style at the left and place its number on the line.

Faulty Behavior Style

_____ Insensitive listening
_____ Assimilation
_____ Pseudolistening
_____ Ambushing
_____ Stage hogging
_____ Insulated listening
_____ Filling in the gaps
_____ Selective listening
_____ Defensive listening

Definition of Poor Listening

1. Gathering information to use in a later attack on the speaker
2. Making up what you don't hear or can't remember
3. Taking any off-handed comment as a direct personal attack
4. Appearing to listen when you are really "a thousand miles away"
5. Distorting what someone says because of what you've heard about their topic in the past
6. Shutting out any reference to a topic
7. Taking over the conversation at every possible opportunity to express your ideas
8. Not being able to sense the unspoken clues behind the spoken words
9. Responding only to what you are interested in

Sample Essay Question: Which of the poor listening habits are your friends guilty of? Are you guilty too? Describe in a paragraph the way you or a friend are guilty of one of these habits.

Understanding a Sequence of Events

23

Sensing a Sequence in Paragraphs

When an author presents facts in their chronological order, the author is giving the reader events in a logical sequence. The order in which things happen is often important and should be noted and remembered. In the example, mark the words that signal a chronological order. Then check the set of notes that reflects the most logical way of remembering the facts.

Example

The alarm clock didn't go off on time. Jim awoke with a start and rushed through his morning routine. First, he washed and dressed. Next he joined his family and gulped down a quick breakfast. He then grabbed his coat and ran to the bus. After all this, Jim got to work on time but was completely exhausted.

_____ A. The Things Jim Does

1. had breakfast
2. washed and dressed
3. rushed routine
4. tired at work
5. awoke with a start
6. ran to bus
7. alarm didn't work
8. grabbed coat

_____ B. Events in Jim's Morning

1. alarm was late
2. awoke suddenly
3. rushed routine
4. washed and dressed
5. breakfast with family
6. grabbed coat
7. ran to bus
8. tired at work

Sensing that the paragraph follows a specific sequence of events, you can put that understanding to use by including the word "events" in your written main idea and by noting the details in a chronological order. Not only should you remember what Jim did, but you should also remember those facts in the order in which they occurred. The "B" main idea and details are concise, clear, and useful; they indicate that you will want to remember a sequence of "events."

Your understanding and recall of text material can sometimes depend on the order in which the information is presented. If you change that order, the facts are no longer logical and correct. If ideas are presented in **sequence**, the main idea usually reflects that sequence. For example, the main idea contains phrases like "the steps in," "the process of.". . . The details are the steps in that sequence.

Understanding a Sequence of Events 113

> The following words should be remembered as some typical signals of a sequence. They often appear in detail sentences.
>
> | after | when | first | next | then | last | dates |
> |-------|------|-------|------|------|------|-------|
> | finally | numbers | today | later | early | since | before |

Practice: Read this paragraph and complete the notes that accompany it. Use the word steps in the main idea and list the details in their correct chronological order. The words that signal a sequence are marked for you.

Notes

The SQ3R Study (Method,) if practiced, develops greater reading efficiency. The student must (first) survey, or preview, the assigned reading. (Next,) he questions his knowledge of general ideas. The 3Rs come (next.) These are: read the passage, recite major ideas, and (finally) review the material. Thus, the title SQ3R applies to a specific system of study.

A. Steps in _____
  1. _____
  2. _____
  3. _____
  4. _____
  5. _____

or

Steps in	•
	•
	•
	•
	•

Practice: As you take notes on the following paragraphs, use a phrase such as steps in or the process of in the main idea. Then list the details in their correct order and mark any words that signal a sequence in the paragraph.

Notes

1.   Blood follows a path through the human body. It starts through the aorta and passes into the arteries, arterioles, and capillaries. It then flows into the veins, proceeds through the vena cava into the right auricle, and then into the right ventricle. It next flows through the pulmonary vein. The blood continues into the left auricle, then goes through the left ventricle into the aorta. This completes a very basic description of the flow of blood in the body.

2.   An army programmer created an entirely new (although imaginary) military base staffed by 200 nonexistent people. He then opened 200 checking accounts for their paychecks and the money rolled in. Everything went so smoothly that it took him several

Notes

months to realize that he would probably never be caught as long as the base continued to operate. He had become—in a few months—a self-made millionaire but could think of no way to close the base! An accidental bombing, mass food poisoning, or 200 desertions all seemed too unbelievable. So finally he simply turned himself in.

(Boone and Kurtz, 367)

3.   An auto dealer who receives a shipment of new cars may sign an agreement with a local commercial bank or other financing agency for a loan in the amount of the shipment. Title to the cars passes to the lender, but the cars themselves (the inventory) remain with the dealer. The lender periodically checks the dealer's inventory to make sure that all the required collateral is still in the borrower's hands. As cars are sold, the dealer pays a portion of the sales price plus interest to the lender.

(Boone and Kurtz, 476)

4.   Groups stand the best chance of developing effective solutions to problems if they begin their work by identifying the problem, avoiding the mistake of failing to recognize hidden needs of individual members. Their next step is to analyze the problem, including identification of forces both favoring and blocking progress. Only at this point should the group begin to develop possible solutions, taking care not to stifle creativity by evaluating any of them prematurely. During the implementation phase of the solution the group should monitor the situation carefully and make any necessary changes in its plan.

(Adler and Rodman, 267)

Practice: As you take notes on the following paragraphs, use a sequence phrase in your main idea and be sure that the details follow logically. Mark any words or phrases that signal a sequence in the paragraph.

Notes

1.   Among the cells which migrate to the inflamed area are macrophages, large cells with a large, round nucleus. These cells have the ability to engulf small particles, including microorganisms, and to bring them into the cell in a little vacuole. The products of the digested microorganisms are released and taken up by smaller cells with eccentrically placed nuclei. These lymphoidal, as they are called, then undergo rapid, successive cell division. Some of the descendants manufacture proteins, called antibodies, in response to the digested fragments taken up by their forebears. The antibody is released into the bloodstream and has the ability to recognize the microorganism from which the original fragment came. The antibody unites specifically with the microorganism to try to destroy it. The fragments of the microorganism, as well as the microorganism itself, are traditionally called antigens. The union of antigen with antibody, which removes or destroys the invading antigen, is one form of the immune response.

(Mayer, 213)

2.   Once the problem is defined and refined, the next step is to develop a research plan that will provide the necessary information for its solution. The first step is to determine the objectives of the research—that is, what is to be accomplished. The second step is to determine the specific information desired. Care in this task will prevent the problem of ending up with useless information. Step three is to determine the possible sources for the required information, considering, for example, the experimental or descriptive methods or a combination of them. Each method must be weighed in the light of such factors as cost, time, accuracy, dependability, and completeness. The fourth step is to write a formulation of the research plan in complete detail; the complexity of this written report depends of course on the complexity of the planned research. This report becomes the working plan for the research. Frequently, it is submitted for approval before the research is undertaken.

(Mandell, 124)

3.   Throughout a child's early years, society imposes a set of expectations for that particular sex. The parents give the baby either a girl's name or a boy's name and wrap it in either a blue or a pink blanket. At home, they raise the baby either as a girl or a boy, with toys and regulations they consider appropriate for its sex. From the beginning, parents behave differently with baby girls and baby boys; they tend to talk more to a baby girl and roughhouse more with a baby boy. Such different treatment contributes to the child's growing sense of masculinity or femininity—and eventually to that of the adult he

Notes

or she will become. As the child behaves more like one sex or the other—displaying growing gender identity—then, more and more, this behavior elicits appropriate reciprocal behavior from others. When a small girl, for example, begins to flirt with her father, he may flirt back. Or when his small son begins to play with a ball, he may play catch with him. Such responses, in turn, further reinforce the child's gender identity. By the age of three or four, most children have developed a strong gender identity and have begun to learn their gender roles; that is, they have learned to imitate the behaviors their society considers appropriate for their sex.

(Grawunder, Pruitt, and Steinman, 57)

4.   All traffic offense adjudication systems involve seven separate elements. Law enforcement begins the process by apprehending the motorist and issuing a complaint and summons. Identification and case preparation follows, providing the transition from enforcement to adjudication by clerical processing. The motorist is notified of his rights and responsibilities, a plea is entered, and, if necessary, a formal trial or hearing is conducted resulting in a judgement during the decision-making phase. The next step is sanctioning, which sets the penalty for violating the traffic laws. Compliance involves actions such as the collection of fines and enforcement of other sanctions which assure the authority of the adjudicatory agency. The review phase gives the motorist an opportunity to appeal adverse decisions. Finally all actions taken against a motorist are brought to the attention of the State Department of Motor Vehicles (or Registry) during the driver licensing and control phase.

(Law Enforcement Assistance Administration, 6)

Anticipating Test Questions

When you understand the sequence-of-events pattern in a subtitled section or chapter, you will be able to organize your notes for future recall. A sequence of ideas requires that you remember the steps or order in which things happen. To note or recall facts in proper sequence reflects an understanding of the important relationship of ideas. When you sense a sequence of events, you can note ideas logically, and you can anticipate test questions. In the following example, notice how the sequence of events appears in the questions.

Example

Sigmund Freud

Freud was born in 1856 in what is now Czechoslovakia, but he lived for almost 80 years in Vienna. After taking his degree in medicine in 1881, Freud spent many years in the laboratory studying the human nervous system. He was almost 40 when he married. And since being a laboratory scientist didn't pay much money (then or now), Freud went into private practice in order to earn enough to support a family. Much of his theory of psychoanalysis grew out of the observations he made on these patients.

Around 1885, Freud spent several months in Paris, studying hypnosis with Charcot. Freud's interest in personality theory seems to have begun about this time. He returned from Paris believing that hypnosis might be useful in curing some types of insanity.

(McConnell, 482)

Notes

I. Sigmund Freud
   A. His early years
      1. born 1856
      2. Vienna life
      3. medical degree
      4. studied human nervous system
      5. married at 40
      6. began private practice
   B. Beginning interest in hypnosis
      1. 1885 studied with Charcot
      2. developed interest in personality theory
      3. believed hypnosis might help cure some insanity

Here are key words and phrases that signal a sequence of events in matching questions, fill-ins, multiple choices, and true-false statements.

1. **Rearrange the order of events** to show Freud's early years.
2. **List the steps** that led Freud to believe in hypnosis.
3. **Before** Freud arrived in Paris, he _____
4. **Match** the event in Freud's life with the correct year.

Here are key words and phrases that signal a sequence of events in essay test questions (see Chapter 29).

1. **Trace the events** that led to Freud's use of hypnosis.
2. **Develop the order of events that led to** Freud's introduction to hypnosis.

When you sense that the author is presenting facts in a special sequence, use the phrase **steps in** (or another phrase signaling sequence) in your written main idea. Be sure that the details are listed in the correct order.

When studying, use the sequence-of-events pattern to anticipate a test question beginning with one of these typical key words or phrases:

trace	**rearrange the order**	**develop**
give the steps	**diagram**	**number**

Practice: Read each selection and mark any phrases that signal a sequential ordering of ideas. Your notes on the following selections should include a phrase that indicates a <u>sequence</u> in the main idea and details that follow in a logical order. Then develop a short-answer question and an essay question that you could use as an aid in studying the material.

Notes

1.   During the second week of its life, the embryo grows to 1.5 millimeters in length, and its major body axis begins to develop. (In this and subsequent measurements, the fetus is measured from crown to rump.) As it elongates, a primitive streak forms, very similar in appearance to the primitive streak of the chick. Cells migrating through the primitive streak form the mesoderm, establishing the three-layered embryo. The dorsal part of the body can be seen to be divided into somites.

During the third week, the embryo grows to 2.3 millimeters long, and most of its major organ systems begin to form: the neural groove . . . , which is the beginning of the central nervous system (spinal cord and brain), the first organ system to develop; the heart and blood vessels; the primitive gut; and the muscle rudiments.

(Curtis, 624)

Short-Answer Question

_____

_____

Essay Question

_____

_____

Notes

2.   **Stages of an Interview**

Opening. This beginning stage serves two important functions. Most importantly, it establishes the tone of the relationship between interviewer and subject: formal or informal, relaxed or tense, serious or humorous. Just as the first stages of a date or party will generally shape what comes later, the success or failure of an interview is often determined before the first question is asked. Besides setting the tone, a good introduction will also give the interviewee a preview (or reminder) of the interviewer's goals and what subjects will be covered.

The usual format for an opening begins with some sort of greeting, which includes any introductions that are necessary. A period of informal conversation sometimes follows, in which the interviewer and subject talk about subjects of mutual interest not necessarily related to the interview topic. This period gives both people a chance to get settled and acquainted before getting down to business. This greeting stage may sound artificial—which it often is. But there's no need to discuss obviously trivial subjects or act phony here: the idea is to sincerely establish some common ground between interviewer and subject.

In the final stage of the opening the interviewer should preview topics of discussion and brief the subject on plans for proceeding: "I appreciate your giving me the time. I expect my questions will take about forty-five minutes. I'd like to start by learning how you got started, then go on to talk about what you've learned during your career, and finish by asking for any suggestions you have which might help me in my career."

Body.   This middle stage of the interview is the longest. It's here that the interviewer asks the questions that were planned before the meeting.

While the list of questions is important, it's sometimes a mistake to follow them precisely. Some areas will need more exploration, while others won't seem worth pursuing. The trick in the body of the interview is to focus on all the important content areas in a way that seems most comfortable to both interviewer and subject. (We'll have more to say about the roles of each party shortly.)

Closing.   In many ways the closing is similar to the opening. Instead of previewing, however, the conclusion is a time for reviewing what's occurred during the interview. This helps ensure that the interviewer has correctly understood any points that might be unclear and has gotten the general tone of the subject matter correctly.

The closing is also a time to establish the future of the relationship between interviewer and subject: to decide if any future meetings are necessary, possibly to set a date for them. Finally, it's usually good to conclude the interview with an exchange of sincere pleasantries.

(Adler and Rodman, 214)

Short-Answer Question

_____

_____

Essay Question

_____

_____

3.   The United States was an importer of textiles and apparel from its beginnings. Early in our history, before the American Revolution, we did not have the capability to produce our own cloth. At that time, English law prohibited textile craft or machinery from reaching these shores. Textiles had to be imported until Americans learned how to make machines in the late eighteenth century. Until the end of World War II we were complacent about the importation of many categories of apparel: styles from Paris, cashmere sweaters from Scotland, sweaters that reflect the art of Norway and Ireland, and leather goods from Italy. These were high-priced fashions considered status symbols for those who could afford them. The apparel industry was not concerned, since there was no serious inroad into the core of its business. The United States fashion industry's strength has always been as a mass producer for mass acceptance, and the importation of nominal amounts of high-styled merchandise was really a positive factor, since some of the styles could be copied and sold at moderate or popular prices.

     After World War II the picture changed. The jet airplane brought easy and fast access to world markets, and retailers started to explore the capabilities of foreign makers. At first their approach was cautious. American retailers traveled to Europe and purchased principally shoes and sportswear. This merchandise was not exactly trouble-free, despite newness of styling and a willingness on the part of consumers to accept it. The difficulties were that foreign specifications were not always suitable for American customers, the delivery periods were extended, goods were not usually received in time for seasonal retail selling, and the stock composition was frequently out of balance—for instance, too many jackets for the number of skirts in outfits that were designed as inseparables (coordinates designed to go together, not sold as separate units). But, in the main, the results were sufficiently satisfactory for retailers to continue the practice.

(Packard, 147)

Short-Answer Question

_____

_____

Essay Question

_____

_____

4. Science as a "Detective Story"

Science is, to a great extent, the fine art of solving mysteries. Nature gives us a puzzle—human or otherwise. For some reason—perhaps due to our own peculiar nature as human beings—we are motivated to solve the puzzle. We can either use our "hunches" and make wild guesses about the answer—which is what people did for most of the history of civilization. Or we can adopt a logical process of some kind in trying to find the solution to the puzzle.

Even today, most people prefer using their guesses and their *subjective* feelings when trying to unravel any mystery that they encounter. And that's fine—as a starting point. But ever since the Middle Ages—when the scientific method was first developed—a growing number of individuals have tried to apply a logical, *objective* approach to the solution of human problems.

This objective approach is called the *scientific method,* and it is based on the belief that most mysteries have *natural* or *measur-*

able causes. To use the scientific method properly, you must follow several steps:

First, you have to recognize that a mystery of some kind exists that needs solving, and that the mystery probably has a natural cause. We might call this step *perceiving the problem.* Then you make as many *initial observations* about the mysterious circumstances as you can. And you try to make your observations as exact and complete as possible.

You use the results of your initial observations to come up with a *tentative solution* or "first guess" as to what the answer is. Scientists often call this step "making an hypothesis." The solution you pick, however, will be determined by how you view the problem—and the world. If you think events that take place in the world around you are affected primarily by *supernatural powers,* then the scientific method won't help you much. But if you believe that a mysterious event might have a *natural cause,* then perhaps you can state your "tentative solution" or hypothesis in a way that will help you determine what that cause is.

Next, you draw up a plan for *testing objectively* whether or not your first hunch about the solution was correct. This test may merely involve making further observations about the puzzling affair. Or it may involve performing an experiment in which you "do something" to the puzzle in order to get a reaction of some kind.

Whether you merely observe things, or whether you undertake an experiment of some kind, you then look over the data and try to decide as unemotionally as possible whether your tentative solution to the problem was right or wrong. If your initial hypothesis was wrong, you will revise it and make some more observations. But if your first hunch was correct, you probably will refine your solution to the mystery by *testing it again and again.* And to do so, you will again need to make predictions about future events.

If these further predictions turn out to be accurate, then most likely your solution to the puzzle was correct. But if your predictions were incorrect, you should realize that you goofed up somewhere along the way. And you will have to start the problem-solving process all over again.

(McConnell, 6–7)

Short-Answer Question

_____

_____

Essay Question

_____

_____

5. Daily Operation of the System

On a day-to-day basis, the operation of the system begins with the reservation clerk. Let's assume that we are watching a clerk who has just received a call from a customer requesting a reservation for three on Flight 713 for December 22. As the clerk turns to the terminal, he is about to engage in a conversation with the computer; a copy of this conversation is shown. . . .

The clerk starts by pressing an ATTENTION button on the terminal; in response, within (usually) a fraction of a second, the computer causes the words "ENTER FLIGHT?" to be printed on the terminal (the question mark is the computer's way of asking the clerk to enter some data). The clerk types the flight number and date, and hits the RETURN button on the terminal keyboard. The flight and date are then printed, under control of the computer, for visual verification by the reservation clerk, and the status of the flight—capacity, number of seats assigned, and number of seats available—is printed. This information is followed by a question, "DO YOU WISH TO MAKE A RESERVATION?", after which control returns to the clerk.

The reservation clerk responds by typing "YES" or "NO"; in this example, the response was "YES," followed by the hitting of the RETURN key. The computer asks "HOW MANY SEATS?" The clerk responds with the number of seats requested, after which the computer confirms the reservation and asks for the passenger names. Once all the names have been entered, the computer thanks the clerk, and moves on to the next transaction. Total elapsed time for this transaction was in the neighborhood of 30 seconds.

(Davis, 332–334)

Fill in this chart to show the sequence of the "conversation" between the clerk and the computer.

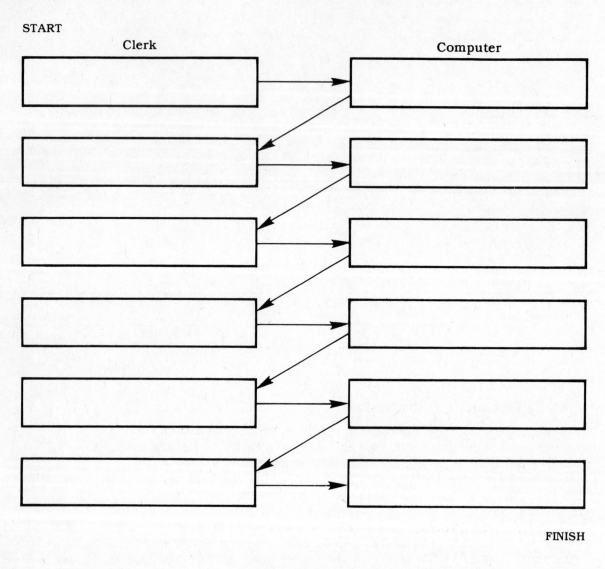

Short-Answer Question

_____

_____

Essay Question

_____

_____

Practice with Longer Selections: Read the following passages carefully. After you take notes on the material, answer the questions.

Customer Execution

Introduction

"Customer Execution" is a term signifiying the complex process by which a broker will carry out a customer's order to buy or sell a specific stock. Actually, this system involves many people operating in varied locations. Customer Execution is a fairly routinized process through which millions of stock shares are exchanged daily. The smooth operation of stock exchanges is but one example of the complex individual skills and procedures vital to effective functioning in big business.

First Steps in the Broker's Office

The customer first calls the broker with an order to buy, for example, 100 shares of IBM stock. A special order ticket is filled out by the broker, who relays this to the order clerk. He, in turn, clocks the time on the ticket. Available to the clerk are phones connecting to the stock exchange. A call to buy IBM shares is put through the firm's clerk at the exchange. At this point the action shifts from the brokerage office to the firm's representatives at the exchange.

Steps at the Exchange

A second order ticket is prepared by the floor clerk, who carefully notes the time on it. The clerk then calls the company's trader through a special code. The trader takes the order and proceeds to the trading area. The trader voices the order to the person conducting the trades. The buy order of 100 IBM is matched to a sell order at the best possible price at that time. Thus, the stock has been purchased.

Completing the Procedure

The floor trader receives the traded price and informs the floor clerk, who in turn relays the information back to the office clerk. He reports the purchase to the broker, who can then call the customer to report the specific price paid.

Shortly, the buyer will receive written notification of the transaction, along with a statement of monies owed. Up to this point, no money has changed hands. The procedure is based on a system of oral communication used by stock companies and exchanges throughout the world. When the monies are paid, the customer will receive the actual stock certificates. Thus, Customer Execution has been completed.

Customer Execution

Vocabulary: Using the context, define the following words.

1. Customer Execution: _____

2. routinized: _____

3. brokerage: _____

Sample Question: Arrange the following steps in their correct sequential order according to the passage.

_____ The clerk calls the floor trader through a special code.
_____ The broker reports the purchase to the customer.
_____ The customer receives the stock certificates.
_____ The order clerk relays the buy order to the floor clerk.
_____ Buy and sell orders are matched at a trading price.
_____ The company order clerk clocks the time on the ticket.
_____ The customer gets a bill.
_____ The floor clerk clocks the time on the ticket.
_____ The broker writes a purchase ticket.
_____ The trader takes the order to the trading area.
_____ The customer places an order for 100 IBM shares.
_____ The order clerk receives a ticket from the broker.

Sample Essay Question

What question might your instructor ask about "Customer Execution" on an essay test? _____

_____

Administrative Adjudication

A Case History

Joan M. was driving up Sixth Avenue early one morning when she was suddenly forced to swerve sharply to her left to avoid colliding with a reckless taxi. Somewhat agitated and preoccupied with what might have been a serious accident, she failed to notice the change of traffic signals and proceeded through a red light at Thirty-eighth Street.

A traffic officer observed the infraction and directed Joan to pull her car to the side of the road. Joan received a summons which explained that she could plead "guilty," "guilty with an explanation," or "not guilty" of the alleged offense.

Joan Pleads Guilty

Joan decided to plead "guilty." She simply mailed the citation with the prescribed fine to the Central Office. Her plea was accepted, her record was updated, and her payment processed. However, if the computer had found that she had too many "points" on her record due to prior traffic violations or other irregularities such as outstanding summonses, her "guilty" plea would have been rejected. If that had happened Joan would have been required to appear in person at the Manhattan office, where the hearing officer would have determined an appropriate sanction.

Joan Pleads Guilty with an Explanation

Joan felt that her near accident was a mitigating factor and should be considered in determining her penalty, so she decided to plead "guilty with an explanation." She appeared in person at the Manhattan hearing office. The police officer was not required to appear. Joan was given approximately five minutes to present her explanation. After listening to her and reviewing her past record, the hearing officer imposed an appropriate sanction. Joan accepted the sanction and her driving record in Albany was immediately updated through a computer terminal located in the hearing room. If Joan had rejected the sanction, it would have been reviewed by an administrative appeals board.

Joan Pleads Not Guilty

Joan decided to plead "not guilty" because she honestly believed that the light was still yellow when she entered the intersection. When she received her summons to appear for a hearing, the date and time had been scheduled by the police officer, based on the availability of hearing rooms and the police officer's schedule. This reduced the time that Joan and the officer had to wait before the case was heard. It was set for 3–4 weeks after the incident while details of it were fresh in Joan's mind. It could have been rescheduled at her request.

The hearing took place in the Manhattan AAB office, presided over by the hearing officer. Joan and the police officer were sworn. The officer presented the case for the prosecution and was questioned by the hearing officer and cross-examined by Joan, who could have retained legal counsel if she had wished. Then Joan testified and was questioned by the hearing officer and the police officer. After the evidence was presented Joan was permitted to make a statement in the form of a closing argument. All this took about twenty minutes.

The entire hearing was tape recorded. Although rules of evidence were not strictly applied, evidence which was in the nature of a privileged communication, violated Joan's constitutional rights, or referred to her past driving conduct was excluded. This permitted Joan to present her case effectively without the aid of counsel.

The hearing officer found Joan "guilty." He accessed the Department of Motor Vehicle's computerized data base using a telephone hook-up, and her driving record was displayed on a TV screen. (Prior to reaching his decision, this information would not have been available to the hearing officer.) Based on the nature and circumstances of the violation and Joan's driving record, he then imposed an appropriate sanction, in this case a fine. He could have suspended or <u>revoked</u> her license, assigned her to rehabilitative driving classes, or imposed a combination of these sanctions.

Joan Appeals

Joan was dissatisfied with the decision, and she appealed it to a three-member administrative appeals board. The tape recording of her proceedings was transcribed and submitted for review to the appeals board. Within 60 days the board reaffirmed the decision. Joan was still dissatisfied and requested judicial review of her case. The court upheld the administrative decision. Joan was not permitted to make a personal appearance before the appeals board but was allowed to comment on the transcript in writing.

(Law Enforcement Assistance Administration, 9–13)

Vocabulary   Using the context, determine the meaning of the underlined words in the selection.

1. infraction: _____

2. agitated: _____

3. alleged: _____

4. sanction: _____

5. mitigating: _____

6. revoked: _____

Sample Essay Question

What question could your instructor ask about this passage for an essay test?

_____

_____

Administrative Adjudication

Fill in the following chart by listing the steps required in each type of action.

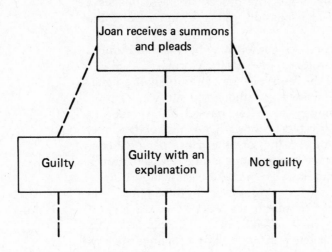

Stages of Communicable Diseases

Transmission and Infection

Transmission is the process whereby a disease is "caught." In this process the pathogen is carried in some way from its source and enters the body in an area where it can cause infection. Infection is the process that establishes a pathogen as a parasite in the body. Transmission and infection require the following:

1. Pathogen. The pathogen, as discussed earlier, may be one of a number of viruses, rickettsia, bacteria, fungi, protozoa, or parasitic worms.

2. Source. The source, also called the reservoir, may be human or animal, soil, water, food, or an object that will allow the pathogen to survive.

3. Method of transmission. Pathogens are often passed from person to person or animal to person by direct or indirect contact. Transmission by direct contact can occur as a result of touching, kissing, or other close personal contacts. Indirect transmission takes place when pathogens are released during coughing, breathing or talking. Transmission also can take place when contaminated food or water is taken into the body. Many diseases are transmitted only by the bite of a specific vector, such as a mosquito or a tick.

4. Portal of entry. The pathogen must get into the body. This occurs as the result of a vector bite, a wound, or entry through body openings such as the nose, mouth, eyes, genital openings, and skin and mucous membranes.

5. Susceptible host. A susceptible host is an individual who is unable to resist the pathogen and its effects.

Should all five links in the cycle be present, then infection will occur and the cycle may begin again. If any link in the cycle is broken, however, the disease will be prevented.

Incubation Period

Once a communicable disease has been caught, it progresses through an incubation period, the interval between the time of infection and the appearance of the first symptoms. During this time, the pathogen multiplies in numbers until it is abundant enough to overcome the body's defenses and produce the disease.

The incubation period may be as short as a few hours or as long as several months or years, depending on the disease. Most diseases have an incubation period of a few days to a few weeks. Generally, diseases are not contagious during the early part of the incubation period, but they do become highly contagious at the end of the period, just before the symptoms appear.

Prodromal Period

The prodromal period is the time during which vague, nonspecific symptoms of a disease appear. This period lasts from a few hours to several days and is characterized by fever, headache, and various aches and pains. Many diseases are highly contagious during this period.

Typical Illness Period

After the prodromal period a group of specific symptoms will appear. This is the typical illness period during which a recognizable disease is present. (The term syndrome often is used to indicate a group of symptoms characteristic of a given disease.) In this period the person is usually ill enough to stay home, so the number of people exposed is sharply reduced.

Recovery Stage

The recovery stage begins when the body defenses start to overpower the pathogens and the symptoms disappear. It is important to remember that the pathogens are still present in the body during the recovery or convalescence stage. If a <u>convalescent</u> person resumes full activity too soon, the body defenses will be weakened, and there may be a <u>relapse</u> (return of the symptoms of the disease).

(Jones, Shainberg, and Byer, 417, 419)

Notes

Stages of Communicable Diseases

Vocabulary   Using the context, give technical meanings for the following.

1. transmission: _____

2. pathogen: _____

3. infection: _____

4. reservoir: _____

5. vector: _____

6. incubation period: _____

7. prodromal period: _____

8. convalescent: _____

9. relapse: _____

Sample Question: Number the stages at the left in their correct sequence. Then match each stage with its corresponding symptom(s). (Some stages will be matched with more than one symptom.)

_____ Prodromal
_____ Recovery
_____ Transmission and Infection
_____ Typical Illness
_____ Incubation

_____ recognizable symptoms appear
_____ pathogens move into a host
_____ pathogens are overcome by body defenses
_____ a host can't resist pathogens
_____ pathogens overpower body defenses
_____ many diseases become highly contagious
_____ indirect contact releases a pathogen
_____ nonspecific symptoms appear
_____ pathogens multiply in the host
_____ relapses may occur
_____ pathogens get into point of entry
_____ exposure to new hosts is reduced

Sample Essay Question

What essay question could an instructor ask about this selection? _____

_____

Understanding Causes and Effects

24

When an author writes about the reasons for an idea or action or the results of an idea or action, the author is presenting causes and effects. You should be able to recognize and distinguish between causes and effects.

Example

The extreme heat led to the buckling of the sidewalk.
        (cause) ⟶ (effect)

Here, the cause is the extreme heat; the effect is the buckling sidewalk. The effect may in turn cause something else.

Example

The extreme heat led to the buckling of the sidewalk, which caused a traffic jam for several hours.

    (cause) ⟶ (effect)

extreme heat ⟶ buckling sidewalk ⟶ traffic jam
                    (cause) ⟶ (effect)

The buckled sidewalk, a result of extreme heat, directly causes the traffic jam. Also, the extreme heat indirectly causes the traffic jam.

> When one occurrence leads directly, or sometimes indirectly, to another, we say it **causes** something. What it causes is called the **effect** or **result.**

Example

The bridge gave way due to heavy flooding.
        (effect) ⟵ (cause)

Here the collapse of the bridge is the result of heavy flooding. The effect is stated before the cause in this sentence.

> Although the event that is the cause always occurs before the effect or result it produces, the cause does not have to be stated before the effect. Sometimes the effect is stated first.

Practice: Read each sentence below. Highlight the cause and circle the effect.

1. People have done tremendous damage to the environment.
2. Your insurance rates may rise after you have an accident.
3. Poor grades are the result of not devoting enough time to one's studies.
4. Coming upon the accident, he was horrified at the sight before him.
5. The author revised his manuscript according to the critics' suggestions.
6. Since we were cautioned to drive carefully, we were able to avoid the accident, which tied up traffic.
7. The end of the war signaled a time of prosperity in which we could once again buy the luxuries we desired.
8. At last we could rest easy; we had passed those terrifying final exams.
9. Speaking before an unfamiliar audience, I was armed with the key facts to support my position. I was rewarded by a tremendous ovation.
10. Getting the worst dormitory rooms, registering last, and knowing no one was the price I had to pay for being a lower freshman.

Sensing Causes and Effects in Paragraphs

When you recognize that an author makes a statement about an idea or a subject and develops that statement with reasons (causes) and/or results (effects), you can make that understanding work for you. Use that pattern in stating the main idea, for example, "the causes of" or "the results of.". . . The details will then be a listing of those causes or effects.

Example

Each year, thousands of students drop out of high school for a variety of reasons. Educational surveys uncover many contributing causes. Some students see little relationship between class work and vocational goals. Economic pressures at home may force the teenager to seek full- or part-time employment. In addition, family responsibilities may demand much of the student's time. The daily school routine presents an unchanging and often boring schedule. Associated with this problem is the inability of school personnel to develop new programs and methods designed to meet the needs of potential dropouts. In addition to these factors, the student's own problems and needs may lead the student to drop out.

Notes

A. The reasons why students drop out of high school
 1. little relationship between classwork and jobs
 2. economic pressures at home
 3. family responsibilities
 4. school is boring
 5. no new school programs or methods to meet needs of potential dropouts
 6. student's own problems

Sensing that the paragraph gives the reasons or causes for high school students dropping out, you can put that understanding to work by using the word "causes" or "reasons" in the main idea. The details are a list of those causes. The restated main idea and details are concise, clear, and useful; they indicate that you will want to remember "the reasons."

When an author organizes information to show the reasons for something or the results of something, the author is using a **cause-effect pattern**. Here the author makes a statement and supports it with either the reasons for or results of that statement.

The following are some of the words that signal **cause** or **effect** in paragraphs or longer passages:

causes	makes	effects	therefore
leads to	affects	results	because of
thus	brings about	as a result of	outcome
	determines	consequence of	

Practice: As you take notes on the following text selections, use either phrase—causes for or effects of—in your main idea. Also, mark any words that signal either the causes or effects described in the paragraphs. The first one is started for you.

Notes

1.   The emotional (effects of) divorce are greater than the average person who has never been through it realizes. Both parties involved usually find it a painful experience emotionally, socially, and financially. It usually does not solve the basic human problems that were its true cause. New problems are created for both the divorced couple and any children they might have had. There is often a mixture of feelings of guilt and resentment. For some, the readjustment demanded is severe enough to call for the outside help of friends, clergymen, or a psychiatrist.

(Jones, Shainberg, and Byer, 356–357)

A. Emotional <u>effects</u> of divorce
   1. _____
   2. _____
   3. _____
   4. _____
   5. _____

or

Emotional <u>effects</u> of divorce	• • • • •

2.   Alcohol acts as a depressant on the central nervous system. This fact is the overall reason for the changes that result from drinking. Physiologically, it first depresses a part of the brain that is involved in coordinating various parts of the nervous system. It also interferes with the processes that control inhibitions and depresses the function of nerves, muscles, including the heart muscle, and many other body tissues. We do not know precisely how alcohol exerts these effects.

(Insel and Roth, 260)

3.   Selection of a specific drug (heroin, marijuana, alcohol) is generally dictated by factors such as availability, practices of friends, and social environment. Individuals tend to have drug experiences related to their own basic emotional needs. Drug users who never progress beyond social, occasional use may suffer physical discomfort (hangover, withdrawal, shakes, and so on) but they are able to control their emotional reaction to drugs. Psychological processes can override physical drug effects. Emotional factors are less important as use becomes heavier and more compulsive. For example, depressant drugs remove an individual from stresses and anxieties. Heroin does this very quickly; alcohol, slowly, but for a longer period of time. Hallucinogenic drugs and cocaine can compensate for a lack of "peak" or "high" experiences, can help control emotions, or can help someone deal with the frustrations leading to aggression. Amphetamines help increase output of physical energy.

(Jones, Shainberg, and Byer, 126)

4.   Throughout history, vegetarianism has been a way of life for some people. However, in the late 1960s, the popularity of this eating style rose significantly in the United States. The reasons for choosing a meat-free diet vary. For some, there is an almost religious belief that killing animals is unnecessary to nourish humans. Some feel we must resolve the question of food supply for the hungry masses of the whole world and, therefore, eliminate the high level of protein waste in the meat-centered American diet. Just consider one fact alone—it takes 16 pounds of grain and soy to produce 1 pound of beef. Others are concerned about the hormonal, antibiotic, and toxic additives to beef and fowl in the marketing process. Still others see industrial wastes contaminating our fish with mercury, mirex, or polychlorinated biphenyls (PCB) and want no part of this contamination. For example, the breast milk of nursing mothers who are vegetarians contains fewer pesticide residues. Whatever the reasons, the pursuit of this eating life style seems here to stay.

(Sinacore and Sinacore, 196)

5.   The era of the cowboy came to an end as the combination of factors that gave rise to it changed. The long cattle drives from Texas ended as more and more homesteaders and railroad lines interfered with them, and as new breeds of cattle derived from English and Scottish stock proved themselves superior to the longhorns, especially in the north. Then, too, the amount of open rangeland, most of which was government owned, diminished as railroads and homesteaders gobbled it up for themselves and as sheepmen competed for the remaining grazing land. Ultimately, the seemingly limitless rangelands proved quite limited. Barbed wire fences protected remaining grazing lands, while windmill-pumped tanks eliminated the need to range over vast areas for water.

(Haviland, 425)

Practice: Take notes on the following five passages and answer the question that follows each one.

Notes

1. Unions have great influence on the American economy, for several reasons. First, the largest unions, such as the Teamsters, have the power to bring the economy virtually to a standstill by calling a major strike. Second, the actions of organized labor set the pace for treatment of most other workers. For example, suppose organized labor wins a contract calling for higher wages, better fringe benefits, or more time off. In time, nonunion enterprises, because they compete for workers with unionized organizations, must offer their workers better employment packages also.

Third, many employers of nonunion workers want them to stay unorganized. These employers then may offer their employees as much—sometimes more—than union workers receive, hoping to remove the main incentives for joining a union.

(Mauser and Schwartz, 278)

What three effects do unions have on the American economy?

_____

_____

_____

2. Automation is spurred on by several factors. First, human labor is expensive. As employees demand higher wages, management turns more and more to automation. Second, many jobs have become too com-

Notes

plicated for human beings to perform competently and efficiently. Some industrial operations are much too rapid for the human eye to observe and react to. Third, some industrial activities are harmful or unsafe. Chemical industries, munitions factories, and nuclear energy installations, especially, have potential hazards. Automation reduces the potential number of accidents.

(Mauser and Schwartz, 302)

What factors encourage automation to occur?

_____

_____

_____

3.   Among the situational factors affecting the child's adjustment and progress within the school setting, probably none is as important as the teacher-pupil relationship. The kinds of teachers a child has will determine in great measure his school experience, will foster his overall development or will simply increase his difficulties and frustrations. Having the right teacher may help a child to overcome handicaps and make the most of his talents and interests, while having a teacher who is ill-suited to working with children generally, or with a particular child or group of children, may have serious and sometimes disastrous consequences. This may be especially true of teachers working with socio-economically disadvantaged, minority-group children, as will become evident later.

(Mussen, Conger, and Kagan, 491)

What effect does having the right kind of teacher have on a child?

_____

_____

_____

4.   Some of the manifestations of psychological problems in childhood are relatively easily understood. The child whose efforts at mastery behavior have met consistently with criticism or ridicule for his ineptness may be anxious and uncertain in the face of new and challenging situations and inclined to withdraw and avoid them. The child who has been subjected to an endless series of injustices or rejections, has had only harsh, arbitrary, or inconsistent discipline, and has not developed strong internal superego controls may emerge as angry, rebellious, unmanageable, and generally lacking in conformity to the social patterns one would expect of his age group. The child with overly meticulous, compulsive, overprotective parents who inhibit any evidence of spontaneous emotion and who place great emphasis on being controlled, orderly, and cautious may well end up being overly meticulous, cautious, and lacking in spontaneity himself.

(Mussen, Conger, and Kagan, 452)

What causes a child to be anxious and uncertain in new situations?

_____

_____

_____

_____

5.   According to the 1976 *Uniform Crime Reports,* crimes against the person are highest during the summer months and, with the exception of robbery, crimes against property also reach their peak during the summer months. Traditionally, these differences in crime by months have been explained as follows. Crimes against the person, such as murder and forcible rape, increase during the hot summer months when people are more visible and less clothed. More people are outdoors for such purposes as swimming, sunbathing, and other recreations. The violent crime of murder, which peaks in the month of July but is also very high in December and January, is attributed to the increased drinking over the holiday season and the congregation of relatives with resulting family disputes. Crimes against property peak in December or August, in the latter because people are away on vacation leaving their property more vulnerable, and in the former because of the need for an additional access to property during the holiday season. We noted that the FBI, in reporting that the rates

Notes

of serious crimes in this country for the last quarter of 1976 and the first quarter of 1977 were lower than at any other comparable period suggested that the decrease might be due in some measure to the bitterly cold winter.

(Reid, 81)

Why do property crimes increase in December and August?

_____

_____

_____

_____

Anticipating Test Questions

When you understand the cause-effect pattern in a subtitled section or chapter, you will be able to organize your notes for future recall. Understanding cause-effect relationships requires that you remember the reasons for or the results of something. You should now be able to study material with a specific goal in mind: to remember facts in a cause-effect relationship. When you sense a cause-effect relationship, you can note ideas logically and anticipate test questions. In the following example, notice how the effects appear in the sample questions.

Example

Wind affects sensible temperature because it makes us feel cooler by increasing our loss of body heat. Thus at high temperatures, wind will make us more comfortable, while at lower temperatures wind can make us very uncomfortable. The faster the wind speed and the lower the temperature, the greater will be the chilling effects caused by the wind.

(Gabler, Sager, Brazier, and Pourciau, 241)

Outline

A. The <u>effects</u> of the wind
   1. affects sensible temperature
   2. makes us feel cooler by increasing loss of body heat
   3. high temperature makes us comfortable
   4. lower temperature makes us uncomfortable
   5. faster wind and lower temperature, greater chilling effects

Here are several key words and phrases that signal cause-effect in multiple-choice, fill-in, and true-false questions.

1. What **effect** does the speed of the wind have on body temperature?
2. Low temperatures **will lead** to _____ comfort.
3. T-F: The loss of body heat **results from** high winds.

4. Which of the following **is not affected** by wind:
   a.
   b.
   c.
   d.

   Here are key words and phrases that signal cause-effect in essay test questions (see Chapter 29).

1. Describe the **effects** of wind on our body temperature.
2. How does wind **make us** feel uncomfortable on a cold day and **bring about** comfort on a hot day?

When you sense that the author is presenting facts in a cause-effect relationship, use the phrases **causes of** or **results of** in your written main idea. The details will be a list of those causes or results.

When studying, use the cause-effect pattern to anticipate a test question beginning with one of these typical key phrases:

give the reasons for	**what are the effects of**
what affects	**what is the outcome of**
what determines	**what results in**

Practice: As you take notes on the following selections, use either phrase—causes of or results of—in your main idea. Also, mark any words or phrases in the selections that signal either causes or effects. Finally, complete the questions that follow each selection or write typical questions an instructor might ask.

                                                        Notes

1.   **Union power.** Many people feel that unions are responsible for inflation. Their reasoning is as follows. Unions decide to demand a wage hike that is not warranted by increases in their physical output. Since the unions are so powerful, employers must give in to union demands for higher wages. When the employers have to pay these higher wages, their costs are higher. To maintain their usual profit margin, these businesspeople raise their prices. This type of cost-push inflation seemingly can occur even when there is no excess demand, even when the economy is operating below capacity at under full employment.

     The union-power argument rests on the unions having monopolistic or market power in their labor markets. In other words, some unions are so strong that they can impose

Notes

wage increases on employers, even when those wage increases are not consistent with increases in the productivity of their labor.

(Miller, 154)

Short-Answer Question

_____

_____

Essay Question

_____

_____

2.   What affects the price of a stock? You might say that people's psychological feelings are the only things that matter. If people think a stock's going to be worth more in the future, they will bid up the price. If they think it will be worth less in the future, the price will fall. However, that is not a very satisfactory theory. What are psychological feelings based upon? Usually, such feelings are based upon the stream of profits that the company is expected to make in the future. Past profits may be important in formulating a prediction of future profits. However, past profits are bygones and bygones are forever bygones. A company could lose money for 10 years and then make profits for the next 15.

     If a company gets a new management with a reputation for turning losing companies into winning ones, people in the stock market might expect profits to turn around and go up. If a company develops and patents a new product, one would expect the profits to go up. If a company has a record number of sales orders given to it for future months, one might expect profits to go up. Whenever profits are expected to rise, we typically find a rise in the value of the stock. That is, people bid up the value of the stock. Any information about future profits should be valuable in assessing how a stock's price will react.

(Miller, 409)

List five factors that influence the price of a stock.

_____

_____

_____

_____

_____

Essay Question

_____

_____

3.   We have affected our environment both directly and indirectly. We can divide our direct effects into three categories. First, we have had an impact on the animal population of the world, even eliminating certain species such as the bison or the whooping crane from their natural habitats (that is, from their natural homes or environments, though we may still be able to find some living in zoos). We have killed animals for food, for fun, and from fear. We have increased the populations of other species, such as cows, horses, cats, chickens, water buffalo, and sheep, that we use for food, play, or work. In fact, we reintroduced the horse to the new world where it had once existed, but had become extinct. Over-population of certain animals has occurred sometimes when we have introduced an animal to a new environment in which it has no natural enemies. It is partly for this reason that, once introduced, the rabbit population in Australia and the deer population in New Zealand expanded so rapidly. Rats have become one of the most widespread mammals and they have traveled from continent to continent as uninvited and unwelcome passengers on our ships. Other animals like flies, cockroaches, and pigeons have increased in number because, like ants, they can live on our garbage.

      Secondly, we have had effects upon the earth's vegetation similar to those we have had on animals. In the United States and many other countries large tracts of forest have been cleared, not just for timber but also to provide land for farming. . . . And certain grasslands like the pampas of Argentina or the midwestern prairies of the United States may not be the original vegetation at all, but may be the result of fires set in the past by human beings to drive out game.

And every time we have set out to farm the land we have changed the natural vegetation to one of our own making.

The third way we have directly affected our environment is through inorganic means. That is, every time a road is constructed or a mine dug or a dam built we change our natural surroundings. A city, where we walk on pavement all day, is one of the prime examples of our direct alteration of the natural world, as are the Dutch farmlands that would be beneath the sea if it were not for a system of dikes and dams.

(Gabler, Sager, Brazier, and Pourciau, 14–15)

In your opinion, have society's organic or inorganic environment controls been more damaging to the environment? Give examples to back up your answer.

Practice with Longer Selections: Read the following four selections. Take notes on each and answer the questions that follow.

Other Factors Affecting Consumption

Education.   Education affects consumer demand in two ways. First, it increases the number of wants. Until people know that a thing exists, they have no desire for it. Education brings one into contact with more customs, products, ideas, and ways of doing things, and these increase one's desire for material as well as nonmaterial things.

Second, education changes the character of wants. It tends to make individuals more discriminating, harder to please. Preferences in music, literature, recreation, and style change with increased education. Even color preferences may be affected: It was once found that college graduates tend to prefer pastels and subdued colors; those with less schooling usually like bright primary colors best.

Climate.   Manufacturers who sell nationally realize that differences in climate materially affect demand. The types of clothing worn in northern states differ in weight, weave, color, and frequently style from those worn in the South. Demand for sporting equipment, heating systems, air conditioners, and, to a certain extent, food, is affected by climate.

Retailers are usually more concerned with weather than with climate, for during extremes in weather, such as heat waves, consumers tend to postpone buying. Retailers in northern cities have learned that snow before Christmas stimulates buying, whereas warm weather depresses sales. A mild autumn results in fewer sales of winter clothing and a prolonged winter adversely affects spring clothing sales.

(Mauser and Schwartz, 386)

Other Factors Affecting Consumption

Sample Question: Place a check in front of the answer or answers that best complete the statement. Use the information in the passage to determine the answers.

1. Increased education leads to
_____ a. differences in northern buying patterns.
_____ b. differences in the desire for material goods.
_____ c. differences in the types of goods desired.
_____ d. differences between northern and southern buying patterns.
2. Retailers are chiefly concerned about
_____ a. weather patterns.
_____ b. future sales patterns.
_____ c. climate patterns.
_____ d. educational patterns.

Sample Essay Question: If you were opening a retail business in the United States, what factors would influence your purchasing and stocking of certain types of items?

Suicide

Suicide is the tenth leading cause of death in the United States today. The "official" annual suicide rate is about 12 per 100,000 population, and over 25,000 deaths are recorded as suicides each year. The actual suicide rate is probably closer to double the official rate, as many suicides are disguised as accidents or natural deaths to avoid loss of insurance money or stigmatization of survivors.

No group or class of people is free of suicide. Every person is a potential suicide, and almost everyone at some time gives some consideration to the possibility of suicide. However, the risk of suicide does relate to certain individual characteristics.

The most significant pattern in the incidence of suicide is the increase with advancing age. Suicide is rare among those under 14 years of age. The rate rises sharply in adolescence and sharply again among college students, for whom suicide is second only to accidents as a cause of death. Several factors are commonly associated with college suicides, the most frequent of which is academic failure. Failure brings not only the disappointment and disapproval of parents, but a shattering of personal self-confidence as well. The second leading cause of college suicide is the end of a love affair. When romance ends, there is more than just disappointment; there is the tumultuous feeling of being rejected and abandoned, the complete loss of self-esteem. College suicides often involve the reserved, <u>introverted</u>, or shy students who, lacking social contacts, tend to <u>internalize</u> their problems. Despite the alarming college suicide rate, many colleges offer little or no on-campus therapy for emotional problems.

The suicide rate rises again in middle age when the male realizes that his career goals have not been attained and are in fact now unattainable. The middle-aged woman may turn to suicide in reaction to menopause, if she feels "finished" as a woman, or upon the departure from home of her children, after which she may no longer feel useful and needed.

Finally, the suicide rate reaches its peak among the elderly, who today suffer from a host of emotionally crippling influences. Our society now emphasizes youth and young ideas. After a forced retirement at age 70, many people feel useless, lonely, bored, and frustrated. In addition, they may suffer great financial insecurity, physical pain from chronic aliments, or may have terminal illnesses. For persons over age 85, the suicide rate is 26 per 100,000.

For the United States in general, the suicide rate among men is greater than among women, though on the West Coast there are more female suicides than male.

(Jones, Shainberg, and Byer, 78)

Notes

Suicide

Vocabulary: Use the context of the selection to help you define these words.

1. introverted: _____

2. internalize: _____

Sample Question: Circle the answer that better completes each statement, based on the selection.

a. Lack of personal self-confidence can be the result of (the end of a love affair / academic failure).
b. Rejection and feelings of abandonment can be caused by (academic failure / the end of a love affair).
c. Many (middle-aged / college) persons suffer emotionally because they realize that their life goals are unattainable.
d. Retirement may result in (emotional frustration / new upward strivings).

Sample Essay Question: Write a question an instructor might use to test a student's understanding of this selection.

_____

_____

Smog and Temperature Inversion

The Los Angeles type smog is composed mainly of partially burned gasoline, which is the result of extensive automobile use in that city. We also know that these hydrocarbons, when released into the atmosphere, can be converted by sunlight into more damaging and more reactive substances. Any city with a substantial amount of <u>vehicular</u> traffic will experience a certain amount of the Los Angeles smog.

In 1956, the Clean Air Act was passed as a result of the 1952 smog catastrophe that killed thousands. This Act created smoke-control areas where only authorized fuels could be burned (thus prohibiting the use of soft coal). In 1968, the Clean Air Act was amended to make its application even more effective. These legislative measures have increased the number of sunny days in London by 80 percent and the quality of the atmosphere has improved significantly. In addition, the number of deaths from chronic bronchitis in the large urban areas has decreased.

An atmospheric condition known as temperature inversion contributes to critical periods of air pollution. During an inversion, warm air makes up the upper level of the atmosphere, keeping the cold air closest to the ground. This combination results in air pollutants being held down by the cold air. Because of their inability to escape into the upper atmosphere, these pollutants increase in concentration over a city. It was during inversion periods of this type that the disasters of Meuse Valley, London, and Donora, Pennsylvania occurred. Where industrial areas are located in valleys with high hills on either side, they are particularly <u>prone</u> to periods of temperature inversion. It has been shown that inversion periods occur about 100 days each year in Los Angeles. This city is particularly prone to this kind of condition because the cool sea air moves in under the warm desert air and an inversion layer is produced. It is only when the warm air rises high enough to permit the cool air to escape that the inversion "lid" is lifted.

(Sinacore and Sinacore, 416, 419)

Notes

Smog and Temperature Inversion

Vocabulary: Define the following words.

1. vehicular: _____

2. prone: _____

Sample Question: Complete each of the following statements based on your understanding of the facts in the selection.

1. The inversion lid lifts when _____

_____.

2. _____

are particularly prone to temperature inversions.

3. _____ air holds pollutants close to the ground during an inversion.

4. The _____ contributes to the Los Angeles type of smog.

5. A reaction to the 1952 smog catastrophe was the passage of the _____.

Sample Essay Question: Consider the following statement and list five supporting reasons that you could use in developing a short paragraph.

It is dangerous to live in an industrial town located in a small valley.

1. _____

2. _____

3. _____

4. _____

5. _____

The Jet That Crashed Before Take-off

Beirne Lay, Jr.

Jet fighter Number 313 taxied onto the end of the runway, cleared for take-off. The Pilot, a young major, fastened his safety belt, set his brakes, and ran up 100 per cent rpm on his engine—a huge, long corncob that made up nearly all of his airplane. Then he released his toe brakes. The wheels rolled the first inch. And in that first inch, the Pilot of Number 313 was doomed. In effect, he was already dead.

A mile and a half of smooth, white concrete runway narrowed into the distance in front of the nose of the gleaming, javelin-sleek, swept-wing fighter—8,000 feet of it, more than ample for the 6,700-foot take-off distance calculated in the flight plan.

The weather was good, a clear bright morning with a hot sun beating down on the shimmering California desert. Surface winds were nearly dead calm. The J-79 engine was in perfect condition and turning up normal thrust. No mechanical defect lurked anywhere within the complex innards of the aircraft. The Pilot was highly experienced and could point to a spotless safety record and superior past performance. The mission, like every mission in the Air Force, had been minutely planned: gross weight at take-off figured to the pound; runway temperature, surface-wind velocity, and every other factor to insure the mathematical certainty that the wheels of Number 313 would unstick from the runway after a roll of 6,700 feet. No one connected with the planning or preparation for the mission was guilty of a fatal blunder.

Only one thing was wrong. A series of minor errors, already irrevocably committed, not one of which was fatal in itself, when added together spelled out a stark fact: Number 313 could not possibly get off the 8,000-foot runway safely.

She needed 8,100 feet, instead of 6,700 feet.

Why?

How could this happen in a precision organization like the United States Air Force, where hundreds of heavily loaded jet aircraft take off every day without incident? The Air Force emphasizes "flying safety" second only to accomplishment of its primary mission and has achieved a consistently lower accident rate each year since World War II.

Part of the answer is that each "routine" take-off is not really routine. Rather, it is a kind of triumph, endlessly repeated, over an unseen enemy always lying in wait to prove that an accident is "no accident." It is a triumph, illustrated in reverse, so to speak, by the case of Number 313, which highlights one of the new facts of life in the jet age: a jet take-off is more critical than the familiar take-off in a propeller-driven aircraft. Far more so.

Perhaps the simplest way to visualize the situation that confronted Number 313 is to think of the Pilot's safety margin—that 1,300-foot surplus between his estimated 6,700-foot take-off distance and the 8,000-foot runway—as money in the bank. As long as he had any or all of those 1,300 feet, he was in the black. But a series of petty thefts could conceivably put him in the red. Number 313 was the victim of four such thefts, plus two other contributing factors.

Theft number one: As the fighter was taxiing out, the control tower reported practically a dead calm, a zero wind, as forecast in the flight plan. However, by the time Number 313 actually started her take-off, she had a four-knot tailwind. This was so small a change that the tower operator either did not notice it or did not consider it important enough to relay it to the Pilot. Certainly this was no drastic windshift. But it cost the Pilot

310 feet of added take-off distance required. Unknown to him, it brought his bank balance down to 990 feet. Still plenty of margin.

Theft number two: Take-off had been planned for 11:15 a.m., at which time the runway temperature was forecast to be, and actually was, 97 degrees. But Number 313 had taxied out half an hour late because of a valid delay while the crew chief double-checked a malfunctioning fire-warning light and replaced a bulb. During this delay and later, while the fighter was taxiing for over a mile from the parking ramp to the end of the runway, the temperature rose slightly to 101 degrees. A prolonged delay, say of an hour, would have automatically necessitated a revised flight plan, but the Pilot followed common procedure, in view of the shorter delay, when he followed his original flight plan. This unforeseen and seemingly negligible rise of four degrees of temperature robbed him of another 190 feet, since hotter air adds to the take-off roll of a jet in two ways. The engine develops less thrust, and the wings need a higher take-off speed in the thinner air. As he released his toe brakes, the Pilot did not know that his bank balance was now down to 800 feet.

Theft number three: The Pilot was executing his first take-off from an unfamiliar air base, having arrived the previous day as a transient. Therefore he was unaware of an optical illusion that confronted him as he stared down the runway at the desert floor, rising gradually from the far end of the runway toward a distant mountain range. To his eyes, the runway appeared to slope slightly downhill in contrast with the rising ground beyond. Actually, there was an imperceptible uphill grade, placing the far end of the runway 260 feet higher than where he sat, and requiring a take-off roll—under existing conditions of a tailwind and high temperature—of an additional 550 feet. Now, unknown to the Pilot, his bank balance had shrunk to 250 feet. It was still enough, but it was getting close to bankruptcy.

Theft number four: Lack of sleep for the Pilot, as a result of an unexpected change in the weather during the previous night, became a pertinent factor. Confident he would be weathered in for a couple of days until a cold front passed, he had left the base on the evening before to enjoy a night on the town with a clear conscience.

His family and his girl lived not far from the air base, and their convivial reunion lasted into the small hours. He was awakened after three and a half hours of sleep by a call from the base notifying him of a break in the weather. Since he was under orders to return to his home base as soon as possible, there was nothing for it but to bolt a cup of black coffee, hustle on out to the base, and start wheeling and dealing.

You don't just leap into the cockpit of a supersonic jet fighter and take off, unless you are an interceptor pilot on twenty-four-hour alert duty. This was an extended navigational mission requiring careful planning, preflight inspections, and attention to the check lists. And there is where the lack of sufficient rest led to the final withdrawal from the already slim bank account of Number 313.

The Pilot arrived to find that the Assistant Operations Officer, an old pal, had lent a hand and figured the weight of fuel in the main tanks and the auxiliary wing-tip tanks, based on servicing performed the night before. It had been a cold night—an important factor. In arriving at the correct weight, it is necessary to apply a correction for temperature. This his friend had done, but inadvertently he had applied the correction the wrong way, subtracting it instead of adding it. A gallon of fuel will weigh more when it is cold and dense than when it is warm and expanded—just a fraction of a pound more, but it adds up when you're dealing with thousands of pounds of fuel.

The Pilot checked over his friend's figures. Partly because of confidence, based on past experience, in the other man's accuracy and conscientiousness, and partly because lack of rest had affected his alertness, the Pilot failed to spot his friend's slip-up. Thus, when the wheels of Number 313 rolled that first inch, the aircraft weighed slightly more than the Pilot thought she did. Under any other circumstances, it might not have been a costly error, but it was enough in this case to add a disastrous 350 feet to the distance Number 313 must travel before she could become airborne, thereby chipping away the remaining 250 feet still left in the bank—and then some.

Now the Pilot was in the red. By one hundred feet. Number 313 was bankrupt and prepared to drag down with her a million-dollar fighter and the life of an invaluable combat pilot.

Only two hopes of reprieve for this Pilot still lived. First, if it became apparent in the final stage of take-off that he'd never make it, he could jettison his tip tanks and lighten his load by approximately one ton of the extra fuel. Secondly, at a given point down the runway, he would have an opportunity of recognizing that he had not reached a predicted airspeed. Then he could yank the throttles back and abort the take-off in time

for a safe stop. But this second safeguard had already been taken out of his hands through an error of omission, committed by someone now far removed from the scene.

The runway, originally, had been 7,600 feet long. Recently, 400 feet had been added to the end from which Number 313 took off. But the runway markers—large signs placed at 1,000-foot intervals alongside the runway to enable the Pilot to see at a glance during take-off how much runway he still has left—were in their original locations. The fact that they were scheduled to be moved back 400 feet the next day was just twenty-four hours too late.

Black smoke pouring from her tail pipe, Number 313 rolled forward, gathering momentum slowly, the thunder of her departure ricocheting off the buildings along the flight line. When the Pilot passed the first 1,000-foot marker, he was really 1,400 feet down the runway. The same misinformation was waiting to mislead him at the 2,000-foot and the 3,000-foot markers, depriving him of his last chance to judge whether or not his take-off was proceeding according to plan.

He reached his maximum refusal speed of 106 knots at the 4,000-foot marker. Had his airspeed been appreciably below the briefed speed at this juncture, here is where he could—and undoubtedly would—have refused to take-off. But he saw that his airspeed was indicating within two knots of the desired speed. He continued. What he didn't know, because of the hidden extra 400 feet he had covered, was that he should have been going eight knots faster at the critical moment of decision.

Now the end of that once endless-looking ribbon of white concrete began to unreel alarmingly fast. It was too late to stop. The Pilot pressed the release button to jettison his tip tanks. Nothing happened. Malfunction in the circuit. Consuming precious seconds, he resorted to hand operation of the manual release. The tanks dropped clear.

But Number 313 was still solidly on the runway, still below the minimum take-off speed of her stubby, razor-blade wings as the last foot of the concrete blurred in under the nose. Reacting out of automatic desperation, the Pilot pulled back on the controls. Number 313 staggered a few feet into the air. Instantly he retracted the landing gear, fighting to reduce the drag and gain that two or three knots of airspeed that might still spell the difference. Quivering right at her stalling speed, the heavy fighter squashed back onto the rough, rising terrain beyond the runway, plowing ahead at 140 knots. Seconds later came the explosion.

For Number 313, time and distance had run out. And for her Pilot, in that master ledger where no mistakes in the ultimate arithmetic of cause and effect are permitted to occur, the account was now forever closed.

Notes

The Jet That Crashed Before Take-off

Sample Essay Question: Write a question that an instructor might use to test a student's understanding of the selection.

_____

_____

Now, answer your question.

Understanding Comparisons and Contrasts

25

When an author describes the characteristics of two or more subjects—people, places, events, or ideas—for the purpose of showing their similarities or differences or both, the author is giving the reader a comparison or contrast of them. Noting whether the subjects are similar or different with respect to a particular trait will help you to focus on the important ideas you will want to study.

What do these two pictures show? If you were called upon to explain this pair of pictures, what traits would you want to be sure to discuss?

Example

Photos courtesy of New York Convention and Visitors Bureau

The author who uses a comparison-contrast method of presenting information is showing the similarities or differences between two or more subjects based on a common or shared trait.

Consider the following statement. If you were called upon to discuss the subjects, what trait would you want to discuss?

Example

Jean's hair is brown and Bob's is blond.

In this example you should note the characteristic, hair color, and then determine whether there are similarities or differences between Jean's and Bob's hair color. Here you can note differences: brown versus blond. In this example, the author states <u>one</u> characteristic shared by both subjects.

Now consider this example:

Example

Jean and Bob both own ski jackets, but only Bob owns his own skis.

Here, two characteristics are stated: owning ski jackets and owning skis. Jean and Bob are alike in the ownership of a ski jacket. Jean and Bob are different in the ownership of skis.

Authors can focus on one <u>or</u> several traits to show how subjects are similar or different. You must **identify the trait** or characteristic being discussed and determine whether the subjects are similar or different. Then consider the next trait presented.

Practice: In each sentence, mark the trait (characteristic) that is discussed. Then determine whether the subjects are alike or different with respect to that trait. The first one is done for you. (Notice that some sentences have more than one trait to consider.)

alike **1.** Grace and Sylvia both have an extreme dislike of snakes.
_____ **2.** When compared with today's rising costs, 1940s prices seem lower.
_____ **3.** Unlike his predecessors, today's king has little power in the societal structure.
_____ **4.** Open any paper, and you'll read about more acts of cowardice than of bravery.
_____ **5.** The applicants both had acceptable skills, but one had a better work record.
_____ **6.** Jazz, like the symphonic form, makes specialized use of certain instruments.
_____ **7.** This sponge cake has more eggs than the other and is lighter and fluffier.
_____ **8.** Many machines can perform tasks faster and cheaper than humans.
_____ **9.** Thank goodness for blue skies again after yesterday's dreary overcast!
_____ **10.** Single-handed, this brave soldier took the hill where everyone else had failed.

Sensing Comparisons and Contrasts in Paragraphs

Once you understand the comparative pattern, you can apply it to taking notes. Use the pattern in the main idea sentence by stating "a comparison of" or "the differences between." The details will then be a list of the similarities or differences stated in the main idea.

Example

Notes

There are several differences between plant and animal cells. First, plant cells are generally larger. They are surrounded by a cellulose wall. Animal cells are not. Plant and animal cells possess vacuoles, but, in the animal cell, the vacuoles are more numerous than those of the plant cell, where there is one large vacuole. Plastids are found in plant cells.

A. The <u>differences between</u> plant and animal cells
   1. plant cell larger
   2. plant cell—cellulose wall
   3. animal cell vacuoles—small and many
   4. plant cell vacuole—large one
   5. only plants—plastids

Sensing that the paragraph is comparative, you can put that understanding to use by including the phrase "the differences between" in your written main idea and by listing those differences in the details. The restated main idea and details are concise, clear, and useful; they indicate that you will want to remember "the differences."

When an author organizes information to show the differences between or the similarities shared by two or more subjects, the author is using a **comparison-contrast pattern**. What you will want to remember are the similarities and/or differences between the subjects.

Following are some of the words that signal comparisons or contrasts in passages:

compare	contrast	different	similar
like or	on the other hand	also	but

Practice: As you take notes on the following passages, use the phrase <u>similarities of</u> or <u>differences between</u> in your main idea. Also, mark any phrases that signal either comparisons or contrasts in the passages.

Notes

1.   Government procurement differs in three respects from purchasing by private business. First, the government buys goods mainly for use, not for resale or for use in production. (An exception is the purchase by the government of many consumer goods for resale through post exchanges and commissaries.) Second, government purchases are not motivated by a desire for profit. Third,

A. The differences between government and private business purchases
   1. _____
      _____
   2. _____
      _____
   3. _____
      _____

or

government purchasing is subject to many legal and budgetary restrictions intended to safeguard the expenditure of public funds.

(Mauser and Schwartz, 299)

2.   Two types of advertising agency are available to the industrial advertiser: the general advertising agency and the industrial advertising agency. Carefully chosen, each can afford the advertiser expert counsel. The criteria for making a choice of agencies are the same as the criteria for choosing an agency for consumer goods advertising. . . . Many general advertising agencies maintain staff personnel to render service specifically to industrial advertisers, while the smaller number of industrial advertising agencies deal with industrial accounts exclusively. However, because general agencies are geared to consumer goods accounts, with large portions of their budgets specified for commissionable media, they generally are not attuned to any but large industrial accounts that may also have considerable commissionable media schedules. The industrial agencies, on the other hand, are geared to the needs of the industrial advertiser and, therefore, find it possible to operate profitably for the agency and effectively for the client.

Whereas general agencies typically operate on a commission compensation plan, industrial agencies more frequently do not.

(Mandell, 654)

3.   Chimpanzees and gorillas, which form closely related genera, are more adapted to terrestrial existence. Chimps spend much of their time on the ground, although they sleep in the trees and move through them easily by brachiation. Gorillas are almost entirely terrestrial, sleeping and feeding on the ground. Both chimps and gorillas can stand erect on two legs, but on the ground they usually move quadrupedally, on the soles of their feet and the knuckles of their hands. Both are mainly vegetarians, but the chimpanzees supplement their diets with meat. Chimpanzees also use simple tools. Members of both genera are social, living in groups that move through territories generally separate from the feeding ranges of other groups of the same species. The groups of chimpanzees are less well knit, however, and territories are not aggressively defended. Groups are socially structured, with dominance hierarchies. Gorilla groups are always led by an older

Differences between government and private business purchases	• • •

male. Although basically similar in many characteristics, gorillas and chimpanzees differ in size, with chimpanzees averaging about three feet and 100 pounds compared to the six foot height and 350 to 450 pound weight of the adult male gorilla. They also differ in personality; chimpanzees are noisy, rowdy, gregarious, and curious, whereas gorillas are shy, apparently gentle (despite occasional fearsome threat displays), quieter, less curious, and more retiring.

(Curtis, 933)

4.   The variables of sex, race, socioeconomic status, and age, which we have observed to be important in the understanding of crime rates and the administration of criminal justice, also are important in the implementation of punishment. Specifically, blacks often get the blunt end of justice where punishments are concerned. They are more likely to receive long prison terms and less likely to be paroled or placed on probation, although this is not the case for all crimes. As we have noted, blacks may not be prosecuted for crimes against other blacks. Blacks less frequently receive pardons than whites; blacks are more often executed for capital crimes; and they less frequently receive commutation of a death sentence. And although no empirical evidence is available for analysis, they probably are more frequently subjected to physical punishment within prisons than are whites.

Punishments also vary by age, with less severe punishments imposed on young offenders. This, of course, is the philosophy behind the establishment of the juvenile court. Punishment may be more severe for recidivists, and some jurisdictions have statutes that provide for an automatically increased penalty for such individuals. Punishment may vary by sex, with women often receiving less severe penalties than men for the same crime. Women, for example, less frequently receive the death sentence when it could be imposed. Finally, milder penalties are often imposed on members of the middle and upper classes than on those from the lower classes.

(Reid, 577)

Sensing Comparisons and Contrasts in Longer Passages

In single paragraphs, it is fairly easy to see the similarities or differences between two subjects. The author usually shifts back and forth presenting first a trait of one and then a contrast in the other.

Multiple paragraphs may also follow the comparative pattern. However, the author sometimes presents all the facts about one subject before presenting the facts about the second subject. Consider this passage:

Example

Characteristic being contrasted ←

        The two major forms of test evaluation are the objective-type and the essay examinations. Instructors select the type of exam best suited to evaluate both specific and general knowledge in the particular subject area.

First subject ←

        Objective, short-answer exams focus on the ability to remember a wide range of factual material. The more details students can remember and understand, the better equipped they are for this type of test. The students must read directions and answer questions accurately. Their range of factual knowledge is tested by multiple-choice, completion, true-false, and matching questions.

Second subject ←

        The essay exam requires more than just a mere recall of facts. Students must analyze the question and be prepared to organize both general and specific information in their responses. Emphasis is placed on the students' insights and organizational abilities. Their interpretation, evaluation, and discussion of subject material provides the instructor with a meaningful measure of the students' knowledge.

    In this example, objective and essay tests are being contrasted on the basis of the type of knowledge and skills needed by the student. After the introduction, the author presents the types of skills needed by students taking objective tests. In the next paragraph, the author presents the types of skills needed by students taking essay tests.

> **In longer passages, the author may present similarities or differences together. However, many authors first present facts about one subject and then facts about the next subject. It is often up to you to put the ideas together to see what is really different or similar about the two subjects.**

Example

	Objective exams (Subject 1)	**Essay exams (Subject 2)**
Knowledge and skill tested (Characteristic)	Recall stated facts Follow directions Fill in or choose answers Remember details	Interpret and evaluate ideas Analyze questions Organize ideas as a response Use insight

Like all the passages in this book, the preceding passage can be outlined. However, another form of note-taking especially helpful for the comparison-contrast pattern of organization is the **chart form,** as in the preceding example. In this set of notes, the trait being discussed is identified, and the similarities or differences are noted for each subject.

Remember that if you sense that a passage is comparative, you may want to use the chart form of note-taking. It is perfectly acceptable to switch to this form of note-taking because the method can help you study better. Again, these are your notes. They should be written in the most convenient way of putting ideas on paper for future recall.

Practice: Make an outline or a split-page set of notes for each selection. Also, practice writing the notes in chart form. The first passage has been started for you.

1.　　Despite the changes of recent years, there is still a strong consensus in the United States about the personality traits that are most desirable for each of the sexes. The American woman is still widely expected to be conformist, passive, affectionate, sensitive, and dependent. She is not supposed to be too assertive, ambitious, or interested in sports, politics, and economics. She should not take the initiative in sexual relationships but instead should entrap the male by shrewd psychological manipulation. She is expected to be deeply concerned about her physical appearance, and her life should revolve primarily around the home. The self-image of a woman comes not from any achievement in the occupational world but rather from a satisfactory fulfillment of a nurturant (role) for her children and a supportive role for her husband.

　　The American man, on the other hand, is still expected to be self-reliant, competent, independent, and in certain circumstances aggressive. He should keep his emotions under fairly strict control and is expected to have opinions on public affairs. In his relationships with the opposite sex he is supposed to take the initiative, and be more often interested in sexual gratification than romantic involvement. He may give some authority in the home to his wife, but on major domestic issues, such as relocating in a different neighborhood, his decision is final. His self-image comes mainly from his achievements in the outside world, and his work is a major focus of his life. He has a moral duty to be the family breadwinner, and his self-image may be severely undermined if his wife takes this role, or even if she earns more than he does.

(Robertson, 300)

Outline

A. Personality traits of the American woman
   1. She is expected to be
      a.
      b.
      c.
      d.
      e.
   2. She should not
      a.
      b.
      c.
   3. In sex, she should
      a.
      b.
   4. Her self-image should
      a.
      b.
      c.
      d.
B. Personality traits of the American man
   1. He should be
      a.
      b.
      c.
      d.
      e.
      f.
   2. In sex, he should
      a.
      b.
   3. His self-image
      a.
      b.
      c.
      d.
      e.

Chart

Personality Traits

	What is expected	Not expected	In sex	Self-image
American woman				
American man				

Notes

2.   To conclude this discussion of production, some of the major contrasts between industrial and nonindustrial economies will be summarized. It is often—and accurately—said that the factory worker in the contemporary United States or Western Europe is alienated from the item he produces; that is, he feels no strong personal identification with it. This is not so among nonindustrial populations, where the manufacturer, that is, the individual worker, usually sees his work through from start to completion and feels pride, or at least accomplishment, in the finished item.

Another contrast involves relationships between co-workers. In nonindustrial societies, the economic relationship is merely one aspect of the social relationship. In the industrial nation, people usually do not work with their kinsmen and neighbors. However, if their colleagues are also their friends, the relationship is usually founded on their common occupation rather than on a broader tie of kinship or fictive kinship.

(Kottak, 166–167)

	Personal identification with product	Relationship of co-workers
Workers in industrialized countries		
Workers in nonindustrialized countries		

3.   There are major differences between the nuclear family and descent groups. Descent groups are permanent units which continue to exist even though their membership changes over time. The nuclear family, on the other hand, is impermanent. It lasts only as long as parents and their children reside together. When the parents die or all the children move away, the nuclear family dissolves.

There is another contrast between the nuclear family and descent group organization. Status as a member of a descent group is often ascribed at birth. An individual is born a member of a given descent group and remains a member throughout his life. On the other hand, he is normally a member of at least two different nuclear families at different times in his life. He is born into one consisting of his parents and siblings. Anthropologists call this the *family of orientation*. When he reaches adulthood, he normally marries and establishes a nuclear family which includes his spouse and eventually their children. Anthropologists call this the *family of procreation*. Since divorce exists in most human societies, some people may establish more than one family of procreation.

(Kottak, 76)

Chart

Anticipating Test Questions

Understanding the comparative pattern can help in two ways: you can take more effective notes and you can anticipate test questions from which to study. If you sense a comparison or contrast between two subjects, use this as a basis for study. You are now studying with a specific goal in mind: to remember the similarities or differences between things. Consider this passage and notice how the similarities and differences appear in the questions.

Example

Comparison of Plant and Animal Cells

Plant and animal cells are alike in their most basic features. They differ, however, in these five general ways:

1. *Size.* Plant cells as a rule are larger than animal cells.
2. *Cell wall.* Plant cells but not animal cells are surrounded by a rigid cellulose wall.
3. *Sap vacuole.* Most mature plant cells possess a large central vacuole. Vacuoles in animal cells are small and frequently numerous.
4. *Plastids.* Plastids, especially the chloroplasts, which characterize many of the cells of green plants, are not found in animal cells.
5. *Division of the cytoplasm.* Cytoplasmic cell division in plant cells is accomplished by the formation of a cell plate, whereas in animal cells the cytoplasm is divided by a constriction.

(Johnson, Delanney, Cole, and Brooks, 24)

Notes

Comparison of Plant and Animal Cells

	Size	Cell wall	Sap vacuole	Plastids	Division of cytoplasm
Plant	Larger	Surrounded by rigid cellulose wall	Mature—one large central vacuole	Characteristic chloroplasts	Form cell plate
Animal	Smaller	No cellulose wall	Small vacuoles Many of them	Not found	Division by constriction

Here are several key words and phrases that signal comparison-contrast in multiple-choice, fill-in, and true-false questions.

1. One **distinguishing** feature **between** plant and animal cells is

   _____

2. The cell **which does not have a** cellulose wall is the
   a. plant cell.
   b. animal cell.

3. T-F: **A characteristic not shared** by plant and animal cells is the presence of chloroplasts.

Here are several key words and phrases that signal comparison-contrast in essay test questions (see Chapter 29).

1. How are plant and animal cells **different?**
2. **Distinguish between** plant and animal cells in the following characteristics: size, cell wall, and plastids.

When you sense that the author is presenting facts in a comparative manner, use the phrases **similarities of** or **differences between** in your written main idea. The details will list those similarities or differences.

When studying, use the comparison-contrast pattern to anticipate a test question beginning with one of these typical key phrases:

show the differences	**compare**
show the similarities	**contrast**
how are these the same	**distinguish between**
how are these different	

Practice: Read the following selections and use the form of note-taking that will give you the most help in studying. Selections one and two require you to write a short-answer question and an essay question. Selection three is followed by questions that you should answer.

Notes

1. Jung versus Freud

Freud emphasized the role of biology in personality development. Jung preferred to think that humans could rise above their animal natures. Freud believed that happiness often came from escaping pain or reducing anxiety, and he tended to attract patients who were highly anxious or pain-ridden. Many of Jung's clients were artists, mystics, or wealthy individuals who felt the need for spiritual guidance "outside the church." Freud focused on the early, developmental years, which he saw as determining the entire structure of an individual's personality. Jung worked to a great degree with older patients, and never did offer a complete account of how the personality is formed.

Perhaps the most telling difference of all between the two men, though, lay in their use of language. Freud was a superb writer who was a serious contender for the Nobel Prize in literature. Jung's books and articles, however, were filled with obscure images and symbols. His greatest influence was perhaps not on psychology, but on art and mysticism.

(McConnell, 491)

Short-Answer Question

_____

_____

Essay Question

_____

_____

Notes

2.   We are told by some alarmed observers that youth today is more rebellious, more troubled emotionally, more promiscuous sexually, less idealistic, more critical of the values and standards of the adult culture, and more "disengaged" from those values than youth in earlier times. All manner of plausible sounding "evidence" has been cited in support of this "distressing" state of affairs: demonstrations on college and high school campuses; lack of respect for authority; confrontations with police and public officials; riots in minority-group ghettos; increased use of drugs, from "pep" pills and glue sniffing to marijuana, "speed," LSD, and even "hard" narcotics; pregnancy among adolescent girls; venereal disease; and suicide. Even adolescent music and fashions in dress and personal appearance have been cited as examples of this presumably deteriorating state of affairs.

    In contrast, we are told by other observers, and with equal assurance, that adolescents today are brighter and better informed than their parents; less sentimental, but more genuinely idealistic; more serious; no more promiscuous in sexual behavior than their elders were at adolescence, but more open, honest, and tolerant; and less hypocritical, obsessed, or troubled in their sexual attitudes and beliefs. We are informed that youth are more concerned about the fundamental purposes of education and less satisfied merely to "get by" with acceptable grades; that they feel a greater sense of social responsibility and concern for the welfare of others; and that, if anything, they come closer to having a sense of their own identity and are less emotionally conflicted than their parents were at the same age.

(Mussen, Conger, and Kagan, 542–543)

Short-Answer Question

_____

_____

Essay Question

_____

_____

3. Dumb Aussies, They Say

Bernard Sloan

While living in Australia, I discovered that banks do not return canceled checks. Having tossed away receipts on the assumption that our checks would come back, I asked the teller what evidence we would have for the tax department.

"Not to worry," he said with a smile, "you just show the stubs in your checkbook."

"But I could write in any amount," I said.

He pondered that for a moment and replied, "I suppose one could, couldn't one?"

He had to be kidding, I thought. How dumb could they be?

Can you imagine the Internal Revenue Service's accepting the amount we write on our check stubs? Why, the entire country would go on a spree of stub-padding that would send sales of ball-point pens soaring.

Yet this prospect has eluded the entire Australian Government and its people. And that's just one instance. Every day I was dumbfounded by behavior that Americans would consider plain dumb.

The Aussies sell soft drinks in return bottles, but require no deposit. They expect people to return the empties without monetary reward, and they do—placing them neatly in boxes set out for the purpose. At events like the Sydney Royal Easter Show, picnic areas with cauldrons of boiling water are provided for people to brew their own tea—missing the whole American point of forcing captive consumers to buy refreshments at inflated prices. They don't even inflate prices. We paid no more for soft drinks or meat pies in a stadium than in a street shop.

I was the smart American advertising man who came to show them how to sharpen their marketing, American-style. A lost cause.

Incredibly, packaged products are sold in containers of uniform size and shape, violating the first law of American marketing: Befuddle the consumer. Comparing prices was absurdly simple. They wouldn't even entertain the idea of the big economy size posing as a bargain. "If it isn't a saving, how can you imply it is?" asked a client, the leader of a giant soap company.

Hopeless.

Why, I once worked with one of America's corporate giants that spent a fortune designing a bottle to look larger yet contain less than its competitors. That tall bottle with the pinched-in middle made them millions. "Women don't read if it's 28 or 32 ounces," the product manager said, beaming, "as long as it looks bigger."

Australian salespeople actually try to save customers money. When we tried to buy shoes for our son, only after half an hour of torturous fittings did the salesman confess to having "dearer" shoes in the stockroom. Let the lad break in the cheaper ones, he urged. A far cry from the American gambit of shaming customers into buying the high-profit item.

Australian doctors are appallingly ignorant; their fees are so low that they live no better than other college-educated members of the populace. Lawyers don't know enough to pressure for a tax system that only lawyers can untangle. The Australian tax form is a five-minute exercise with a few basic deductions.

Why, in the United States the densest college student quickly figures how to get food stamps. And how many of us have gleefully outsmarted unemployment compensation? Landlords cleverly burn buildings for the insurance; tenants burn them for the welfare money. We cross class lines as we spot opportunities. To save an ancient tree, Australian unions refused to dig an underground parking garage, striking themselves out of a work project. At this very moment, New York unions are pressing for a highway regardless of its effect on the environment.

Before leaving, I attempted to settle my electric bill. Without batting an eyelash, the authorities said they would mail it to the United States. When it finally arrived, I did exactly what they expected. I paid. And don't think it was easy converting American money into an Australian money order. "Why didn't you just forget it?" friends asked. "If they're dumb enough to . . ."

I guess I wasn't smart enough.

Notes

Re-entry wasn't easy. One startling thing followed another. Odd-size packages on store shelves. Utilities charging more for less. A $50 eye checkup. Dollar candy bars in theaters, and drinking fountains replaced by attendants hawking watery orange drink on the easy-payment plan. Every night on TV another mob screaming for theirs—bus drivers, teachers, welfare recipients. And the tax form with no end of possibilities to test one's cleverness.

But that's okay. I have a smart tax man, and I'm saving all my canceled checks. You bet I am.

Dumb Aussies, They Say

Vocabulary: Which of these new words refer to Americans and which refer to Australians?

_____ padding
_____ befuddle
_____ dearer
_____ gambit
_____ not to worry

1. American
2. Australian

Essay Questions: The author compares and contrasts American and Australian ways of life. The following are some of the traits considered:

Group A

Bank procedures
Soft-drink sales
Food sales at sporting events
Marketing of packaged goods

Group B

Salesmanship
Doctors' and lawyers' attitudes
Attitudes about the environment
Trust

Choose one trait from group A and compare or contrast American and Australian practices.

_____

_____

_____

_____

_____

_____

_____

Choose one trait from group B and compare or contrast American and Australian practices.

_____

_____

_____

_____

_____

_____

_____

_____

Practice with Longer Selections: Read the two selections and complete the chart that follows each. Then answer the questions.

Forms of Private Ownership

Sole Proprietorships

Sole proprietorship is the original form of business ownership. It is also the simplest, since there is no legal distinction between the sole proprietor as an individual and as a business owner. A **sole proprietorship is an organization owned and usually operated by a single individual.** Its assets, earnings, and debts are those of the owner.

Today, sole proprietorships are still the most common form of private business ownership in the United States. While they are used in a variety of industries, they are concentrated primarily among small businesses, such as repair shops, small retail outlets, and service organizations.

Advantages of Sole Proprietorships. Sole proprietorships offer advantages not found in other forms of business ownership, such as retention of all profits, ease of formation and <u>dissolution</u>, and ownership flexibility. All profits—as well as losses—of a sole proprietorship belong to the owner (except, of course, that part going to the government for personal income taxes). If the firm is very profitable, this can be an important advantage. Retention of all profits (and losses) provides sole proprietors with the incentive to operate the business as efficiently as possible.

A minimum of legal requirements makes it easy to go into (and out of) business. Usually the only legal requirements for starting a sole proprietorship are registering the business name at the county courthouse (this guarantees that two firms do not use the same name) and taking out any necessary licenses. (Restaurants, motels, barbershops, retail stores, and many repair shops require certain kinds of licenses.)

The fact that it is easy to discontinue a business set up as a sole proprietorship is an attractive feature for certain types of enterprises. This is particularly true for businesses that are set up for a limited time period and are involved in a minimum of transactions—for example, the business created by an individual who organizes a rock concert at a local sports arena.

Ownership flexibility is another advantage of sole proprietorships. The owner has no one to consult about management decisions. He or she can take prompt action when needed and can preserve trade secrets where appropriate. Such flexibility can also contribute to the proprietor's personal satisfaction, as exemplified by the common saying "I like being my own boss."

Disadvantages of Sole Proprietorships. Disadvantages associated with sole proprietorships include unlimited financial liability, limitations on financing, management deficiencies, and lack of continuity. Since there is no legal distinction between the business and its owner, the sole proprietor is financially liable for all debts of the business. If the firm's assets cannot cover its debts, the owner is required to pay them with personal funds. A sole proprietor may even be forced to sell personal property—home, furniture, automobile—to pay off business debts. Thus, the unlimited liability of a sole proprietorship can mean financial ruin if the business fails. The financial resources of a sole proprietorship are limited to the owner's personal funds and money that can be borrowed. Sole proprietors usually do not have easy access to large amounts of capital, because they are typically small business people with limited personal wealth. Banks and other financial institutions are often reluctant to risk loans to such small organizations. Thus, financing limitations can retard the expansion of the sole proprietor's business.

The manager of the sole proprietorship is usually the owner. This person has to be able to handle a wide range of managerial and operative activities. As the firm grows, the owner may be unable to attract managerial personnel. Sole proprietorships typically offer little hope of promotion (except for the owner's offspring), fewer fringe benefits than can be found in other organizations, and less employment security. But they do offer employees an excellent chance to learn about a particular type of enterprise. Finally, sole proprietorships lack long-term continuity. Death, bankruptcy, retirement, or change in personal interest can terminate a business organized as a sole proprietorship.

Partnerships

Partnerships are another form of private business ownership. As defined by the Uniform Partnership Act, they are **associations of two or more persons who operate a business as co-owners by voluntary legal agreement.** Partnership has been a traditional form of ownership for professional service organizations of such people as doctors, lawyers, and dentists.

General partnerships are those in which all partners carry on the business as co-owners and all are liable for the business's debts. Some states also permit **limited partnerships** composed of one or more general partners and one or more limited partners. (A limited partner is one whose liability is limited to the amount of capital contributed to the partnership.)

Joint ventures, another type of partnership, occur when two or more people form a temporary business for a specific undertaking—for example, a group of investors who import a shipment of high-quality wine from France and then resell it to wine dealers in the United States. Joint ventures are often used with real estate investments.

Advantages of Partnerships. Partnerships offer the advantages of ease of formation, complementary management skills, and expanded financial capability. It is relatively easy to establish a partnership. As with sole proprietorships, the legal requirements usually involve registering the business name and taking out needed licenses. Limited partners must also comply with state legislation based on the Uniform Limited Partnership Act.

It is usually wise to establish written articles of partnership specifying the details of the partners' agreement. This helps clarify the relationship within the firm and protects the original agreement upon which the partnership is based.

A common reason for setting up a partnership is the availability of complementary managerial skills. If the people involved were to operate as sole proprietors, the firm of each might lack some managerial skills; but by combining into a partnership, each can offer the firm his or her unique managerial ability. For example, a general partnership might be formed by an engineer, an accountant, and a marketer who plan to produce and sell a particular product or service. If additional managerial talent is needed in the business, it may be easier to attract people as partners than as employees.

Partnerships offer expanded financial capability through money invested by each of the partners. They also usually have greater access to borrowed funds than do sole proprietorships. Since the individual partners are subject to unlimited financial liability, financial institutions are often willing to advance loans to partnerships. Involvement of additional owners may also mean that additional sources of loans become available.

Disadvantages of Partnerships. Like other forms of business ownership, partnerships have some disadvantages, including unlimited financial liability, interpersonal conflicts, lack of continuity, and complexity of dissolution. Each partner is responsible for the debts of the firm, and each is legally liable for the actions of the others. This holds true not only for debts in the name of the partnership but also for lawsuits resulting from any partner's malpractice. As with sole proprietors, partners are required to pay the total debts of a partnership with private sources if necessary. In other words, if the debts of a partnership exceed its assets, then creditors will turn to the personal wealth of the partners. If only one general partner has any personal wealth, that person may be required to pay **all** the debts of the partnership. Limited partners lose only the amount of capital they invested in the firm.

Interpersonal conflicts may also plague partnerships. All partnerships, from barbershops to rock groups, face the problem of personal and business disagreements among the participants. If these conflicts cannot be resolved, the partnership is sometimes best dissolved, since the continuation will adversely affect the business. Continuity of a partnership is disrupted when a partner is no longer able (or willing) to continue in the business. The partnership agreement is terminated, and a final settlement is made.

It is not as easy to dissolve a partnership as it is to dissolve a sole proprietorship. Instead of simply withdrawing the investment in the business, the partner who wants to leave must find someone (perhaps an existing partner or perhaps an outsider who is acceptable to the remaining partners) to buy his or her investment in the firm. Sometimes it is very difficult to transfer an investment in a partnership to another party.

Corporations

A **corporation** is *"an association of persons created by statute as a legal entity (artificial person) with authority to act and to have liability separate and apart from its owners."* Since corporations are legal organizations apart from their owners, the liability of each owner is limited to the amount that person invests.

Corporate charters are granted through state legislation. Corporate ownership is represented by shares of stock in the firm. (Types of stock and their issuance are discussed later in the chapter.) Anyone who holds one or more shares of a corporation's stock is considered a part owner of the business. Shares can usually be bought and sold readily on the open market.

Advantages of Corporations. Corporate ownership offers considerable advantages, including limited financial liability, specialized management skills, expanded financial capability, and economies of larger scale operation. Since corporations are considered separate legal entities, the stockholders (owners) have limited financial liability. If the firm fails, they can lose only the amount of their investments. Personal funds of owners are not touched by creditors of the corporation.

The limited liability is clearly designated in the names used by firms throughout the world. U.S. corporations often use the designation "Incorporated" or "Inc." Corporate enterprises in Canada and the United Kingdom use "Limited" or "Ltd." In Australia, limited liability is shown by "Proprietary Limited" or "Pty. Ltd." This limited liability is the most significant advantage of corporate ownership over other forms of ownership.

The managerial ability of sole proprietorships and partnerships is usually limited to that provided by the owners. Corporations can more easily obtain specialized managerial skills, because they offer longer-term career opportunities for qualified people. Employees can also concentrate their efforts in some specialized activity or functional area because of the corporation's large size.

Expanded financial capability is usually another advantage of corporate ownership. This factor may in turn allow the corporation to grow and become more efficient than it would if the business were set up as a sole proprietorship or partnership. Since corporate ownership is divided into many small units (shares), it is usually easier for a firm to attract capital. People with both large and relatively small resources can invest their savings in corporations by buying shares of stock. Corporate size and stability also make it easier for corporations to borrow additional funds. Large, financially strong corporations can often borrow money at lower rates than can smaller businesses.

(Of course, not all corporations are large; many very small firms also choose the corporate form.)

The larger-scale operation permitted by corporate ownership has several advantages. Employees can specialize in the work activities they perform best. Many projects can be internally financed by transferring money from one part of the corporation to another. Longer manufacturing runs usually mean more efficient production and lower prices, thus attracting more customers. . . . The three [largest U.S. industrial corporations]—General Motors, Exxon, and Ford—employ more workers than the combined populations of Alaska, Vermont, and Wyoming.

While corporate size may be an advantage from a business viewpoint, some economists, attorneys, political figures, and business executives have begun to question whether there should be limits to corporate size to protect the interests of society.

Disadvantages of Corporations. Some disadvantages are also inherent in corporate ownership. Corporations are the most difficult and costly ownership form to establish, they are usually at a tax disadvantage, they often face a multitude of legal restrictions, and their impersonality can alienate some employees.

Each state has different incorporation laws, some of which are quite technical and complex. Establishing a corporation usually requires the services of an attorney and legal fees. States also charge incorporation fees that add to the cost of setting up this type of business. Delaware, however, has traditionally attracted corporations because it has relatively easy requirements and low costs for incorporation.

Corporations are subject to federal and state income taxes as separate legal entities. Thus, corporate earnings are taxed, and then any **dividends**—*payments from earnings*—to stockholders are taxed on an individual basis. From the viewpoint of stockholders who receive dividends, this is effectively double taxation of corporate earnings. By contrast, the earnings of sole proprietorships and partnerships are taxed only once, since they are treated as personal income. Many states provide tax relief to corporations meeting certain size and stock ownership requirements by recognizing them as **Subchapter S corporations.** These corporations can elect to be *taxed as partnerships while maintaining the advantages of incorporation.*

Corporate ownership faces a multitude of legal problems not encountered by sole proprietorships and partnerships. Corporate charters restrict the type of business activity in which the corporation can engage. Corporations must also file various reports about their operations. The number of laws and regulations affecting corporations has increased dramatically in recent years.

Big corporations, like other large organizations, sometimes suffer from the impersonality of management. Employees become <u>alienated</u> because they do not feel any close ties with the corporation or its management. Many specialized jobs within a corporation cause the worker to lack a sense of identity with the firm. Some managers lack the initiative and sense of self-achievement found in sole proprietorships and partnerships. Employee morale, productivity, volume, and profitability can all be affected if steps are not taken to reduce the problem.

(Boone and Kurtz, 53–61)

	Definition	**Advantages**	**Disadvantages**
Sole proprietorship			
Partnership			
Corporation			

Sample Essay Question: You have discovered an efficient way to produce a tasty salad dressing. You have always wanted to be your own boss, but have some hesitations about "going it alone." Would you open your own business, go into partnership, or sell the idea to a corporation and become involved in the corporate structure? Discuss your choice and present arguments for and against each possible business arrangement.

Socialism and Communism

Socialism

While there is little agreement on a precise definition of **socialism,** it is generally held to be *an economic system in which the country's major resources and industries are owned by the government.* These include minerals (coal, oil), communications (radio, telephone, television), transportation (railroads, airlines, shipping), utilities (gas, electricity), and major manufacturing establishments (steel, automobiles). Whereas under capitalism the government intervenes in business primarily to *further* competition (on the theory that competition enhances efficiency and stimulates progress), under socialism the government tries to *eliminate* most forms of competition (on the theory that competition is ruthless and wasteful).

Under socialism, individuals are permitted to own personal property, small businesses, and land, and they are free to choose their own occupations. However, since the major parts of the socialist economy are controlled by the state, government leaders have much greater power over industries than do government leaders in capitalistic countries.

What Are Socialism's Advantages? Advocates of socialism claim that it has four major advantages over capitalism. First, they believe socialism results in more stable employment. According to socialist theory, the government can control the number and types of jobs available, since it is free to regulate the kind and amount of goods and services provided.

Second, socialists argue that their system eliminates the wastes of competition. Socialists believe that capitalism encourages too many competing stores, factories, airlines, and other forms of business. They ask why there should be four competing stores in one shopping center when one would be sufficient. They contend that their system is more efficient because it eliminates duplication of effort.

Third, advocates of socialism maintain that the system results in a more equitable distribution of wealth. Large inheritance taxes, maximum wage ceilings, and limitations on profits are some of the ways in which socialism tries to equalize the distribution of wealth.

Fourth, proponents contend that socialism is better able to provide for the welfare of all the people. For example, they feel that it is the obligation of the state to provide hospital and medical care, housing, and transportation systems.

What Are Socialism's Weaknesses? Critics of socialism say that it has three major weaknesses. First, government managers tend to be less efficient than managers in privately owned businesses, since many are appointed for political reasons. Once they are in positions of power, these appointees may run their enterprises on the basis of favoritism and indulge in bureaucratic empire building. Thus, executive leadership tends to be weak. Under capitalism, leaders are selected by the competitive process. Employees compete with employees until the best-qualified eventually direct the enterprise.

Second, even if government managers are competent, a sizable bureaucracy is needed to make, control, and administer the plans of the state. Such a bureaucracy tends to favor the status quo and is expensive to maintain—factors that may substantially reduce the efficiency of the system.

Third, socialism is less effective than capitalism in stimulating individual incentive. People generally work harder and produce more if they know they will reap the full rewards of their efforts. Thus, capitalism stimulates people to develop their skills and abilities. Under socialism, an "I don't care" attitude can develop because individual effort is not related directly to reward. This tends to result in laxness, a lessening of self-reliance, and less stress on innovation. A prominent European socialist who was asked to review this section responded with this highly revealing statement, lamenting socialists' lack of entrepreneurial spark: "The big failure of socialist economies is that they are satisfied dealing with sunset industries when they should be preoccupying themselves with sunrise industries."

When socialism's weaknesses are pointed out to socialist supporters, they are inclined to reply that the price that private enterprise pays for its superior productivity and efficiency is too great. To make his point, a socialist from a Scandinavian country that is largely socialistic said, "If forced to choose, traditional [private] enterprise Americans would prefer property rights over human rights, competition over cooperation, secrecy over openness, technology requirements over human needs, and puritanism over hedonism. The ideal of socialism is to reverse these choices.''

Communism

Communism *is an economic system in which all industries and resources are owned by the government, and individuals have little economic freedom.* It relies to an even greater degree than socialism on a planned and controlled economic order. A completely communist society is one in which all property, including most farms and distribution facilities, is owned by the state. The U.S.S.R. and China, the leading communist nations, permit virtually no private ownership of property. The state dictates not only what will be produced but who will produce, and labor has no freedom to strike.

What Are Communism's Advantages? Advocates of communism claim that when the system is working properly, it results in equitable distribution of a nation's wealth; that there is even less wasted effort and inefficiency than under socialism; and that the system enables a nation to grow more rapidly because the government can ensure that wealth is invested in technology rather than spent on consumer products.

What Are Communism's Weaknesses? The chief weakness of communism is the severe limitations that are placed on individual freedom. The state allows little opportunity to remove those in power from office. Individuals must conform to what the state prescribes. While capitalism makes each person a center of initiative, communism makes the individual a part in a vast plan. Under capitalism, consumers dictate to business what is to be provided in the marketplace; under communism, state planners dictate the nature of all economic activity.

Other weaknesses of communism include all those inherent in a planned state. Government managers are often ineffective, for the same reasons as under socialism. Furthermore, government agencies frequently fail to anticipate the amounts and types of products that will be needed. As a result, there may be oversupplies of some goods and severe shortages of others. While this problem may also occur in a capitalistic economy, the private enterprise system seems, on balance, to result in fewer gross errors in resource allocation. Further, personal service is often poor because there is no incentive to urge customers to patronize a business.

(Mauser and Schwartz, 19–22)

	Socialism	Communism	Capitalism
Definition			
Employment stability			
Waste			
Distribution of wealth			
Welfare of the people			
Efficiency of managers			
Bureaucracy			
Individual incentives			

Vocabulary: You can derive the meaning of each of the following words from the context of the selection. Use each of the words in a sentence.

1. enhance: _____

_____

2. ruthless: _____

_____

3. equitable: _____

_____

4. indulge in: _____

_____

5. reap the rewards: _____

_____

Sample Question: Assume you are an instructor and have assigned this reading. What are five short-answer questions you might ask to test your students' understandings about communism, capitalism, and socialism?

1. _____

2. _____

3. _____

4. _____

5. _____

Sample Essay Question: Write an essay question based on the topics and main ideas in the selection.

_____

_____

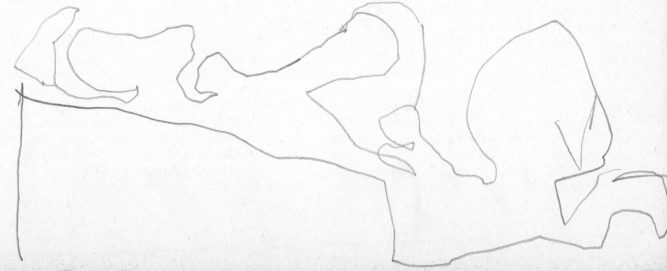

Applying Mixed Patterns

26

Previously, you identified the ways an author organizes facts: in a sequence, in a descriptive listing, by comparisons or contrasts, and with causes or effects. In this chapter, you will read a variety of text passages. As you read each passage, determine the author's method or methods of organizing the key facts, note those facts, answer questions about them, and create a sample essay question about each. Finally, you will take a practice exam based on all five selections.

Practice: Each of the following five selections follows a <u>different</u> and sometimes <u>mixed</u> pattern of organizing ideas. As you read each selection, identify the pattern(s) of organization used by the author. Be sure your notes reflect the important facts organized in a way to help you study. Then answer the questions that follow.

Selection One

The Juvenile and Criminal Court Systems

The juvenile court, with its emphasis on individualized treatment, was originally visualized as a social agency or a clinic, not a court of law. That vision was later to encounter much criticism. The court was to be a social institution designed to protect and rehabilitate the child, not a court designed to try the child's guilt. The purpose was to treat, not punish. Clearly, then, the juvenile court was to differ from the criminal court. In fact, the basic purpose of the juvenile court was to protect the child from the <u>stigma</u> attached to the proceedings in a criminal court. Even the vocabulary of the courts differed. Children would not be "arrested" but "summoned"; they would not be "indicted," but a petition would be filed on their behalf. If detention were necessary, they would be detained in facilities separate from adults but not in jails. They would not have a "trial" but a "hearing," which would be private and in which juries and prosecuting attorneys would rarely, if ever, be used. Nor would they usually have counsel. The hearing would be informal, for the ordinary <u>trappings</u> of the courtroom would be out of place. Judges would not act as impartial observers as was their function in the criminal court. Rather, they would act as wise parents disciplining their children in love and tenderness, deciding in an informal way what was best for those children.

It was extremely important, in the implementation of this philosophy, that a judge be well trained. The founders of the juvenile court emphasized that judges should be trained as lawyers, that they love children, that they be able to understand the point of view of the child. They should have the patience and wisdom necessary to seek the cause of the child's problems and design a plan for individualized treatment.

Juveniles would not be "sentenced" as the concept is known in the criminal court. Rather, after the hearing they would be "<u>adjudicated</u>." A <u>disposition</u> would be made only after a careful study of the juvenile's background and potential, and the decision would reflect the best interests of the child. The relationship between the child and the judge was seen as that of a counselor- or doctor-patient relationship.

The juvenile court hearing differed from the criminal court in procedure as well as in theory. Rules of evidence that characterize the criminal court were not applied to the juvenile court. For example, the juvenile did not have the right to cross-examine his or her accusers. Indeed, there was no need for that safeguard since everyone was assumed to be acting in the best interests of the child. Hearsay evidence, which would be excluded from the criminal court, would be admit-

178

ted in the juvenile court. Judges needed all the information they could get for an adequate disposition of the case, and it was not considered that the information might be false. The emphasis in the juvenile court was not on what the child did but what the child is. The court was to be concerned mainly with a total diagnosis of the child which would enable the judge to "save" the child from a criminal career through proper treatment, in contrast with the criminal court's concern with the narrow issue, during trial, of the guilt or innocence of the accused.

(Reid, 534–535)

Notes

The Juvenile and Criminal Court Systems

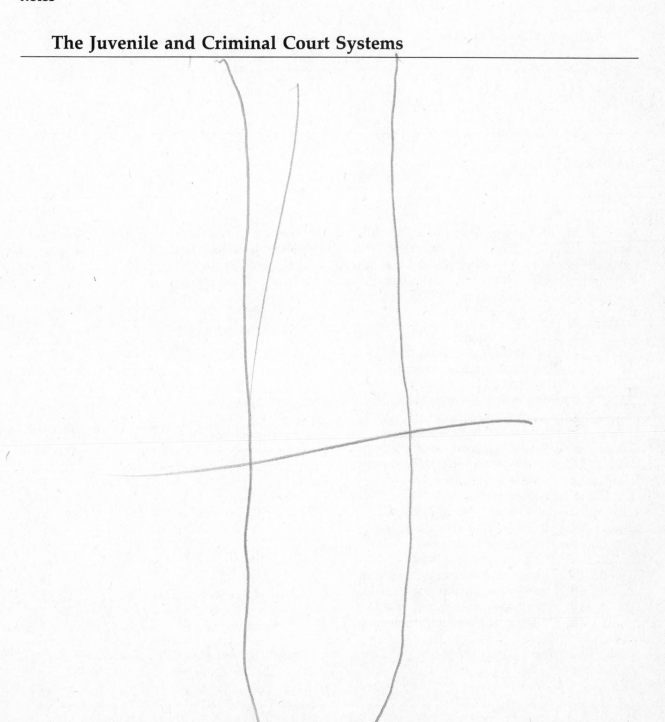

Pattern: Reid uses a _____
pattern of organization to present the facts.

Vocabulary: You can derive the meaning of each of these words from the
context of the passage. Use each of these words in your own sentence.

1. stigma: _____

_____

2. trappings: _____

_____

3. adjudicated: _____

_____

4. disposition: _____

_____

Sample Short-Answer Question: Based on your reading of this passage, you should have an understanding of the criminal and juvenile court
systems. Following are several phrases that describe one or the other system.
If the phrase describes the criminal system, put a **C** on the line. If the phrase
describes the juvenile system, put a **J** on the line.

_____ **1.** No jury
_____ **2.** Treatment emphasized
_____ **3.** The person's guilt is on trial
_____ **4.** The accused has a hearing
_____ **5.** The accused has a trial
_____ **6.** Punishment is emphasized
_____ **7.** No cross-examination
_____ **8.** The accused is summoned
_____ **9.** Hearsay evidence is admitted
_____ **10.** The judge is an impartial observer
_____ **11.** There is a jury present
_____ **12.** The person is adjudicated
_____ **13.** Rehabilitation is emphasized
_____ **14.** The judge takes an active role
_____ **15.** The accused is arrested
_____ **16.** The person is sentenced
_____ **17.** The accused may cross-examine
_____ **18.** Hearsay evidence is not allowed
_____ **19.** A counselor relationship exists
_____ **20.** Prosecuting attorneys are present

Essay Question: Write an essay question an instructor might ask about
this selection.

_____

_____

Radio

For the advertiser today, radio is largely limited to spot announcements. Preparing a radio commercial can be most challenging, because it is limited to words and the possible accompaniment of music and sound effects. There are no embellishments, such as artwork and layouts. Therefore, the copy written for a good print advertisement may not be at all suitable for a radio commercial.

Production of Radio Commercials: Live or Transcribed

There are several useful ways of classifying radio commercials. One distinction is between live and transcribed commercials. Live commercials have several possible advantages. For one thing, they more readily permit delivery by a station or network "personality," someone who is likely to have a sizable audience. Such personalities may add a kind of endorsement value merely by presenting the advertiser's message. Live commercials also add a sense of immediacy by their very nature. It is also possible to make very late changes in the commercial when it is live. Live spot commercials can tie in with local situations. Finally, live commercials can be less expensive. On the other hand, live commercials run the risk of error and poor delivery.

Transcribed commercials offer the advertiser complete control over his advertising, short of an equipment failure. They permit more complex scripts, calling for musical accompaniment, sound effects, and a number of voices. However, because they are usually more complex and involve the additional steps of transcribing, they are usually more expensive than live commercials.

Types of Radio Commercials

Commercials may also be classified by the kind of copy approach used. The straight commercial, as the name suggests, is simply an announcement about the merits of the product, delivered by an announcer without the aid of any special effects or music. Because it is a problem to get attention with only a limited time for presenting a message, there are many who argue that this technique leaves something to be desired. Nevertheless, it is frequently used and is probably the simplest to write.

Another variety is the dialogue commercial, a conversation about the product by two or more persons, one of whom is usually the announcer. These may be real people or imaginary characters. The conversation is usually an endorsement of the product in testimonial form. Although this technique can be used effectively, it presents a problem in creating believability and not sounding like a well rehearsed play.

Still another approach to radio commercials is the dramatic commercial. This is a form of playlet with a brief story plot, generally employing professional actors. Usually it is followed by an announcer who gives a straight commercial finish. Its main virtues are its strong attention-getting value and its ability to create interest. In both dialogue and dramatic commercials there is a choice of playing it straight or using humor.

Finally, there is the singing commercial. This technique has been much criticized by listeners, probably because some very poor commercials have been made using this technique. Some of the better singing commercials have been very popular. The Boston Pops Orchestra has even made symphonic arrangements of them that never fail to bring a huge favorable response from the audience. One variation of the singing commercial that has been rather successful in recent years has been the musical theme that uses no lyrics but is accompanied by a straight announcement. As the theme is repeated in a number of commercials, it becomes identified with a particular product. In most situations, music with or without lyrics becomes a part of a commercial using one of the other forms mentioned above.

(Mandell, 542–543)

Radio

Pattern: Mandell uses a _____
pattern of organization to present the facts.

Vocabulary: The following words appear in the selection. Define them according to the context in which they appear.

1. embellishments: _____

2. copy: _____

3. playlet: _____

4. virtues: _____

5. lyrics: _____

Sample Short-Answer Question: Match the commercial at the left with its characteristic(s) at the right. Each type of commercial may be used more than once.

1. Live commercial
2. Transcribed commercial
3. Straight commercial
4. Dialogue commercial
5. Dramatic commercial
6. Singing commercial

_____ Is the easiest to write
_____ Has an attention-getting plot
_____ Uses a tune plus an announcement
_____ Is very costly and complex
_____ Allows for last-minute script changes
_____ Has an endorsement-type conversation
_____ Announces the product simply
_____ Can be serious or humorous
_____ Can be delivered by a network star
_____ Sounds overly rehearsed at times
_____ Is usually not very expensive
_____ Uses current situations

Essay Question: Write an essay question an instructor might ask about this selection.

_____

_____

Selection Three _____

Preparing the Retail Advertisement

The Plan

The preparation of a retail advertisement starts with the advertising plan. About two weeks before the publication date, the buyer is asked to submit certain information on copy fact forms. The form will indicate the item to be advertised, the date of the advertisement, the newspaper, and the space. The buyer fills in important copy facts about the merchandise, including colors, sizes, and prices. He also indicates any special requirements, such as the use of a manufacturer's logotype, the use of brand name in the headline or copy, or inclusion of mail order information. The form also contains a due date for the form to be returned to the advertising department.

The Advertising Manager

When the copy fact forms are returned to the advertising department, together with samples of the merchandise to be advertised, the advertising manager makes a last review of the advertising plans to be sure that the right merchandise is being promoted. Then he issues instructions to his staff for the execution of the advertisements. At this point, the advertising manager may rough out a layout and then turn the assignment over to a copy supervisor or copywriter; he may turn the advertisement responsibility over to the copy supervisor or copywriter without preparing the rough layout; he may have the art director or a layout artist prepare a rough layout and turn the copywriting task over to the copy supervisor or copywriter. Finally, he may call for a coordinated effort, assigning the advertisement to the layout artist and copywriter simultaneously, expecting them to work together on copy and layout.

The Copywriter

After the layout is prepared, the copywriter, working with the buyer, goes over the copy fact form for any additional information and to <u>ascertain</u> the best approach to advertising the merchandise. The copywriter also may turn to other sources, such as the manufacturer and reference books, for additional information. When the copy and layout have been prepared, they are sent to the advertising manager for approval. Frequently it is checked by the buyer as well.

In Production

The advertisement is now ready for production. Artwork will be assigned either to staff artists and photographers or to <u>freelance</u> artists and photographers. The production manager will mark up the copy and layout to specify sizes and kinds of type and sizes of illustrations. This information is then sent to the newspaper, where the advertisement will be composed. The newspaper sets the display lines and copy, makes the photoengravings, and composes these elements according to the layout. <u>Wait order proofs</u> are then made and sent to the advertising department, where they are proofread by the advertising staff and the buyer and returned to the newspaper for corrections. A second set of corrected proofs is then sent, and if no further corrections are necessary, a day or two before the advertisement is to appear in the newspaper the advertising department proofreader issues a <u>release order</u> for publication of the advertisement.

The Final Steps

The task is by no means completed at this point. The advertising department now sends proofs of the advertisement to the buyer to remind him to have the merchandise available for sale and also to inform the salespeople in the department about the advertisement.

After the advertisement has been published, the advertising department will prepare complete records of the occasion. Copies of the advertisement and competitive advertisements are filed. Data on sales resulting from the advertisement are also gathered and filed. Finally, records are made of costs so that the appropriate departments can be charged, and bills are prepared for resources when cooperative advertising is used.

(Mandell, 642–647)

Notes

Preparing the Retail Advertisement

Notes (continued)

Pattern: Mandell uses a _____
pattern of organization to present the facts.

Vocabulary: Using the context, determine the meanings of these words.

1. copy fact forms: _____

2. logotype: _____

3. ascertain: _____

4. freelance: _____

5. wait order proofs: _____

6. release order: _____

Sample Short-Answer Question: Number the following statements to show their sequence in the selection.

_____ The ad manager assigns the work to a layout artist and a copywriter simultaneously.

_____ The advertising manager approves the copy and the layout.

_____ The production manager orders size and typeset.

_____ The buyer submits information about the item to be advertised.

_____ The staff reads proofs.

_____ The buyer and the copywriter determine the best advertising approach based on the preliminary layout.

_____ The proofreader releases the ad for publication.

_____ The advertising manager makes a rough layout of the ad.

_____ The newspaper composes and sets the ad.

_____ The ad is filed along with competing ads and sales data.

Essay Question: Write an essay question an instructor might ask about this selection.

_____

_____

Selection Four _____

Earlier Business Cycle Theories

The Sunspot Theory

In the late nineteenth century, some economists believed that sunspots caused changes in business activity. Inane as this theory may sound, it did have some scientific basis. Sunspots affected the weather, and the weather affected the output of farmers. Since agriculture was such a large part of business activity, a change in agricultural output would affect overall business conditions. Historically, there was a fairly high correlation between sunspot cycles and agricultural cycles, but, unfortunately for the theory's advocates, the correlation seemed to disappear just as the theory was gaining ground. The sunspot theory would have been a very useful predicting tool had the relationship between weather and business activity held, since we can predict sunspot activity accurately. Given the high accuracy of that prediction, the link to business activity could have been quite useful. Meteorological data would have led to sunspot prediction, which would have enabled weather prediction, which finally would have allowed business-activity prediction.

The Innovation Theory

We all know about some of the great inventions that have been made—the cotton gin, the telephone, and many others. An invention is the creation of something new. Once the invention is made, businesses have to figure out how to use it. That's where innovation comes in. We define innovation as the adaptation of an invention to actual production techniques. Many inventions never lead to innovations because they are never put to use; think about all the unsuccessful home inventors with their gadgets piled high to the basement ceiling.

The idea behind the innovation theory was

that innovations caused <u>fluctuations</u> in investment, which ultimately caused ups and downs in business activity. As soon as one <u>entrepreneur</u> decided to innovate (use an invention), many businesspersons would hop on the bandwagon. In so doing, they'd also invest in the new production process, and we would see a rise in overall business activity as all this investment took place. Soon the new investment rage would die down, and <u>aggregate</u> business activity would slow down as a consequence. Hence, <u>sporadic</u> innovations would cause ups and downs in economic activity.

There is an important difference between the innovation theory and the sunspot theory. Sunspot activity is predictable; however, we don't know how to predict when innovations will occur. After the fact, we can hypothesize which ones caused the particular "take off" in economic activity, but we wouldn't have known beforehand what to predict. The innovation theory is therefore useful for explaining cycles, but not for predicting the timing of them.

Notes

The Psychological Theory

The psychological theory holds that the psychological reactions of businesspersons to changes in political, social, and economic events result in business-activity cycles. These decision makers ride waves of optimism, depending on the prospects for peace or war, on new discoveries of natural resources, and on many other factors.

Many stock market analysts maintain that swings in stock prices are due to psychological factors. The psychological theory may indeed prove useful in explaining stock market waves. Be careful, though: A dip in the stock market doesn't always precede a recession. In fact, one astute observer noted that the stock market has predicted nine of the last five recessions!

(Miller, 130–131)

Earlier Business Cycle Theories

Pattern: Miller uses a _____
pattern of organization to present the facts.

Vocabulary: Using clues in the passage, determine the meaning for each
of the following general or technical words.

1. inane: _____

2. correlation: _____

3. innovation: _____

4. fluctuation: _____

5. entrepreneur: _____

6. aggregate: _____

7. sporadic: _____

Circle the word that better completes each sentence.

1. The (inane / aggregate) effect of three days of rain was widespread flooding.

2. (Fluctuation / Innovation) in industry leads to an upward trend in stock prices.

3. (Entrepreneurs / Correlations) usually risk large amounts of capital.

4. The critic's (sporadic / inane) reviews of new books led me to question his value as a professional.

5. (Sporadic / Aggregate) visits to the library showed his lack of interest in reading.

Sample Short-Answer Question: Match the correct theory with its basis.
(A theory may match more than one basis.)

_____ Based on physical occurrences   **1.** Psychological theory
_____ Based on human creativity   **2.** Sunspot theory
_____ Based on human reactions   **3.** Innovation theory
_____ Based on predictions
_____ Based on events after the fact

Essay Question: Write an essay question an instructor might ask about
this selection.

_____

_____

Selection Five

Crime as the Cost of American Creativity

As the recent *Newsday* series on crime pointed out, though crime rates have dipped in the past year or two, over the long range of the past 20 years they have been dramatically increasing. Even before those two decades, the rates of crime in the United States were significantly higher than they were in the western European countries. Why is crime so prevalent in the United States? Several explanations are usually offered.

One primary theory tries to explain the motivation to commit crime by social conditions: poverty, unemployment, discrimination. If this theory were correct, giving everyone a guaranteed annual income to keep above the poverty line would solve our crime problem.

Although eliminating poverty would be a desirable goal in itself, I doubt that giving everyone a guaranteed income would do very much to lower the crime rates in the United States. The typical criminal does not commit a burglary in order to go to the supermarket and buy dinner for his family. The typical criminal is more likely to be a youth under the age of 20 who steals to pay for drugs, cars, expensive clothing or other nonnecessities.

A second popular explanation for our high crime rate is the failure of our criminal justice system. The courts—this theory holds—are too lenient on convicted criminals and permit plea bargaining, putting dangerous criminals back on the streets quickly. If this were true, we could reduce the crime rate by changing our criminal justice system and really getting tough with convicted criminals. Although long-term sentences for repeat offenders might do good, as Nassau County District Atttorney Dennis Dillon recently pointed out, most criminals never get caught. One reason the criminal justice system has not been effectively changed to stop crime is that such a reform would change the very nature of our society. Conceivably, we could triple the number of judges, prosecutors, policemen and jail cells. But do we want to have a society with a policeman on every corner and a large group of people in prisons? Polls have suggested most Americans do not want to see a police state instituted in order to eliminate crime.

In order to understand the high crime rate, we must look at the factors that prevent people from committing crime. Sociologists call these "social control mechanisms." Society has two basic mechanisms for maintaining social order or keeping people from crime. First, there is the threat of force: People who commit a crime can be sent to prison. But much more important, in most societies, is the second mechanism: The learning by the people of a set of norms or social rules that make them believe it is wrong to commit crimes. It is my hypothesis that the primary reason we have high crime rates in the United States lies in the substance of our culture that emphasizes the rights of individuals over the needs of society.

Of all the large societies in the world, the United States is perhaps the one that places the greatest emphasis on individual rights and the least on collective needs. This emphasis on individualism and the protection of individual rights is the source of some of the social problems that we have today, such as crime, and at the same time the source of what makes this society the envy of many people around the world: great personal freedom and opportunity.

How does the emphasis on individualism interfere with the operation of social control mechanisms? Let us first consider the use of force or punishment. Because we are so concerned with the rights of individuals, we hesitate to make use of severe punishment. One of the reasons that many people oppose capital punishment is the possibility that an innocent person might be executed. It is better to have a thousand real murderers get prison sentences than to mistakenly execute one innocent person. Thus our emphasis on individual rights makes it difficult to use punishment as a means of controlling crime.

The same emphasis on individualism appears in our criminal justice system. It is run under a system of protection of civil liberties that makes it very difficult to convict known criminals. Many persons known by the police to have committed crimes are walking about free because our strict rules of evidence exclude from the courtroom many incriminatory facts. In some cases, the difficulty of obtaining admissable evidence leads prosecutors to settle for guilty pleas to charges lesser than the crimes the persons committed, thus again sending these persons back onto the streets sooner than they would otherwise be there.

But the emphasis on individual rights that makes it difficult to prosecute and punish criminals also gives Americans a degree of civil liberty not found in most other countries. It is true that there have been many serious cases in the United States of abridgment of civil liberties. We tend to take for granted the freedom we have and complain about infringements on that freedom. Although some of us might not appreciate this freedom, its value is not lost on the people of countries like Poland, where civil liberties are nonexistent and a government is maintained in power by force alone.

Our emphasis on individualism also makes the other mechanism of social control, the internal one, weaker. Our society is one in which there is not a tremendous amount of respect for authority. Americans are used to criticizing everything from our national leaders to our schools to our local laws. Law violators are frequently portrayed as heroes in American popular culture. Our cinema has hundreds of examples of the glorification of law violators from Butch Cassidy to the Godfather. This lack of respect for authority means that many people in the United States do not internalize a strong belief that it is wrong to violate the law. This is true not only of poor people but of rich people who commit white-collar crimes, which in terms of the amount of money stolen dwarfs the type of crime committed by poor people.

It is easy to condemn the lack of respect that Americans have for authority and the law. And we should do so. But again there is another side to the coin. The same attitude toward authority, the same loose commitment that we have to social rules also allows for great innovation and creativity. The stronger the norms or social rules are, the more likely people will be to learn them as children, and then follow them later as adults. But societies that do not tolerate nonconformity will generally have both low crime rates and low levels of creativity. Examples are the Soviet Union and Communist China. The United States is a society that has fostered a tremendous amount of creativity. Since the end of World War II, our scientific establishment has led the world in almost every area of science. I am not trying to say that crime is good. I am trying to point out that the same type of culture that leads to a high crime rate also leads to many good things such as great personal liberty and much creativity.

A final illustration of the relation of crime to the attitude toward authority appears in the issue of capital punishment. Would the death penalty cause a reduction in the number of homicides? I believe it would, for two reasons. First, there are some, although probably not very many, who would not commit a crime if they knew they might face the electric chair. Since most homicides are not committed by rational people who engage in a cost-benefit analysis before committing the act, this would probably only have a minor impact on the homicide rate. The second reason that the death penalty probably would decrease homicide is much more important.

I believe that the homicide rate has been rising in the United States over the past 20 years because more and more American children are growing up believing that it is *not* wrong to kill someone. Children learn directly and indirectly. At home and at church, they may be told directly that it is wrong to kill people. But they also see how society actually treats murderers. They see that many people who commit murder are treated leniently. In the case of juvenile murderers, the penalty frequently consists of no more than being sent to a reform school for a few years. They see someone like John Hinckley Jr., who attempted to kill President Reagan, acquitted on the ground of insanity. They see mass murderers like Charles Manson become cult heroes.

The adoption of the death penalty and the occasional execution of a convicted murderer is a powerful and effective way to teach children that murder is wrong and that society believes it to be wrong. The punishment of violators of rules is a way of strengthening the commitment to those rules. The homicide rate will go down when more people believe more firmly that it is wrong to kill.

Even if my analysis of the possible effects of the death penalty is correct, there still remains a serious question about whether it should be reinstated. If we move toward the type of society that places a stronger emphasis on meeting collective needs and maintaining social order, there is danger that we may be losing some of what is great about America: our individual freedom and a society that encourages diversity and creativity.

(Cole, 55)

Notes

Crime as the Cost of American Creativity

Notes (continued)

Pattern: Cole uses two major patterns of organization to present facts in this selection. The two patterns are _____ and _____.

Vocabulary: Look back at the selection. Mark ten words that appear difficult. List those ten words in the spaces provided. Use the context of the selection to determine the meanings of the ten words. If you cannot determine a meaning, use your dictionary.

Words   **Meanings**

1. _____   _____

2. _____   _____

3. _____   _____

4. _____   _____

5. _____   _____

6. _____   _____

7. _____   _____

8. _____   _____

9. _____   _____

10. _____   _____

Sample Short-Answer Questions: Answer each of the following based on your understanding of the facts in the selection.

_____ **1.** According to the author, eliminating poverty in the United States would
  (a) guarantee everyone access to non-necessary items.
  (b) have no effect on the crime rate.
  (c) lower the crime rate.
  (d) greatly affect the typical criminal.

_____ **2.** The author believes that the high crime rate is related to
  (a) society's leniency toward criminals.
  (b) tripling the police force.
  (c) the fact that most criminals are never caught.
  (d) the plea bargaining that is done for most criminals.

_____ **3.** The author states that there is a direct relationship between
  (a) individualism in the United States and the high crime rate.
  (b) the threat of force and low crime rates.
  (c) learning a set of society's rules and low crime rates.
  (d) none of the above.

_____ **4.** The effect of incorrectly executing an innocent person
  (a) is minimal if a thousand real murderers are executed.
  (b) is a factor in the opposition to capital punishment.
  (c) is a factor in the numbers who have voted for capital punishment.
  (d) has no effect on the average American.

_____ **5.** The individual rights that are guaranteed in America are
  (a) directly related to the difficulties experienced in the criminal justice system's attempt to convict known criminals.
  (b) greater than those known in other countries.
  (c) taken for granted.
  (d) all of the above.

_____ **6.** Individualism in America
  (a) strengthens the concept of punishment for crimes.
  (b) weakens the internal social control mechanisms.
  (c) weakens one's belief in the immorality of committing a crime.
  (d) strengthens the internal and external social control mechanisms.

_____ **7.** A high rate of crime
  (a) leads to greater personal creativity.
  (b) occurs in all creative cultures.
  (c) is related to personal liberty and creativity.
  (d) is found in highly structured societies.

_____ **8.** Most murderers would not kill if they
  (a) were well aware of the legal penalties.
  (b) were less rational.
  (c) could find creative releases for their energies.
  (d) none of the above.

_____ **9.** Children are affected by seeing and hearing about
   (a) criminals who receive lenient penalties.
   (b) convicted juvenile murderers who are sentenced to reform school.
   (c) convicted criminals who are acquitted on the basis of insanity.
   (d) convicted murderers who are accepted by the public.

_____ **10.** Individual freedom and social order
   (a) have little to do with the homicide rate.
   (b) are lost in a creative civilization.
   (c) are two mechanisms that keep people from committing crimes.
   (d) are easily attained by most societies.

Essay Questions: Write two essay questions an instructor might ask about this selection.

1. _____

   _____

2. _____

   _____

Practice Quiz: The following essay questions test your understanding of the five preceding selections. Write your answers on separate paper.

1. Discuss the important features of the juvenile and criminal court systems and show how they relate to one another.
2. Distinguish between live and transcribed commercials. Then discuss why a client might choose each of the four types of radio commercials.
3. When a buyer contacts an advertising agency to develop a promotion for a product, many people become involved. Relate the role of each person to the creation of a successful ad campaign.
4. Briefly present the relationships between the three business theories and possible business trends. Illustrate each theory-trend relationship.
5. Explain the increase in United States crime statistics in relation to the major social control mechanisms.

Taking Tests

Introduction

27

You followed a procedure when reading a text assignment:

- Preview specific parts of the chapter.
- Read for an understanding of the important ideas.
- Determine the meanings of new words as you read.
- Organize the important ideas in notes.
- Anticipate test questions according to the ways in which the author organized the information.

At this point the instructor usually wants to determine whether or not you have learned the material successfully. When you understand the text and lecture material and when you take well-organized notes on that material, you have set the stage to study. Now you must demonstrate a mastery of the coursework. Tests are the most common measures that instructors use to determine how much students understand. Here are some helpful general study procedures.

The first two items relate to your instructor:

1. Ask the instructor to identify which material, chapters, and readings the test will be based upon. Perhaps the instructor only wants to include a portion of the course syllabus.
2. Ask the instructor what types of questions will appear on the quiz. Will there be essay questions, multiple-choice questions, short-answer questions, true-false questions, or a combination?

The next four items relate to your notes:

3. Plan to begin studying well in advance of the test. "Cramming" is usually not productive and is easily exhausting.
4. Study all your notes. Use your lecture notes and review the patterns of organization noted in the chapters. Good notes that follow an established pattern of organization can prove their worth as you study.
   - If the chapter notes follow a simple-listing pattern, study all listed facts pertaining to the main ideas.
   - If the chapter notes are organized sequentially, study the sequence of dates, steps, or processes.
   - If the chapter notes are organized according to causes and effects, learn the facts according to the reasons for or the results of an event or idea.
   - If the chapter notes follow a comparative organization, study the differences and/or similarities between subjects.

5. Be sure that all subject definitions are understood; 3″ by 5″ index cards can help. Write the word or phrase on one side and the definition on the reverse.

Side 1	Side 2
pandemic	*a widespread epidemic disease*

6. Use index cards also to summarize key topics and important related details.

Side 1	Side 2
employee benefits	*1. group life insurance* *2. medical or disability insurance* *3. pension programs* *4. paid vacations*

The last four items relate to your review of the material:

7. Using the chapter patterns of organization, set up sample test questions, such as "What are the results of . . . ," "List several facts . . . ," "Show the steps in . . . ," or "Show the differences between. . . ."
8. Test yourself. Define the words and discuss aloud the topics and details noted on the cards. Try to answer all sample essay questions aloud.
9. Review information with one or two well-informed classmates. Discuss, question, argue, and explain answers, and develop a variety of possible test questions. Another student may clarify a confusing item.
10. Feel comfortable knowing that you have studied and prepared thoroughly. Most students are nervous prior to an exam. It is normal to exhibit some nervousness in any tense situation. Excessive nervousness due to lack of preparation, however, can waste energy and can cause confusion.

Taking Objective Tests

28

Objective tests measure your recall of factual information and test your ability to understand basic meanings and relationships. Often students understand the course "facts" but do not do well on objective tests. There are several reasons for this. The reasons focus on following test directions, using test time, answering all questions, and experiencing difficulties with specific determiners and items such as true-false, double-negative, and multiple-choice questions.

First, many students do not follow test directions. As a result, they do not have enough time to complete the exam, and they answer some questions incorrectly. The following sections provide guidelines for avoiding these errors.

Following Directions

How carefully do you read directions before answering test questions?

Example

1. Answer <u>ten out of fifteen</u> questions . . .
2. Choose the <u>least</u> likely to . . .
3. All the following <u>except which one</u> have a common . . .
4. Match <u>all</u> examples of . . .
5. Choose the <u>best</u> example and discuss . . .
6. Place the correct <u>letter</u> on the line and . . .

Some students do not read these types of directions carefully. Refer to the six preceding directions and list some common mistakes that students could make.

1. _A student might answer all fifteen questions._

2. _____

3. _____

4. _____

5. _____

6. _____

You should read the directions for each portion of the test. Be aware of **specific directions**.

198

Practice: Test your ability to follow directions by carefully reading each question below. Each one has a very specific direction in it. Read each question and do not answer it. You have two minutes to read the questions.

1. How <u>many</u> textbooks are required for this course? _____

2. On which night of the week do you do the <u>least</u> amount of studying? _____

3. Where do you do <u>most</u> of your studying? _____

4. Write your instructor's name at the <u>bottom</u> of the page. _____

5. What was the <u>most</u> important skill presented in this class? _____

6. What skill was the <u>least</u> important? _____

7. What course do you spend the <u>most</u> time preparing for? _____

8. What course do you spend the <u>least</u> time preparing for? _____

9. How many quizzes have you passed this term? <u>Circle</u> 0 1 2 3 4 5

10. Reread the PRACTICE directions.

Answering All Questions

Do you answer all required questions on exams? Another reason students do poorly on exams is they do not answer all of the questions. Instructors cannot award points for a blank space. In most cases, instructors do not penalize students for guessing. Therefore, attempt every required question on the test. Do not, however, spend so much time on one difficult question that you neglect answering the other questions. Some general guidelines are:

1. **Attempt all questions.**
2. **Don't waste time staring at questions. Leave the difficult questions you cannot answer and go on to the rest.**
3. **Complete the rest of the test.**
4. **Go back to the difficult questions and answer them. Guess if you must.**

Dividing Test Time

How efficiently do you use your time on a test? Students sometimes complain that they are not given "enough time" to complete the test. Sometimes this is true. But more often they are given enough time. The problem may arise from the students' ineffective preparation before the test or from the students' ineffective use of the time provided during the test. There are several ways to use the test time more realistically.

Example

Biology quiz: 2 hours

Part 1:   20 points true-false
Part 2:   30 points multiple-choice
Part 3:   20 points four short essays
Part 4:   <u>30</u> points one of two possible essays
              100 points

Estimation of time

2 hours = 120 minutes

Part 1 =   20% of test =   24 minutes
Part 2 =   30% of test =   36 minutes
Part 3 =   20% of test =   24 minutes
Part 4 =   <u>30%</u> of test =   <u>36 minutes</u>
                100%   120 minutes

Spend

20 minutes + 4-minute review on Part 1
30 minutes + 6-minute review on Part 2
20 minutes + 4-minute review on Part 3
30 minutes + 6-minute review on Part 4

Problems arise when a student does not adhere <u>fairly closely</u> to the allotted times. For example, a student who spends 30 minutes on Part 1, 45 minutes on Part 2, and 30 minutes on Part 3, may do very well on those portions. But simple arithmetic shows that this student has allowed <u>only</u> 15 minutes for the final 30-point question. The student risks failing the test as a whole because he or she has not allowed enough time to answer this 30-point question.

No matter how much time you spend on any single portion of a test, you can only achieve a set score value on that portion, and not a single point higher. You might, however, lose points because you never got to the other questions or had barely enough time to answer a question adequately.

1. **Wear a watch!**
2. **Make a note of the point value for each section of the test.**
3. **Make a note of the total time allowed for the test.**
4. **Divide the point value percentage into the total time to determine how much time to spend on each section.**
5. **Jot down the time allotment for each section.**

Recognizing Specific Determiners

A fourth reason for poor test performance is students' inability to analyze those portions of test questions which influence or sometimes determine a response.

Example

Consider each statement and mark it true or false.
_____ 1. **All** commuters drive to work.
_____ 2. **Some** commuters drive to work.

You cannot say that <u>all</u> commuters drive to work. "All" limits your answer by excluding any possibilities of other means of transportation, such as bus or train. You can, however, say that <u>some</u> commuters drive to work. "Some" leaves room for other possible means of transportation.

Consider the next example. It includes many specific determiners. Read and evaluate each sentence. Then check the statements that could be true.

Example

_____ 1. <u>All</u> college students wear jeans.
_____ 2. <u>Some</u> college students wear jeans.
_____ 3. <u>Most</u> college students wear jeans.
_____ 4. College students <u>never</u> wear jeans.
_____ 5. College students <u>always</u> wear jeans.
_____ 6. College students <u>only</u> wear jeans.
_____ 7. <u>Only</u> college students wear jeans.
_____ 8. College students wear jeans <u>all the time</u>.
_____ 9. <u>Every</u> college student wears jeans.
_____ 10. <u>No</u> college student wears jeans.
_____ 11. <u>Few</u> college students wear jeans.

In the preceding example, sentences 2, 3, and 11 are possible choices. None of the other choices should be checked because the underlined specific determiners create an "all-or-none" situation. For example, one could not state that "all," "only," or "every" college student wears jeans. Nor could one state that "no" college students wear jeans. It is, however, possible to state that "some," "most," or "few" college students wear jeans.

> You should be aware of specific determiners in test questions. **Specific determiners** are words or phrases that usually set up an all-or-none situation or generally determine the required answer.

Practice: Mark the specific determiner in each sentence. Answer true if the sentence is correct or false if the sentence is not correct.

_____   **1.** The Los Angeles Lakers always win on their home court.
_____   **2.** In surveys of popularity, an often-named American car is Ford.
_____   **3.** It never snows in Florida.
_____   **4.** No banks are open after 3:00 P.M.
_____   **5.** Humans will never colonize the other planets.
_____   **6.** Some senior citizens retire at sixty-five.
_____   **7.** Fair wages always insure good working conditions.
_____   **8.** Postcards are always cheaper to mail than first-class letters.
_____   **9.** All birth-control methods are effective.
_____   **10.** Most crimes are a result of unemployment.

Practice: Mark the specific determiner in each sentence. Answer each statement true or false.

_____   **1.** Some factory workers are more productive during the morning shift.
_____   **2.** Without exception, poor grades in high school mean poor grades in college.
_____   **3.** All professional photographers take better pictures than amateurs.
_____   **4.** In the Northeastern part of the United States, it always snows in February.
_____   **5.** All students desire to be well educated.
_____   **6.** Only matriculated students enrol in college courses.
_____   **7.** Jogging is the best exercise for everyone.
_____   **8.** Only teenagers develop acne.
_____   **9.** All children learn to speak before the age of five.
_____   **10.** Preschool education in the United States is never free.

Practice: Answer each statement true or false.

_____   **1.** Doctors always limit their practice of medicine to treating those who are ill.
_____   **2.** Weather conditions rarely affect air travel.
_____   **3.** Surgery always corrects some physical condition.
_____   **4.** Overcrowded living conditions invariably cause the buildup of slums.
_____   **5.** Bank tellers never make mistakes.
_____   **6.** Lawyers usually are more knowledgeable about legal affairs than teachers are.
_____   **7.** Most adults use aspirin to relieve the symptoms of their headaches.
_____   **8.** Some public places now reserve space for the nonsmoker.
_____   **9.** All women are in agreement with the themes of the women's liberation movement.
_____   **10.** Dentists never allow their patients to chew gum.

Answering True-False Questions

Many test questions require true-false answers. On the surface, they may appear easy. However, they can be difficult.

Example

_____ T-F: Students must take prerequisite courses prior to enrollment in other courses, but may take corequisite courses at any time.

This statement is only partly true. Although it is true that students must take prerequisite courses first, it is not true that they may take corequisite courses at any time. The answer is false since the entire statement is not true.

> **For an answer to be marked true, the entire answer must be true.**

Some statements appear true until you carefully test their truth by adding a specific determiner. Here is an example.

Example

_____ T-F: Students who take 12 credits during a semester have fewer class hours than students who take 15 credits.

Although it may be true that <u>some</u> students who take 12 credits have fewer class hours than <u>some</u> students who take 15 credits, it is not true of <u>all</u> students. By adding the specific determiner <u>all</u>, you can understand why the answer is false. Perhaps some students who take 12 credits have lab courses. They will have more class hours than the student taking 15 credits. Therefore, not <u>all</u> students who take 12 credits have fewer class hours than students who take 15 credits.

> **For an answer to be marked true, it must be true without exception.**

Practice: Mark each of the following statements true or false. If the statement is false, choose one of these reasons to show why it is false:

Reason #1: Part of the statement is true and part is false.
Reason #2: The statement has exceptions to it.

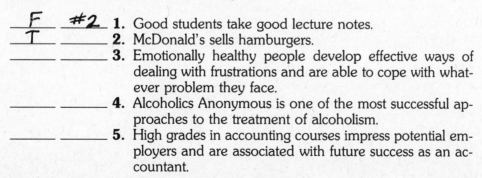

__F__ __#2__ **1.** Good students take good lecture notes.
__T__ _____ **2.** McDonald's sells hamburgers.
_____ _____ **3.** Emotionally healthy people develop effective ways of dealing with frustrations and are able to cope with whatever problem they face.
_____ _____ **4.** Alcoholics Anonymous is one of the most successful approaches to the treatment of alcoholism.
_____ _____ **5.** High grades in accounting courses impress potential employers and are associated with future success as an accountant.

Practice: Mark each statement true or false. If the statement is false, choose one reason to show why it is false:

Reason #1: Part of the statement is true and part is false.
Reason #2: The statement has exceptions to it.

_____ _____ **1.** Businesses with high payrolls employ more people than businesses with low payrolls.

_____ _____ **2.** Fraudulent advertisements contain statements of doubtful honesty.

_____ _____ **3.** English teachers often teach writing skills and are excellent writers.

_____ _____ **4.** Wild animals cannot be domesticated.

_____ _____ **5.** The psychiatrist deals with emotional illnesses and disturbances.

_____ _____ **6.** Good advertisements do not contain fraudulent statements.

_____ _____ **7.** Diseases can be genetically caused.

_____ _____ **8.** Good math students are usually able to solve math problems and can explain their answers easily.

_____ _____ **9.** Triangles are geometric figures that have three sides and one right angle.

_____ _____ **10.** People invest in the stock market for many reasons.

Practice: Mark each statement true or false.

_____ **1.** Plant and animal cells contain chlorophyll.

_____ **2.** Multinational corporations are those operating in several countries.

_____ **3.** Successful lawyers are good public speakers.

_____ **4.** Experienced actors overcome stage fright.

_____ **5.** Unsuccessful salespeople have low sales records.

_____ **6.** Criminals exhibit deviant behavior.

_____ **7.** Distribution of discount coupons brings customers into stores and guarantees low prices.

_____ **8.** Most states have a minimum age requirement for marriage.

_____ **9.** Mental retardation can be caused by physiological problems.

_____ **10.** Hypoallergenic cosmetics are allergy-tested and allergy-free.

_____ **11.** The earth's capacity to provide raw materials is limited.

_____ **12.** Savings banks never offer checking accounts.

_____ **13.** Popular people are more sociable than unpopular people.

_____ **14.** Fad diets are unhealthy.

_____ **15.** The ability to organize information is characteristic of successful students.

Answering Double-Negative Questions

In addition to experiencing difficulty when answering true-false items and questions with specific determiners, students often answer questions incorrectly because they overlook a negative word that changes the meaning of the question or statement.

Example

_____ T or F: Our country has <u>no</u> problems with crime.

If the word "no" is overlooked, the statement appears to be true. The words "problems" and "crime" acquire another emphasis. However, the correct answer is "false." The word "no" cannot be ignored in the statement.

In addition, many students are confused by the following type of sentence:

Example

_____ T or F: The motorist will <u>not</u> break the law if he does <u>not</u> go above the speed limit.

> **Two negatives** in a sentence have the effect of making the sentence difficult to understand. When reading a sentence with two negatives, cross out both negatives. Then determine whether or not the statement is true.

_____ The motorist will n~~o~~t break the law if he does n~~o~~t go above the speed limit.

This sentence becomes:

__T__ The motorist will break the law if he does go above the speed limit.

Example

_____ T or F: All competitive sports are n~~ot~~ ~~un~~harmful.

This sentence becomes:

__F__ All competitive sports are harmful.

**Practice:** Mark each statement true or false. Remember to cross out any double negatives before deciding whether a statement is true or false.

_____ 1. It is not untrue to say that most children enjoy playing games.
_____ 2. The professor was unfair when he graded the tests objectively.
_____ 3. It is not the disinterested passerby who ignores a cry for help.
_____ 4. I did not misunderstand the directions because I knew what to expect.
_____ 5. Nonphysically fit people keep their bodies in shape.

Practice: Mark each statement true or false.

_____ **1.** OPEC nations have no oil supplies.

_____ **2.** Depressed personalities are not unhappy people.

_____ **3.** Some women have no difficulty entering nonmale-dominated industries.

_____ **4.** Museum directors do not often make inaccurate judgments about the value of artwork.

_____ **5.** In some states, possession of small amounts of marijuana has not been decriminalized.

_____ **6.** Innovative thinking is an unmarketable quality.

_____ **7.** Most people can deal easily with the loss of a nonirreplaceable possession.

_____ **8.** It is impossible to balance a checkbook.

_____ **9.** Advertising slogans infrequently misrepresent the product.

_____ **10.** If the Internal Revenue Service does not find any miscalculations in your tax return, they will criminally prosecute you.

Practice: Mark the following statements true or false.

_____ **1.** Employment does not influence a person's buying power.

_____ **2.** For some, it is not difficult to understand the nontechnical aspects of computer technology.

_____ **3.** Skipping rope is not an inexpensive hobby.

_____ **4.** Inefficient machines break down frequently.

_____ **5.** Even a fair-minded person can be unresponsive to a beggar on the street.

_____ **6.** Enthusiastic audiences are not unresponsive.

_____ **7.** A nonrefundable airline ticket policy means the purchaser's money cannot be returned.

_____ **8.** Disrespect for one's elders is not a break in traditional values.

_____ **9.** It is not unusual for an abused child to suffer from emotional problems.

_____ **10.** In most banks, it is not uncommon to find daily instances of depositors' insufficient funds.

Answering Multiple-Choice Questions

Another popular question is the multiple-choice question. As in true-false questions, there may be hidden traps.

Example

_____ **1.** The Dodgers have been known as the home team in which of the following?
   (a) Los Angeles
   (b) Brooklyn
   (c) Denver
   (d) both (a) and (b)

Some students never read past answer (a), "Los Angeles." That answer appears correct, yet the Dodgers have also been known as the home team in Brooklyn. The best choice is (d), "both (a) and (b)."

Some students miss seeing an "all of the above" or "none of the above" response. Also, if two of the responses are definitely correct, the answer must be (d), "all of the above," even if the third answer is unknown.

Example

_____ **2.** Apples are
(a) red.
(b) golden.
(c) green.
(d) all of the above.
_____ **3.** Apples are
(a) sweet.
(b) tart.
(c) succulent.
(d) all of the above.

Consider all alternatives before selecting an answer. Sometimes students see one correct answer and immediately mark that choice without reading the other choices. One of the other choices may be the better response, or "all" or "none of the above" may be correct.

Frequently, two answers appear to be correct.

Example

_____ **4.** Physical fitness for the average person is best accomplished by
(a) jogging twenty miles a day.
(b) following a moderate and continuous exercise program.
(c) swimming once a year.
(d) jumping rope daily.

Answers (a) and (c) are eliminated because each is extreme or absurd. Answers (b) and (d) are possible choices. However, "jumping rope daily" is easily part of "following a moderate and continuous exercise program." The most logical answer is (b), because it is the most complete answer.

Often two answers appear to be correct. A basic guide is to use common sense to eliminate absurd or extreme choices. Narrow the options to the two most logical choices. Then consider the remaining two choices. If one choice is a partial statement of the other, choose the more complete statement.

Practice: Complete each of the following statements by choosing the best answer and by writing its letter on the line.

_____ **1.** The Miami Dolphins are
(a) saltwater animals.
(b) a football team.
(c) a competitive group of men.
(d) two Olympic swimmers.

_____ **2.** The Atlas and the Almanac are
    (a) statues in Rockefeller Center.
    (b) library books.
    (c) reading material.
    (d) reference materials.

_____ **3.** General Motors and Ford are
    (a) names of American cars.
    (b) manufacturing companies.
    (c) car manufacturers.
    (d) American car manufacturers.

_____ **4.** The American Express Card and Master Card are
    (a) credit cards.
    (b) used internationally.
    (c) accepted only in restaurants.
    (d) both (a) and (b).

_____ **5.** Juvenile delinquency is associated with
    (a) broken homes.
    (b) poor school experiences.
    (c) substandard environments.
    (d) all of the above.

Practice: Complete each of the following statements by choosing the best answer.

_____ **1.** Both lawyers and judges
    (a) present evidence at a trial.
    (b) train as trial lawyers.
    (c) are licensed to practice in any state.
    (d) none of the above.

_____ **2.** Psychiatrists and psychologists
    (a) are medical doctors.
    (b) treat emotional problems.
    (c) may prescribe treatment.
    (d) have the same training.

_____ **3.** Scissors are classified as
    (a) dangerous weapons.
    (b) metal objects.
    (c) cutting implements.
    (d) toys.

_____ **4.** A prerequisite is
    (a) a requirement taken before enrollment in a course.
    (b) a requirement successfully completed before enrollment in
        a course.
    (c) a requirement taken along with one or more courses.
    (d) an advanced course taken before a basic course.

_____ **5.** Editorials are newspaper features
    (a) presenting opinions.
    (b) presenting factual information.
    (c) found in daily editions only.
    (d) both (a) and (b).

_____ **6.** Excessive alcohol consumption is characterized by
   (a) increased awareness and drowsiness.
   (b) poor neuro-motor coordination.
   (c) an unsteady walk and sensible conversation.
   (d) slurred speech and clumsiness.

_____ **7.** Cigarette smoking is associated with
   (a) drug dependency.
   (b) health hazards.
   (c) respiratory ailments.
   (d) both (b) and (c).

_____ **8.** Smallpox and polio are diseases that
   (a) have been eradicated.
   (b) are very contagious.
   (c) can be prevented by immunization.
   (d) both (b) and (c).

_____ **9.** The defense attorney
   (a) cross-examines witnesses.
   (b) protects the legal rights of the accused.
   (c) prosecutes the defendant.
   (d) is a court-appointed lawyer.

_____ **10.** Quarks, leptons, and gluons are
   (a) the basic material in the universe.
   (b) the names of three of the seven dwarfs in "Snow White."
   (c) atoms.
   (d) always equal in mass, weight, and motion.

Practice: Complete each of the following statements by choosing the best answer.

_____ **1.** Which of the following statements is true?
   (a) Sleep is necessary for the normal functioning of any animal.
   (b) All animals have the same sleep pattern.
   (c) Lack of sleep increases the retention capacity of the mind.
   (d) all of the above.

_____ **2.** Top positions in large companies are usually held by
   (a) the board of directors.
   (b) chairperson, vice-chairperson, and secretary of the board.
   (c) union representatives from every department.
   (d) stockholders.

_____ **3.** The leaders and members of a meeting must agree that each person should
   (a) talk about one item at a time.
   (b) abide by the will of the majority.
   (c) respect the position and rights of the minority.
   (d) all of the above.

_____ **4.** The elderly often experience a
   (a) decline in creativity.
   (b) lack of interest in learning.
   (c) slowness of movements.
   (d) both (a) and (b).

_____ **5.** The least important quality a newscaster should possess is
   (a) a genuine sense of what is newsworthy.
   (b) an ability to communicate ideas in a clear manner.
   (c) good taste in clothing.
   (d) all of the above.

Taking Essay Tests 29

Another way instructors can determine whether or not you have successfully learned the material is by asking essay questions. Instructors usually ask essay-test questions to determine how students can draw together the facts and concepts studied during the term. They are testing the students' ability to understand and write about relationships rather than to recall isolated facts. Thus, essay-test questions are usually broader in scope than typical objective-test questions.

The key to a good grade on an essay test is being able to organize ideas, develop a line of thinking, and use examples to illustrate a theme. Some students know all the facts, write everything they know, and yet receive little credit for their answers to essay questions. Studying facts in isolation, failing to understand the relationships between ideas, writing tests filled with unrelated memorized facts, not following directions, and not dividing test time properly are common errors. The following section provides guidelines to help avoid these errors.

Following Directions: Answering the Question

Consider the following short essay questions. The phrase that indicates what type of essay is required is marked.

1. <u>Compare</u> the writing styles of Hemingway, Faulkner, and Steinbeck.

For an answer to this question you are required to write about the differences or similarities in authors' styles. A student who first writes about Hemingway's style, then Faulkner's, and finally Steinbeck's has recorded many facts. However, this student has neither answered the question nor demonstrated the knowledge required by the instructor. To do so, the student must draw together readings from many sources to show similarities and differences in the writers' styles; that is, in their prose structure, themes, and character development.

2. <u>Trace the development of</u> the insect's life cycle.

The key relationship you must understand here is the sequence of steps in the insect's development from birth to death. Your knowledge is demonstrated by recording the order of development, and not by listing the stages randomly. To do so is to list only isolated facts that neither answer the question nor demonstrate the knowledge required by the instructor. To demonstrate a real understanding, the student must show the sequential development of the insect's life.

3. <u>What are the results of</u> waste-dumping in our major rivers?

An answer to this question calls for an understanding of the relationship among waste-dumping, water pollution, and killing of fish. The student who lists general ideas about water pollution has put many facts on paper, but this student has failed to describe the causal relationship required in this answer. This student has neither answered the question nor demonstrated the knowledge required by the instructor. To do so, the student must show the causal relationship between existing river conditions and waste-dumping.

4. <u>Name five</u> uses for aspirin.

An answer to this question requires you to recall a list of facts about a topic. The student who writes about one fact, such as aspirin's chemical makeup, has not grouped the information. This student has memorized random facts and has failed to see the common bond that unites these facts. This student has neither answered the question nor demonstrated the knowledge required by the instructor. To do so, the student must draw a specific group of facts, the uses, from the information read about aspirin.

Understanding Terms Used in Essay Questions

Every instructor uses a variety of terms to elicit specific responses on essay tests. Be familiar with the terms and know what your instructor requires for each one. The following terms are grouped according to the <u>general</u> type of information required in the response.

Terms used in essay questions	What is required
1. compare contrast relate	Show the differences and similarities between ideas, people, events, or objects.
2. develop diagram trace	Show a step-by-step movement from one event, stage, occurrence, or idea to another.
3. list name state	Name several key ideas, people, events, or things. No explanation is required.
4. define describe discuss explain illustrate summarize	Give the idea, event, or subject and a definition and an example. This shows an understanding of the meaning and its application.
5. criticize evaluate justify prove	Present the author's viewpoint and discuss the way in which it is expressed and its validity and relevance; possibly add your opinion.

Organizing Ideas

It becomes easier to organize ideas once you understand what the question requires. You can allot a specific amount of time for each essay question. In addition, you can use two basic techniques when answering essay questions: writing a brief outline of the intended answer and beginning the essay with an introductory statement.

> **You can write a mini-outline for each essay question. The mini-outline briefly lists the major points intended for discussion.**

The mini-outline is a guide to be followed as you work through the essay. With a mini-outline, it is less likely that you will forget a key idea midway through the essay, stray from the topic, or lose sight of the direction the essay should take.

If you do not complete the essay, the mini-outline shows the instructor ideas you planned for discussion but did not elaborate.

> **You can begin the essay with an introductory statement identifying the key points for discussion.**

Examples

1. There are three major steps in Customer Execution: steps occurring in the broker's office, steps occurring at the exchange, and steps relaying information back to the customer.
2. There were four major reasons for the auto crash: bad road conditions, faulty traffic signals, improper headlights, and faulty driver judgment. In my opinion, _____ was the major cause of the crash.

In the first example you set up the sequence of facts you will discuss. In the second example you show the instructor a knowledge of all the causes and then proceed to choose one for discussion, as required by the instructor's question.

Practice: Consider the following essay questions and, in the space provided, write a mini-outline of your answers. Then, on separate paper, develop each answer in one or two paragraphs.

1. Compare your two favorite restaurants.

_____

_____

_____

_____

_____

2. Define the five types of context clues presented in this text.

_____

_____

_____

_____

_____

_____

_____

3. Discuss the suggestions for taking essay tests presented in this chapter.

_____

_____

_____

_____

_____

_____

4. Trace the steps to follow in studying for a weekly quiz.

_____

_____

_____

_____

_____

_____

_____

5. Describe the effects of noise on studying.

_____

_____

_____

_____

_____

_____

_____

_____

_____

_____

6. Summarize your instructor's most recent lecture.

_____

_____

_____

_____

_____

_____

_____

_____

_____

_____

Practice: Briefly answer the following essay-test questions. Include an introductory statement that identifies the key ideas.

1. Explain the differences between reading over one's notes and studying for an exam.

_____

_____

_____

_____

_____

_____

_____

2. Briefly describe the four major ways text authors can organize their subject matter.

_____

_____

_____

_____

_____

_____

_____

3. Discuss the reasons why some students do poorly on tests.

_____

_____

_____

_____

_____

_____

_____

4. Imagine that you have a text chapter assignment. Trace the steps you follow to mastering the material.

_____

_____

_____

_____

_____

_____

_____

_____

_____

_____

_____

_____

_____

_____

_____

_____

_____

_____

_____

_____

_____

_____

Drawing Inferences

Introduction 30

You have practiced the skills of locating important facts in written material and determining the author's way of organizing the facts. As a result, you read the passages and drew from them the relationships the author intended you to understand. Sensing relationships that are not stated, but implied, by the author is an important aspect of the reading skill called drawing inferences.

Drawing inferences from observed facts or written statements is basic to everyday living. In order to develop this skill, you must be able to recognize the facts from which inferences are logically drawn.

Consider the following picture and statements. Some of the statements are true or false according to observable facts in the picture. Mark them T or F. Mark a statement I (inferred) if it cannot be observed in the picture.

Courtesy of J.P.S. Associates, Inc.

_____ **1.** A can of Crisco is on Nancy's shelf.
_____ **2.** Four knives are hanging on the wall of Nancy's kitchen.
_____ **3.** Bob is trying to balance his checkbook with the help of a pocket calculator.
_____ **4.** There are two people in the room.

_____ **5.** Bob has not finished his coffee.
_____ **6.** The couple subscribes to _New York Magazine_.
_____ **7.** Nancy is cleaning up after dinner.
_____ **8.** Both Nancy and Bob have worried expressions on their faces.
_____ **9.** There are several electrical appliances in this room.
_____ **10.** One part of dinner required oil for cooking.

There is only one statement that should be labeled "true": "There are several electrical appliances in this room." This statement can be shown with the facts in the picture. The remaining statements should be labeled "inferred" because they are not shown directly in the picture.

> **Some statements can be proved factually and are thus known to be true; some can be disproved factually and are thus known to be false. Some ideas can be drawn logically from evidence and are thus known as inferences.**

Using the picture as a guide, list five true statements about the scene.

1. _____

2. _____

3. _____

4. _____

5. _____

Using the picture as a guide, list five false statements about the scene.

1. _____

2. _____

3. _____

4. _____

5. _____

Practice: Imagine that you are an astronaut exploring another planet. You
discover the objects pictured here. What statements can you make about the
civilization that created these objects?

1. _____
   _____

2. _____
   _____

3. _____
   _____

4. _____
   _____

5. _____
   _____

6. _____
   _____

7. _____
   _____

8. _____
   _____

9. _____
   _____

10. _____
    _____

Drawing Inferences from Stated Facts

31

Drawing inferences from what you read is a very important skill. You can sense ideas the author did not directly state yet wanted you to know.

Example

The sky is clear and crystal blue. The sun is warm and shines brightly. The birds sing as they float through the gently swaying trees. A soft breeze fills the air.

Logical Inference: <u>The weather is mild</u>.

Illogical Inference: <u>The weather is nasty</u>.

Can't Tell: <u>The birds are migrating south</u>.

The inferred statement "The weather is mild" can be supported logically with statements (evidence) from the paragraph: "The sky is clear and crystal blue," "The sun is warm and shines brightly," "birds . . . float through the gently swaying trees," "A soft breeze fills the air." It is illogical to conclude that the weather is nasty; the evidence contradicts that idea. When there is not enough information available, the reader can't tell whether or not the inference is logical, as in the statement about migrating south.

> **Facts can be proved or disproved with written, stated, or observed evidence. Inferences are ideas you draw <u>logically</u> from written, stated, or observed evidence.**

Practice: Each of the following short passages is followed by several statements. If a statement can be supported with evidence from the passage, write the evidence in the space at the right, and mark the statement <u>L</u> (logical). If the evidence in the passage contradicts the statement, mark it <u>ILL</u> (illogical). If there is not enough information to make a judgment, write <u>CT</u> (can't tell). The first one is done.

Evidence

1. Trudging from building to building through the snow, Peter wondered if he would get to Physics 202 on time.

    _L_ It is either the beginning of the spring semester or the end of the fall semester. → *trudging through the snow*

    ILL Peter attends an elementary school.

    _CT_ Peter dislikes physics.

2. It is difficult to feel the Christmas spirit in the poorest section of town. The only bright lights are those in the old rundown grocery or in the corner drugstore. Some decorations hang in windows, but these are not enough to cheer up an overwhelmingly dismal scene. Even the children reflect a saddened spirit. They may have wide-eyed stares as they press their noses against a frosted store window, but they will probably never get any of the toys they see there. How can their parents afford the shiny new trucks that cost $27.00 each? The small boy with his face pressed to the pane of glass knows that new toys are not a part of his Christmas.

_____ Only one child stares through the frosted window.

_____ The cost of a new truck equals a day's wages for the parents.

_____ The small boy does not expect a toy truck for Christmas.

_____ The grocery is located at the corner.

_____ The children stare at the toys.

3. The old woman sat at the second-floor window and, for a few moments, watched the activities below: the passersby, the cars and the occasional truck, and the groups of children who raced to meet the school bell. The woman smiled and walked to the stairway, where she petted her sleeping gray Siamese cat. Moving down the flight, she continued to the kitchen side door. Outside she found her bottle of milk on the steps and her newspaper in the driveway. As she started breakfast, she skimmed the paper and quickly located the movie and theater section.

_____ The woman lives in a private house.

_____ The children are playing hooky from school today.

_____ The old woman has children.

_____ She lives alone.

_____ She has regular deliveries made to her house.

Making Assumptions, Conclusions, Generalizations, and Predictions

32

You have practiced drawing inferences from stated material. In each example, you drew a logical inference, and you wrote the stated evidence for it. Inferences can be drawn from other than written material. Everyday survival depends on the ability to make several types of inferences. You can make many kinds of inferences based on either written material or observed facts. One kind of inference is the assumption.

Example

Each of you has volunteered for this dangerous experiment. You have all read the reports of previous test results. I assume you know the risks involved.

Questions

1. Is the assumption a logical one? _____

2. Mark the evidence that supports the assumption.

In this example, all volunteers have read the previous test reports. They have been told that the experiment is dangerous. Based on these facts, it is logical to assume that they are aware of the risks involved.

In addition to making assumptions, you can form conclusions based on either written material or observed facts. Here is an example.

Example

Katie bent down and stroked the tiny, shivering kitten. Holding it in her arms, she comforted the frightened animal. She said, "You're adorable. You'll love living with my pup, Fred, and my four cats, Onyx, Mendy, Fitch, and Blazes."

Questions

1. Can you conclude that Katie is an animal lover? _____

2. Mark the evidence that supports your conclusion.

The fact that Katie strokes the shivering animal, holds it in her arms and comforts it, along with the fact that she has a pup named Fred and four cats named Fitch, Onyx, Mendy, and Blazes is good proof for the conclusion that Katie is probably an animal lover.

You can make another type of inference when you generalize.

Example

Today almost every student in my technology class is carrying a lab manual. Most probably, the majority of tech students who have labs today are carrying lab manuals.

Questions

1. Is it correct to generalize that most tech students are carrying lab manuals? _____

2. Mark the evidence that supports your generalization.

3. Can you make the generalization that most students in school today are

   probably carrying lab manuals? _____

4. Give the reasons for your answer:

   _____

   _____

Consider the facts that lead to the generalization. A statement is made about a small group—the technology class. An observed behavior is noted about that group—almost everyone is carrying a lab manual. This evidence is the basis for generalizing to an equal, larger group—the majority of tech students. However, there is no logical evidence to support the generalization about a different group—most students.

Still another type of inference is the ability to predict outcomes or behavior.

Example

During the first half of the game, the inexperienced freshman squad struggled against the experienced, senior varsity football team. As they went to the lockers for halftime, the score was 21 to 0. During the third quarter, the freshmen scored only three points. By the end of the quarter, the score was 34 to 3. Most of the crowd began to head for the exits.

Questions

1. Were the fans correct to leave before the end of the game? _____

2. What prediction did the fans make? _____

3. Mark the evidence that supports the fans' prediction.

Based on the performance of the freshman squad and the large difference in the teams' scores, the fans were probably correct in predicting the outcome of the game. There is observable evidence to support their prediction.

You can draw **inferences** from a variety of situations such as daily experiences or written materials. It is important to draw those inferences from verifiable evidence. You can make an **assumption,** a logical explanation about behavior, if you base the assumption on observed behavior. Or you can draw a **conclusion** based on facts about a subject. You can make a **generalization,** a statement about the behavior of a large group, if you base it on the proved behavior of a similar, smaller group. And finally, you can make a **prediction,** a statement about probable future behavior, if you base it on evidence of past or present behavior.

Practice: Read the following selection carefully. The questions that follow require you to draw ideas logically from the reading. Be sure that your answers are based on evidence in the selection.

I never learned hate at home, or shame. I had to go to school for that. I was about seven years old when I got my first big lesson. I was in love with a little girl named Helene Tucker, a light-complected little girl with pigtails and nice manners. She was always clean and she was smart in school. I think I went to school then mostly to look at her. I brushed my hair and even got me a little old handkerchief. It was a lady's handkerchief, but I didn't want Helene to see me wipe my nose on my hand. The pipes were frozen again, there was no water in the house, but I washed my socks and shirt every night. I'd get a pot, and go over to Mr. Ben's store, and stick my pot down into his soda machine. Scoop out some chopped ice. By evening the ice melted to water for washing. I got sick a lot that winter because the fire would go out at night before the clothes were dry. In the morning I'd put them on, wet or dry, because they were the only clothes I had.

Everybody's got a Helene Tucker, symbol of everything you want. I loved her for her goodness, her cleanliness, her popularity. She'd walk down my street and my brothers and sisters would yell, "Here comes Helene," and I'd rub my tennis sneakers on the back of my pants and wish my hair wasn't so nappy and the white folks' shirt fit me better. I'd run out in the street. If I know my place and didn't come too close, she'd wink at me and say hello. That was a good feeling. Sometimes I'd follow her all the way home, and shovel the snow off her walk and try to make friends with her Momma and her aunts. I'd drop money on her stoop late at night on my way back from shining shoes in the taverns. And she had a

Daddy, and he had a good job. He was a paper hanger.

I guess I would have gotten over Helene by summertime, but something happened in that classroom that made her face hang in front of me for the next twenty-two years. When I played the drums in high school it was for Helene and when I broke track records in college it was for Helene and when I started standing behind microphones and heard applause I wished Helene could hear it, too. It wasn't until I was twenty-nine years old and married and making money that I finally got her out of my system. Helene was sitting in that classroom when I learned to be ashamed of myself.

It was on a Thursday. I was sitting in the back of the room, in a seat with a chalk circle drawn around it. The idiot's seat, the troublemaker's seat.

The teacher thought I was stupid. Couldn't spell, couldn't read, couldn't do arithmetic. Just stupid. Teachers were never interested in finding out that you couldn't concentrate because you were so hungry, because you hadn't had any breakfast. All you could think about was noontime, would it come? Maybe you could sneak into the cloakroom and steal a bite of some kid's lunch out of a coat pocket. A bite of something. Paste. You can't really make a meal of paste, or put it on bread for a sandwich, but sometimes I'd scoop a few spoonfuls out of the big paste jar in the back of the room. Pregnant people get strange tastes. I was pregnant with poverty. Pregnant with dirt and pregnant with smells that made people turn away, pregnant with cold and pregnant with shoes that were never bought for me, pregnant with five other people in my bed and no Daddy in the next room, and pregnant with hunger. Paste doesn't taste too bad when you're hungry.

The teacher thought I was a troublemaker. All she saw from the front of the room was a little black boy who squirmed in his idiot's seat and made noises and poked the kids around him. I guess she couldn't see a kid who made noises because he wanted someone to know he was there.

It was on a Thursday, the day before the Negro payday. The eagle always flew on Friday. The teacher was asking each student how much his father would give to the Community Chest. On Friday night, each kid would get the money from his father, and on Monday he would bring it to the school. I decided I was going to buy me a Daddy right then. I had money in my pocket from shining shoes and selling papers, and whatever Helene Tucker pledged for her Daddy I was going to top it. And I'd hand the money right in. I wasn't going to wait until Monday to buy me a Daddy.

I was shaking, scared to death. The teacher opened her book and started calling out names alphabetically.

"Helene Tucker?"

"My Daddy said he'd give two dollars and fifty cents."

"That's very nice, Helene. Very, very nice indeed."

"That made me feel pretty good. It wouldn't take too much to top that. I had almost three dollars in dimes and quarters in my pocket. I stuck my hand in my pocket and held onto the money, waiting for her to call my name. But the teacher closed her book after she called everybody else in the class.

I stood up and raised my hand.

"What is it now?"

"You forgot me."

She turned toward the blackboard. "I don't have time to be playing with you, Richard."

"My Daddy said he'd . . ."

"Sit down, Richard, you're disturbing the class."

"My Daddy said he'd give . . . fifteen dollars."

She turned around and looked mad. "We are collecting this money for you and your kind, Richard Gregory. If your Daddy can give fifteen dollars you have no business being on relief."

"I got it right now, I got it right now, my Daddy gave it to me to turn in today, my Daddy said . . ."

"And furthermore," she said, looking right at me, her nostrils getting big and her lips getting thin and her eyes opening wide. "We know you don't have a Daddy."

Helene Tucker turned around, her eyes full of tears. She felt sorry for me. Then I couldn't see her too well because I was crying, too.

"Sit down, Richard."

And I always thought the teacher kind of liked me. She always picked me to wash the blackboard on Friday, after school. That was a big thrill, it made me feel important. If I didn't wash it, come Monday the school might not function right.

"Where are you going, Richard?"

I walked out of school that day, and for a long time I didn't go back very often. There was shame there.

Now there was shame everywhere. It seemed like the whole world had been inside that classroom, everyone had heard what the teacher had said, everyone had turned around and felt sorry for me. There was shame in going to the Worthy Boys Annual Christmas Dinner for you and your kind, because everybody knew what a worthy boy was. Why couldn't they just call it the Boys Annual Dinner, why'd they have to give it a name? There was shame in wearing the brown and orange and white plaid mackinaw the welfare gave to 3,000 boys. Why'd it have to be the same for everybody so when you walked down the street the people could see you were on relief? It was a nice warm mackinaw and it had a hood, and my Momma beat me and called me a little rat when she found out I stuffed it in the bottom of a pail full of garbage way over on Cottage Street. There was shame in running over to Mister Ben's at the end of the day and asking for his rotten peaches, there was shame in asking Mrs. Simmons for a spoonful of sugar, there was shame in running out to meet the relief truck. I hated that truck, full of food for you and your kind. I ran into the house and hid when it came. And then I started to sneak through alleys, to take the long way home so the people going into White's Eat Shop wouldn't see me. Yeah, the whole world heard the teacher that day, we all know you don't have a Daddy.

(Gregory, 43–46)

_____ **1.** Helene Tucker is probably
   (a) a white girl.
   (b) a black girl.
_____ **2.** Richard believes that the relief system
   (a) helps families.
   (b) brings shame to poor people.
_____ **3.** When Richard sits in class, he
   (a) cannot concentrate.
   (b) is able to do the arithmetic.
   (c) can do the work, but doesn't want to.
   (d) often counts his money.
_____ **4.** The teacher responds to Richard's behavior by
   (a) showing great concern for him.
   (b) showing little concern for him.
   (c) making him the teacher's pet.
   (d) allowing him to contribute money to the fund.
_____ **5.** Richard probably sleeps
   (a) poorly each night.
   (b) very well.
   (c) at the Boys' Annual Dinner.
   (d) in wet clothing.
_____ **6.** When Richard receives the jacket, he
   (a) takes great pride in wearing it.
   (b) hates the colors and throws it away.
   (c) hates what it represents.
   (d) gives it back.
_____ **7.** One can conclude that Richard is
   (a) bright, despite his poor performance.
   (b) incapable of doing classwork.
   (c) indifferent about school.
   (d) a troublemaker.
_____ **8.** The author probably believes that people steal because of their
   (a) social circumstances.
   (b) evil natures.
   (c) desperate situations.
   (d) need to possess things.
_____ **9.** The author believes that
   (a) troublemakers should be separated from their peers.
   (b) stealing is unacceptable under any circumstance.
   (c) people should accept gratefully what the system offers.
   (d) even the poorest can achieve success.
_____ **10.** One can conclude that Richard has
   (a) gotten Helene out of his system.
   (b) contacted Helene since he began his stage career.
   (c) achieved success because of his love for Helene.
   (d) never really forgotten what Helene symbolized.

Applying Inference Skills in Text Selections

33

In this section you will have the opportunity to make predictions, generalizations, and assumptions, and to form conclusions based on information in short passages. Remember to base your inferences on evidence in each passage.

Practice: Read each text passage carefully. Then, use evidence from the passage to help you answer the question(s) that follow it.

1.   **Gods and Goddesses.** Gods and goddesses are the great and more remote beings. They are usually seen as controlling the universe, or, if several are recognized, each has charge of a particular part of the universe. Such was the case of the gods and goddesses of ancient Greece: Zeus was lord of the sky, Poseidon was ruler of the sea, and Hades was lord of the underworld and ruler of the dead. Beside these three brothers, there were a host of other deities, each similarly concerned with specific aspects of life and the universe.

(Haviland, 347)

_____ One can conclude that
   (a) the Greeks worshiped three deities.
   (b) all deities rule a specific aspect of the universe.
   (c) the Greeks were the only ancient culture ruled by deities.
   (d) most civilizations are ruled by gods and/or goddesses.

2.   Another development in modern capitalist economies that upsets the assumed natural balance of the marketplace is the growth of *conglomerates*. Conglomerates differ from monopolies in that rather than competitors in the same line of business, other types of firms are taken over. Thus, conglomerates do not necessarily limit competition, but when one large company buys up several other kinds of businesses, decision-making power in several economic sectors is concentrated in just a few dozen central boards of directors.

(Mauser and Schwartz, 13)

_____ Without conglomerates,
   (a) the marketplace would be naturally balanced.
   (b) business decisions would be made by a variety of boards of directors.
   (c) competition would surge in many industrial areas.
   (d) all businesses would be run as monopolies.

3.   Psychopaths are not out of touch with reality. On the contrary, they often can be very charming, friendly, and able to function well in society. Unlike neurotics, who are restricted by their condition, psychopaths are perhaps freer than most people because they are not burdened with the sense of morality or guilt. Accordingly, people tend to like psychopaths at first meeting, not realizing that their friendly behavior is entirely superficial and that they are capable of an almost unlimited range of antisocial acts. Generally, psychopaths go through life getting

involved in a series of impulsive, antisocial acts that may or may not get them in serious trouble. But aside from these incidents, they function well and in fact may be successful in our competitive society if they have developed at least a minimal ability to delay gratification and plan ahead.

Most delinquents and criminals are not psychopaths. They usually have developed a sense of morality, even though it may be somewhat different from that of the rest of society, and they do distinguish between acceptable and unacceptable acts. They may be willing to steal or even to kill, but would not steal from friends, would not be disloyal, would not hurt a woman, or whatever. In other words, they may be willing to break certain laws of society and commit acts that most other people would not, but they do have a code of ethics that may be just as strong as someone else's. In addition, most criminals are capable of forming deep personal relationships, experiencing strong emotions, and so on. In contrast, psychopaths do not experience love or affection. Some criminals are psychopaths, but they are the exception.

(Freedman, 467)

_____ From this passage you can predict that
  (a) psychopaths will probably steal from friends.
  (b) psychopaths will probably form deep personal relation-
      ships.
  (c) criminals often become psychopaths.
  (d) a criminal can move easily to the next stage of mental
      disorder—being a psychopath.
_____ From this passage you can conclude that
  (a) criminals are in touch with reality.
  (b) most criminals are psychopaths.
  (c) psychopaths tend to give unfavorable impressions in so-
      cial situations.
  (d) juvenile delinquents do not understand the laws they have
      broken.
_____ Psychopaths are likely to feel
  (a) guilt concerning social transgressions they commit.
  (b) no guilt concerning social transgressions they commit.
  (c) a need to be loyal to their friends.
  (d) intensely strong emotional bonds with their associates.

4.   It is clear that sleep is necessary for the normal functioning of any animal. A total lack of sleep produces not only fatigue but also much more extreme reactions such as depression, disorganized activity, hallucinations, and eventually even death. An animal that has not slept for a long time will lapse into sleep almost instantly if it is not deliberately kept awake. Keeping a person awake is a particularly vicious form of torture. It has frequently been employed in the so-called brainwashing of political prisoners, in which the goal is to weaken and disorient the individuals to the point that their most basic beliefs and values can be altered.

(Freedman, 320)

_____ You can conclude that
  (a) sleep is unnecessary for most animals.
  (b) without sleep, animals and people cannot think clearly.
  (c) brainwashing is effective only when a person has had ade-
      quate sleep.
  (d) lack of sleep affects people emotionally more than physi-
      cally.

5.   In all human societies, there exist individuals whose job it is to guide and supplement the religious practices of others. Such individuals are highly skilled at contacting and influencing supernatural beings and manipulating supernatural forces. Their qualification for this is that they have undergone special training. In addition, they may display certain unique personality traits that particularly suit them for their job. In societies with the resources to support occupational specialists, the role of guiding religious practices and influencing the supernaturals belongs to the priest or priestess. He or she is the socially initiated, ceremonially inducted member of a recognized religious organization with a rank and function that belongs to him or her as the tenant of an office held before by others. The source of power is the society and the institution in which the priest or priestess functions. The priest, if not the priestess, is a familiar figure in our own society; he is the priest, minister, pastor, rector, rabbi, or whatever the official title may be in some organized religion.

(Haviland, 351)

_____ A priest or priestess is usually
  (a) an official of a religious organization.
  (b) specially trained to communicate with supernatural forces.
  (c) granted temporary power by the society and the institution.
  (d) all of the above.

6.   It is almost impossible to come up with a satisfactory definition of what constitutes a happy or an unhappy marriage. One couple's happy compromise may be another's insurmountable stumbling block. If we cannot define "good" and "bad" marriages, we can hardly expect to come up with figures about how many of each kind occur. But even if we rely on information that does seem to be measurable, for instance the number of marriages that end in divorce, we soon discover how complicated the task is.

(Light and Keller, 430)

_____ From this passage you can conclude that
  (a) the number of good marriages equals the number of bad ones.
  (b) most couples compromise about the same issues.
  (c) more than one factor is responsible for marriage success or failure.
  (d) sociologists use divorce statistics to determine the reasons marriages fail.

7.   **Occupational Roles.** The kind of work we do often governs our view of the world. Imagine five people taking a walk through the park. One, a botanist, is fascinated by the variety of trees and plants. The zoologist is on the lookout for interesting animals. The third, a meteorologist, keeps an eye on the sky, noticing changes in the weather. The fourth companion, a psychologist, is totally unaware of the goings-on of nature, instead concentrating on the interaction between the people in the park. The fifth person, being a pickpocket, quickly takes advantage of the others' absorption to make some money. There are two lessons in this little story. The first, of course, is to watch your wallet carefully. The second is that our occupational roles govern our perceptions.

    Even within the same occupational setting, the different roles participants have can affect their experience. Consider a typical college classroom, for example; the experiences of the instructor and students often are quite dissimilar. Having dedicated a large part of their lives to their work, most professors see their subject matter—whether French literature, physics, or speech communication—as vitally important. Students who are taking the course to satisfy a general education requirement may view the subject quite differently; maybe as one of many obstacles that stand between them and a degree, maybe as a chance to meet new people. Another difference centers on the amount of knowledge possessed by the parties. To an instructor who has taught the course many times, the material probably seems extremely simple; but to students encountering it for the first time, it may seem strange and confusing. Toward the end of a semester or quarter the instructor might be pressing onward hurriedly to cover all the material in the course, while the students are fatigued from their studies and ready to move more slowly. We don't need to spell out the interpersonal strains and stresses that come from such differing perceptions.

(Adler and Rodman, 47–48)

Decide whether the following statements are logical (L) or illogical (ILL) based on facts in the passage.

_____ 1. Botanists rarely notice changes in the weather.
_____ 2. People unconsciously "select" things that they are aware of in their environments.
_____ 3. Professors never understand the reasons why students behave as they do.
_____ 4. Changing one's perception of a difficult situation will ease the interpersonal stresses caused by the situation.
_____ 5. Factors other than occupation affect one's perceptions.

8.   The concept of intelligence and the measurement of IQ play an important role in most of our lives. Children who score high on intelligence tests in grade school are put into advanced classes, while those who score low are often held back. Someone who is supposed to have a high IQ is treated differently by teachers, parents, and even other children. In some countries such as England and France, performance on aptitude tests determines whether you are allowed to go on to college, while in this country scores on the SAT are a major factor in whether or not you are admitted to a particular school. Although they are not strictly speaking IQ tests, the medical and law aptitude tests are merely specialized forms of intelligence tests, as are the graduate record examinations, and all of these to a large extent determine whether a student can get into a particular professional or graduate school. Since intelligence and other aptitude tests are so important, it is essential that we understand as well as possible just how good they are and what they measure. We need to answer three major questions: (1) How reliable are the tests? (2) How valid are they? and (3) How fair are they to different people and groups of people? A related issue of great interest is the role of heredity and environment in intelligence. We shall discuss this in a separate section.

(Freedman, 204)

_____ You can assume that
(a) intelligence tests are losing the appeal and significance they once had.
(b) children are unconcerned about their performance on intelligence tests.
(c) low scores on intelligence tests are evaluated by educators.
(d) in the United States, scores on IQ tests determine whether or not students will go to college.

_____ You can predict that
  (a) children who score high on intelligence tests develop healthy concepts of their abilities.
  (b) children who score low on intelligence tests never go to college.
  (c) children who score high on intelligence tests in grade school will become dentists, lawyers, and doctors.
  (d) there is no relationship between intelligence and success in school.

9.   If men and women <u>are</u> born with distinct interests and talents, how do we account for the fact that 76 percent of the physicians in the Soviet Union but only 6 percent of their American counterparts are female (Sullerot, 1971, p. 151)? . . . The recruitment of Soviet women for employment outside the home is unique in the modern world. Marx, Engels, and other communist thinkers equated the subjugation of women with the oppression of the workers: under capitalism, women were chattel. In the early days of the Soviet experiment, women were seen as natural allies, and their role in the Revolution was idealized. In fact, ideology coincided with need in Russia. War had created a shortage of manpower; if the country was to modernize, women had to work. Indeed, women were doubly valuable—as workers and as mothers, who in bearing children would contribute needed population.

Today a Russian woman who chooses not to work is stigmatized as a kept woman, a parasite. But conditions for women are far from ideal in the Soviet Union. Russian men consider housework degrading; as a result, Soviet women are housewives as well as workers. And although women have entered many professions (the Soviet Union had the first female astronaut), they are under-represented in executive and managerial positions in industry and in the Communist party (Field and Flynn, 1970). Nevertheless, the number of female physicians, engineers, and the like in the Soviet Union shows clearly that society, not biology, determines what women can do.

(Light and Keller, 136, 138)

_____ From this passage you can conclude that
  (a) men and women are born with distinct interests and talents.
  (b) society influences peoples' interests and talents.
_____ From this passage you can conclude that
  (a) American women are not encouraged to be physicians.
  (b) American women prefer to be housewives.
  (c) most Russian women are encouraged to study medicine.
  (d) Russian, not American men, find housework degrading.

10.   Few of us would dispute the fact that computers have revolutionized American industry. But there is little agreement on the effect computer technology has had on the number and type of jobs available in the work place. Whether computers and the automation they create push people out of work or create jobs is an issue that will continue to be debated for a long time.

Many experts link the computer revolution to unemployment among blue-collar and unskilled labor. As the demands of industrial competition force businesses to computerize their traditional manufacturing techniques, semiskilled machine operators are replaced by white-collar technicians.

The plunging cost of mass-produced, programmable microprocessors is accelerating this trend, according to some observers who claim that the technology has developed to the point where it is often as flexible as the retraining of people.

On auto assembly lines, for example, human workers have been replaced by computerized robots that work double shifts at peak efficiency. In offices where productivity has risen only 4 percent in a decade, computers may someday replace secretarial and support staff. Using computerized word-processing equipment, office correspondence can be written, corrected, clean-typed, duplicated, and distributed in a fraction of the time it takes a secretary to do the same job.

There is little room in this picture for file clerks, stenographers, secretaries, and other back-up personnel who many believe will become obsolete and unemployable.

Few disagree with the projection that certain kinds of work will simply disappear in the computer age, but not every expert translates this into higher levels of unemployment. As the number of workers engaged in routine, repetitive, and dangerous work decreases, service and technological occupations will grow, they feel. During the 1950s and early 1960s, for example, when high technology first became a fact of life, employment expanded. The shrinkage in the manufacturing sector of the economy was more than offset by expanding white-collar and service jobs.

Experts assure us that this growth in white-collar service jobs does not mean permanent unemployment for unskilled and semiskilled blue-collar workers. Secretaries, clerks, and stenographers may become co-participants in office decision making along with their bosses. Or, as their skills become obsolete, they may be retrained by their corporations in computer skills so they, too, will be members of the technological elite. "The increased need for more educated manpower," says Harvard University's Program on Technology and Society, "has expanded the opportunities for upward mobility as the bottom level of the employment hierarchy contracts and the upper levels expand."

Recent data from the computer industry tell a story of expanding demand and an inadequate supply of qualified personnel. The industry now employs nearly half a million programmers and systems analysts, up from almost none in 1960. And according to a 1980 finding of the U.S. Bureau of the Census, the number of job openings for skilled computer personnel will grow at a faster rate than the rest of the labor force.

(Boone and Kurtz, 380–381)

_____ You can assume that as computers become part of the workplace,
(a) there will be no change in the unemployment statistics.
(b) the level of unemployment will rise continuously.
(c) all workers will be retrained in computer skills.
(d) the demand for certain skills will increase whereas the demand for others will decrease.
_____ With the rise in technology, office workers will
(a) become obsolete.
(b) become bosses.
(c) retrain for technology careers.
(d) be unemployable.

_____ In the early 1960s,
  (a) the field of computer programming was on the brink of an employment boom.
  (b) no one was interested in entering the field of computer programming or systems analysis.
  (c) there were no jobs available in technology.
  (d) the blue-collar sector was becoming obsolete.

_____ One can conclude that
  (a) machines will soon replace most workers.
  (b) workers must adapt to industrial changes.
  (c) the rise in computer technology has led to great numbers of unemployed workers.
  (d) white-collar jobs are not susceptible to unemployment crises.

Analyzing Passages

34

When you are able to form conclusions and make assumptions, predictions, and generalizations, you can understand more about the passages you read. You can read and understand what the author states, and you can infer ideas the author intends you to understand. Drawing inferences is a skill that is necessary for analytical reading.

Problem

You have just read an assigned selection. Your instructor has asked you to analyze the passage. What will you write about?

When your instructor asks you to analyze a passage, he or she wants more than a retelling of the plot or a description of the characters. Your telling of the plot and description of the characters should only come in as evidence for your inferences.

An author creates characters and situations in order to make statements or to offer views about people and society. The author may suggest many ideas through the narration. As you read, you can begin to draw out ideas that the author intended you to understand concerning people, relationships between people, and society. Using evidence from the selection, you can build a thorough analysis of the reading.

Setting Up Notes

1. First, you must understand literally what has happened in a selection. To make sure you remember the selection for homework, class discussion, papers, and, later on, tests, write a brief summary of the plot.

Title:	Author:
Plot Summary:	*write a brief summary*

2. Next, decide what aspect of society the author is discussing. Is the author using characters or plot to present a view on any of the following or on other social institutions or themes?

Education	Elderly	Politics	Culture
Religion	Technology	Family	Government
Working class	Medicine	Economics	Communications
Traditions	The future	Environment	Leisure
History	Sex roles	Growing up	Peer-pressure

3. Now set up a series of questions about these topics. Using the theme of "Education" as a model, here are some possible questions:

• What is the author's view about the quality of education?
• Is the quality of education poor or good?
• What does education provide for the characters?
• What changes should be made in the educational system?

Consider these questions as you think about the passage. Can you answer the questions based on information in the passage and on your own observations of daily life? Does the plot or character development lead you to any conclusions about education? Note your inferences with the supporting evidence in the chart.

Title:		Author:	
Plot Summary:			
Author's views about	**Inferences from passage**	**Evidence from narrator's description of characters and situations**	**Evidence from your observations of society**
education in society	What ideas about education did you draw from the selection?	Use evidence to support your inferences.	Do you agree? Disagree? Use evidence to support your opinion.
People's natures			
People's relationships			

4. Now you can begin to draw inferences about the nature of people, first through the characters and then through your experience. What does the author intend you to understand about human nature? Here are some questions to guide you:

- What is the nature of the characters in the passage? How do they behave?
- Are people in the passage good or bad, honest or dishonest?
- Do people care about one another?
- Do people experience conflicts?
- How do people resolve those conflicts?

These questions lead you back to the characters. See how the main characters behave. Can you answer the above questions based on the behavior of the characters? Write the inferences in your chart and be sure to include the supporting evidence.

Title:		Author:	
Plot Summary:			
Author's views about	**Inferences from passage**	**Evidence from narrator's description of characters and situations**	**Evidence from your observations of society**
_____ in society			
People's natures	What ideas did you draw about people's behavior from the selection?	Use evidence to support your inferences.	Do you agree? Disagree? Use evidence to support your opinion.
People's relationships			

5. Finally, you can examine people's relationships. What is the author's view about people's relationships? Here are typical questions you can consider:

- How do the characters relate to each other?
- Do people help others?
- Do people try to influence other people?
- Are people loyal to one another?
- Are people competitive?

To answer these and similar questions, you must look at the relationships between the characters in the passage. Again, note your inferences and the supporting evidence.

Title:		Author:	
Plot Summary:			
Author's views about	**Inferences from passage**	**Evidence from narrator's description of characters and situations**	**Evidence from your observations of society**
in society			
People's natures			
People's relationships	What ideas did you draw about people's relationships from the selection?	Use evidence to support your inferences.	Do you agree? Disagree? Use evidence to support your opinion.

Now you have a set of notes in chart form containing both factual information and inferences drawn from the selection. Your class discussion will probably focus on many of the themes and questions mentioned here. Whatever your instructor discusses in class can be added to your chart notes. Any discussion of the author's style of writing, use of imagery, personal history, and so on can also be added.

Title:		Author:	
Plot Summary:			

Author's views about	Inferences from passage	Evidence from narrator's description of characters and situations	Evidence from your observations of society
_____ in society			
People's natures			
People's relationships			

Analyzing Longer Selections

You will now have the opportunity to read and analyze several selections. As you read each selection, be aware that the author probably intended you to understand ideas that are implied but not stated in the selection. Briefly summarize the plot, consider what aspect of society the author is commenting on, and decide what views the author is expressing about society, people, and the relationships between people. Enter these ideas in the chart, and, for each, provide the supporting evidence from the selection and from your own observations of your society and your friends.

1. A Shocking Tale

Russell Baker

The extraordinary events at the Bertle household began innocently enough several years ago when Martha Bertle gave her husband, Ted, an electric razor.

They can't even remember now whether it was a birthday or a Christmas present. In any event, Ted Bertle countered quickly on the next gift-giving occasion by giving Martha an electric carving knife.

It should be clear, of course, that before this exchange, which the Bertles now regard as the take-off point, they had already purchased, over the years, an electric stove, an electric refrigerator, an electric television set, three electric clocks, two electric air-conditioners, an electric freezer, an electric clothes-washing-and-drying unit, three electric radios and a large number of electric lamps.

Also an electric stereo system.

And an electric slide projector.

And an electric toaster.

The electric train which Ted Bertle's parents had given him one boyhood Christmas was also in the house, as were Ted's electric saw and an electric sander and Martha's electric vacuum cleaner.

It was not particularly surprising then that after Ted Bertle, on the occasion of their wedding anniversary, gave Martha an electric burglar alarm system for the house, electricians had to be called to deal with frequent power failures. Eventually they ran more lines into the house.

Thus strengthened for the long haul, the Bertles bought an electric dishwasher. On Father's Day, although Ted Bertle was not yet a father, Martha gave Ted an electric guitar, a sort of musical return for the electric organ Ted had given her on Mother's Day.

With the Fourth of July, Ted replied by giving Martha a pair of electric scissors and an electric sewing machine.

On the fifth of July, without knowing quite why, Martha countered by giving Ted an electric comb. On the sixth of July, Ted struck back by giving Martha an electric hair dryer.

For several days they were content simply to glare at each other, but in late July Martha surprised Ted one evening with an electric toothbrush.

Ted was silent for more than two weeks.

Then, on Aug. 15, Napoleon's birthday, Ted surprised Martha with an electric griddle, an electric mixing bowl, an electric frying pan, an electric rotisserie-broiler, an electric coffee pot and an electric tray for keeping food warm on the sideboard.

Martha became sullen and uncommunicative. On Labor Day she gave Ted an electric blanket, but Ted, who had been expecting something like this, was ready for her.

He immediately retorted with an electric can opener, an electric food blender, an electric coffee grinder, an electric hot-dog cooking machine and a beautiful electric cut-glass decanter imported from Schenectady.

Martha stayed in her room, refusing to see anyone, until Veteran's Day when she surprised Ted with an electric radio-cassette-recorder-player, an electric typewriter, an electric shoe polisher and a bound volume of advertisements by their local electric company on the joys of "electric living."

That night the Bertles had a tender evening together. Martha brought out the electric candles she had secretly bought for herself and they played a game of electric football by electric candlelight.

On Thanksgiving Day, while carving the turkey with his electric knife, Ted Bertle was severely shocked by the electric wishbone, which had not been perfected yet and still had bugs in it. He was taken to the hospital and subjected to a long humiliating course of therapy before it was safe for anyone to touch him without wearing rubber gloves.

When Martha Bertle was admitted to the hospital for the birth of their first child, Ted was not allowed to visit the maternity ward because he still sizzled and crackled so loudly that it woke the other babies. For this reason, he did not learn until Martha came home that he had become the father of an electric son, who requires a change of fuses with each fresh diaper.

With what modern technology has learned about extension cords, the child's electrician assures the Bertles, there is no reason why he cannot live a perfectly normal life, provided he is careful not to get rained upon.

The happy Ted and Martha have already given him an electric teddy bear.

Title:	*A Shocking Tale*		Author: *Russell Baker*

Plot Summary: *For no clear reason, Ted and Martha begin to give each other electrical gifts. This goes on through holidays, birthdays, and so on. Soon they are glaring at each other as they try to outdo the other's gifts. Martha gives birth to an electric son; he gets an electric teddy bear.*

Author's views about	Inferences from passage	Evidence from narrator's description of characters and situations	Evidence from your observations of society
<u>technology</u> in society	1. It makes us physically lazy. 2. 3. 4.	→ ex.-electric shoe polisher, washers and so on.	→ I agree-people take elevators <u>one</u> flight.
People's natures	1. People are dependent on electrical gadgets. 2. 3. 4.		
People's relationships	1. It isolates people. 2. 3. 4.	→ Ted is silent; Martha is sullen and uncommunicative; she stays in her room.	

2. Most People Remember Their First Kiss. Others Remember Bogey's and Ingrid's

Joe Baltake

At some point early in my moviegoing education, I realized that Movies Live Forever. By simply thinking about favorite films and recalling great moments, one can go on a movie spree. It's easy to master: First, think of a particularly memorable movie—say, "E.T.—The Extra-Terrestrial." Now, close your eyes and recall the film's final scene. Relive the moment when E.T., carrying his potted plant, waddles aboard his space ship. Abandon yourself to his final words to Elliott. "Be good." Go ahead, cry. Nobody's watching.

Now that you're in the proper mood, think about "The Best Years of Our Lives," specifically Fredric March's homecoming scene. A classic American moment. It perfectly captures the joy of returning home as one immaculate detail blends into the next—March quietly entering his apartment . . . surprising his son, Michael Hall . . . hushing his daughter, Teresa Wright . . . and finally embracing his wife, Myrna Loy. Probably the most heartfelt—and sexiest—embrace in movie history.

More tears? Okay. "Some Came Running." Frank Sinatra is Dave, the Sensitive Writer. Shirley MacLaine is Ginny, a painted, lovelorn tramp who doesn't understand Dave, but somehow knows how he feels (both have been Emotionally Hurt) and that what he does is special. Unable to express herself but desperate for some affection, Ginny blurts out, "Love me, Dave! Oh, please love me!"

Then there's the moment in "All Quiet on the Western Front" when Lew Ayres as a young German soldier facing death reaches out to clutch an elusive butterfly.

And finally, Maurice Chevalier's death scene from "Fanny." I'm thinking of the moment when his old friend, Charles Boyer, leans over his bed and says, "Tell me. What will you miss the most?" Chevalier thinks for a split second and then responds, "Lunch."

What make such scenes so moving and so memorable is that they seem so natural, almost unpremeditated. And there's something truly intimate about the most memorable moments in movies—Gene Kelly dancing in the rain, Humphrey Bogart saying goodby to Ingrid Bergman at the airport, Richard Widmark pushing a crippled Mildred Dunnock down a staircase. ("Singin' in the Rain," "Casablanca" and "Kiss of Death," as if you had to be told.)

You can't forget these movies. You give in to them and to the lifetime of memories they provide. Ah, the memories. Diane Keaton singing "Seems Like Old Times" in "Annie Hall" . . . the fight between Anne Bancroft and Shirley Mac-Laine in "The Turning Point" . . . Victor McLaglen in "The Informer," offering condolences to the mother of a friend he betrayed.

For thrills, there's Cary Grant being stalked by a crop duster in "North by Northwest," Robert Mitchum as the maniac in "The Night of the Hunter," and Robert Walker as the sociopath Bruno Anthony in "Strangers on a Train."

For laughs, there's the "Springtime for Hitler" number in "The Producers," Bruce Dern as Big Bob in "Smile," and Bill Murray ad libbing his way through "Caddyshack."

For iconography, there's Monroe's skirt billowing up from a subway grating in "The Seven Year Itch" and Edward G. Robinson in "Little Caesar," asking "Mother of Mercy, is this the end of Ricco?"

And, leaving the best for last, there's the first glimpse of color in "The Wizard of Oz," the burning of the fortress of "Gone With the Wind" and the final shot of Chaplin in "City Lights." Memorable moments.

Title:		Author:	
Plot Summary:			
Author's views about	**Inferences from passage**	**Evidence from narrator's description of characters and situations**	**Evidence from your observations of society**
_____ in society			
People's natures			
People's relationships			

3. The Awful Beginning

James A. Smith

I looked across the desk at my big girl. She'd come for help in planning her semester schedule.

"Look," I said, "you have some electives. Why don't you take a course or two for fun? You've worked hard and really should take something outside your major that will be pleasurable."

"Like what?" she asked.

My eyes scanned the college schedule of courses. "Like Dr. Mann's Creative Writing or Dr. Camp's Painting for Beginners or something like that."

She threw back her head and laughed. "Who, me? Paint or write? Good grief, Dad, you ought to know better than that!"

"And this," I thought, "is the awful ending."

It was not always like this. I remembered an early golden September day when I went to my garage studio and gathered together my easel, paintbrushes, and watercolors. I sensed someone was watching me and looked up from my activity to see her framed in silhouette in the doorway. The breeze and the sun tiptoed in the gold of her curls. Her wide blue eyes asked the question, "Whatcha doin'?"

"I'm going to the meadow to paint," I said. "Want to come along?"

"Oh, yes." She bounced on her toes in anticipation.

"Well, go tell Mummy and get your paints."

She was off but returned in no time carrying the caddy I had made to hold her jars of paint and her assortment of brushes.

"Paper?" she asked.

"Yes, I have plenty of paper. Let's go."

She ran down the hill before me, pushing aside the long, soft grasses of the meadow. I watched closely for fear of losing her golden top in the tops of the goldenrod. She found a deserted meadowlark's nest and we stopped to wonder at it. A rabbit scurried from under our feet. Around us yellow daisies and goldenrod nodded in friendly greeting. Above, the sky was an infinite blue. Beyond the meadow, the lake slapped itself to match the blue of the sky.

On the lake, a single white sailboat tipped joyously in the breeze. My daughter looked up and saw it. "Here!" she said.

Trusting her wisdom as I always did, I set up our easels. While I deliberated over choice of subject and color, she had no such problem. She painted with abandonment and concentration and I left her alone, asking no questions, making no suggestions, simply recognizing uncontaminated creative drive at work.

Before I had really begun, she pulled a painting off her easel.

"There!" she said. "Want to see?" I nodded.

I cannot describe the sense of wonder that flooded over me as I viewed her work. It was all there—that golden September day. She had captured the sunlight in her spilled yellows, the lake in her choppy, uneven strokes of blue, the trees in her long, fresh strokes of green. And through it all, there was a sense of scudding ships and the joyousness of wind that I experience when I sail, the tilting and swaying of the deck, the pitching of the mast. It was a beautiful and wondrous thing and I envied her ability to interpret so honestly, so uninhibitedly, so freshly.

"Are you going to give it a name?" I suggested.

"Yep! Sailboats!" she responded, as she taped another sheet of paper to the easel.

There wasn't a single sailboat in the picture.

She began school the following week. One dreary November day she came into my study with a sheet of paper in her hand.

"Daddy," she asked, "will you help me draw a sailboat?"

"Me? Help *you* draw a sailboat?"

My eyes turned to the wall where her golden September painting hung in a frame I had made for it.

"Me? Help you draw a picture of a sailboat? Why, sweetheart, I could never paint a picture like the one over there. Why don't you paint one of your own?"

Her blue eyes looked troubled.

"But, Daddy, Miss Ellis doesn't like my kind of painting."

She held up her sheet of paper in the middle of which was a dittoed triangle.

"Miss Ellis wants us to make a sailboat out of this."

And that was the awful beginning!

Title:		Author:	
Plot Summary:			

Author's views about	**Inferences from passage**	**Evidence from narrator's description of characters and situations**	**Evidence from your observations of society**
in society			
People's natures			
People's relationships			

4. New Yorkers, etc.

Enid Nemy

With a Bit of Guilt, Enjoying Others' Small Tribulations.

There's a little devil in all of us that sometimes makes us feel good when others don't. Some people's devils are bigger than others, but human nature being what it is, there is little doubt that even good and quite decent people get a feeling of gratification over the misfortunes of others. Nothing major, mind you. Very few would be nasty enough to wish serious trouble or calamity on anyone, but a small tribulation is quite another thing. Indeed, some minor misfortunes are just meant for others to enjoy.

The enjoyment in such situations is rarely overt. No gleeful chortles or happy laughter are heard. There is merely a sense of satisfaction, a rather mild and quiet pleasure—and if the person is basically nice, even this is usually tempered by at least a small twinge of guilt.

Take, for instance, the situation on a rainy or blustery day when, by some miracle, you snare the one free cab in a sea of occupied ones. You settle back and look out of the window at the miserable human beings risking their lives standing out in the road, signaling wildly and screaming "Taxi! Taxi!" It's nice to be inside the cab, rolling along over the potholes and, sad to say, it's even nicer when the demand is greater than the supply.

Elevators, particularly slow ones that seem to move at 15-minute intervals, are another source of not-nice satisfaction. Few are the people whose pleasure at being absolutely the last to squeeze in isn't heightened by the plight of those left behind, waiting, waiting, waiting.

Really nice people who get home just before the rain comes pelting down look out their windows and pity the bedraggled unfortunates scurrying along with newspapers over their heads or umbrellas blown inside out. The joy of being dry wouldn't be nearly as intense if others weren't wet.

Talking about weather, if one has to get a cold or sore throat or sprain an ankle and take a day or two off, isn't it wonderful when the elements cooperate and it's really lousy out there? The fact that thousands of others are squeezing themselves into buses and subways makes even the sprained ankle a lot more bearable.

Someone is going to get the damp or grubby newspaper at the top of the rapidly diminishing pile at the newstand. But as you slide your hand under for a pristine copy, you know it isn't going to be you. Too bad about the third or fourth person in line though, isn't it?

Then there are the weekend people who either plan well or just strike it lucky. They arrive wherever they are going without encountering any delays, park the car, put their things away and settle back with a drink to watch a bit of television or listen to the radio. What's that? Massive traffic jams with cars backed up for miles—and on the very highway they've just traveled. A fleeting thought for the poor souls, locked into their vehicles bumper to bumper; it will be a miracle if they get to their destinations before midnight. Somehow that thought makes the drink taste even better.

The movie is especially popular, and when you arrive to buy your ticket 50 people are ahead of you. What a bore. It's enough to spoil anyone's mood and you fidget impatiently. But then you look around and notice that in the last five minutes 100 people have arrived and are standing behind you. It doesn't get you in any faster, but it makes you feel a lot better, doesn't it?

"Satisfaction" may be too mild a word when it comes to being the last to grab something during a sale; how about "triumph"? Isn't that the feeling when scores of hands are reaching out for the smashing handbag that's been marked down from $200 to $49.50 and you're the one who has physical possession? Or you're the one to get the last tube of toothpaste at half price or the only decent head of lettuce at the produce store?

Some women just naturally manage to look immaculately groomed no matter what the circumstance or time. Run into them at the crack of dawn in a supermarket and their hair is properly tied back in neat ribbons, their jeans look worn just enough, their shirts are crisp and they have the right canvas bags to coordinate with their espadrilles or sneakers. On formal occasions the effect is even more stunning. Envy is pointless; such perfection is not for the likes of most. Still, who can be faulted for secretly reveling on the few occasions when a paragon's slip peeks out from under her skirt or a shoulder strap appears where it shouldn't or her pantyhose spring a run.

Should you be nice and tell her? Oh, to heck with it! Let her look like the rest of the world. Just once.

Title:		Author:	
Plot Summary:			

Author's views about	Inferences from passage	Evidence from narrator's description of characters and situations	Evidence from your observations of society
_____ in society			
People's natures			
People's relationships			

5. Commencement Address

Alan Alda

Ever since it was announced that a non-doctor, in fact, an actor, had been invited to give the commencement address at one of the most prestigious medical schools in the country people have been wondering—why get someone who only <u>pretends</u> to be a doctor when you could get a real one?

Some people have suggested that this school had done everything it could to show you how to <u>be</u> doctors and in a moment of desperation had brought in someone who could show you how to act like one.

It's certainly true that I'm not a doctor. I have a long list of nonqualifications. In the first place I'm not a great fan of blood. I don't mind people's having it, I just don't enjoy seeing them wear it.

I have yet to see a real operation because the mere smell of a hospital reminds me of a previous appointment.

And my knowledge of anatomy resides in the clear understanding that the hip bone is connected to the leg bone.

I am not a doctor.

But you have asked me, and all in all I think you made a wonderful choice.

I say that because I probably first came to the attention of this graduating class through a character on television that I've played and helped write for the past seven years: a surgeon called Hawkeye Pierce. He's a remarkable person, this Hawkeye, and if you have chosen somehow to associate his character with your own graduation from medical school, then I find that very heartening. Because I think it means that you are reaching out toward a very human kind of doctoring.

And a very real kind of doctor.

We didn't make him up. He really lived as several doctors who struggled to preserve life twenty-five years ago during the Korean war.

In fact, it's because he's based on real doctors that there is something especially engaging about him.

He has a sense of humor and yet he's serious . . . he's impertinent and yet he has feeling . . . he's human enough to make mistakes, and yet he hates death enough to push himself past his own limits to save lives. In many ways he's the doctor patients want to have and doctors want to be.

But he's not an idealization. Finding himself in a war, he's sometimes angry, sometimes cynical, sometimes a little nuts.

He's not a magician who can come up with an instant cure for a rare disease without sweating and ruining his makeup. He knows he might fail. Not a god, he walks gingerly on the edge of disaster—alive to his own mortality.

If this image of that very human, very caring doctor is attractive to you—if it's ever touched you for a moment as something to reach for in your own life—then I'm here to cheer you on. Do it. Go for it. Be skilled, be learned, be aware of the dignity of your calling . . . but please don't ever lose sight of your own simple humanity.

Unfortunately, that may not be so easy.

You're entering a special place in our society. People will be awed by your expertise. You'll be placed in a position of privilege. You'll live well, people will defer to you, call you by your title—and it may be hard to remember that the word "doctor" is not actually your first name.

I know what this is like to some extent because in some ways you and I <u>are</u> alike. We both study the human being. And we both try to offer relief—you through medicine, and I through laughter—but we both try to reduce suffering. We've both learned difficult disciplines that have taken years to master, and we've both dedicated ourselves to years of hard work. And we both charge a lot.

We live in a society that has decided to reward my profession and yours, when we succeed in them, very highly. It can sometimes be easy to forget that the cab driver also works fourteen or fifteen hours a day and is also drained of energy when he's through. It's easy to think that because our society grants us privilege that we're entitled to it. Privilege feels good, but it can be intoxicating.

As good doctors, you will, I hope, be able to keep yourselves free of toxins.

It's no wonder, though, that people will hold you in awe.

I know I do.

You've spent years in a grueling effort to know the structure and process of human life. I can't imagine a more difficult task. It has required the understanding of complexities within complexities, and there has been more pressure placed on you in four years than most people would be willing to take in a lifetime. I stand here in utter amazement at what you've accomplished. And I congratulate you.

I only ask one thing of you: possess your skills, but don't be possessed by them.

Certainly your training has encouraged you to see the human side of your work, and you've examined the doctor-patient relationship. But still, the enormity of your task has required you to focus to such an extent on technique and data that you may not have had time enough to face your feelings along the way.

You've had to toughen yourself to death. From your first autopsy when you may have been sick or cried or just been numb, you've had to inure yourself to death in order to be useful to the living. But I hope in the process you haven't done too good a job of burying that part of you that hurts and is afraid.

I know what it's like to be absorbed in technique. When I write for "MASH" I'm always writing about people in crisis with what I hope is compassion and feeling. And yet one day I found myself talking to someone who was in a real crisis and real pain—and I remember thinking, "This would make a great story."

Both of these things—becoming set apart and becoming your skill—can make it tough to be a compassionate person.

All right, that's my diagnosis of the problem. Here's my prescription.

I'd like to suggest to you, just in case you haven't done it lately, that this would be a very good time to give some thought to just exactly what your values are, and then to figure out how you're going to live by them. Knowing what you care about and then devoting yourself to it is just about the only way you can pick your way through the minefield of existence and come out in one piece.

It can be a startling experience when you try to rank your values, though. Just ask yourself what's the most important thing in the world to you. Your work? Your family? Your money? Your country? Getting to heaven? Sex? Dope? Alcohol? What? (I don't need a show of hands on this.)

Then when you get the answer to that . . . ask yourself how much time you actually spend on your number one value . . . and how much time you spend on what you thought was number five . . . or number ten. What in fact is the thing you value most?

It may not be easy to decide.

We live in a time that seems to be split about its values. In fact it seems to be schizophrenic.

For instance, if you pick up a magazine like *Psychology Today*, you're liable to see an article like "White Collar Crime: It's More Widespread Than You Think." Then in the back of the magazine they'll print an advertisement that says, "We'll write your doctoral thesis for twenty-five bucks."

You see how values are eroding? I mean, a doctoral thesis ought to go for at least a C-note.

The question is where are their values? What do they value?

Unfortunately, the people we look to for leadership seem to be providing it by negative example.

All across the country this month commencement speakers are saying to graduating classes, "We look to you for tomorrow's leaders."

That's because today's leaders are all in jail.

Maybe we can afford to let politicians operate in a moral vacuum, but we can't afford to let doctors operate under those conditions.

You know how we're feeling these days as the power and fuel monopoly has its way with us. Well, you people graduating today are entering a very select group. You have a monopoly on medical care. Please be careful not to abuse this power that you have over the rest of us.

You need to know what you care about most and what you care about least. And you need to know now.

You will be making life-and-death decisions and you will often be making them under stress and with great speed. The time to make your tender choices is not in the heat of the moment.

When you're making your list, let me urge you to put people first. And I include in that not just people, but that which exists between people.

I suggest to you that what makes people know they're alive—and in some cases keeps them alive—is not merely the interaction of the parts of their bodies, but the interaction of their selves with other selves. Not just people, but what goes on between people.

Let me challenge you.

With all your study, you can name all the bones in my body. You can read my X-rays like a telegram. But can you read my involuntary muscles? Can you see the fear and uncertainty in my face?

If I tell you where it hurts, can you hear in my voice where I ache?

I show you my body but I bring you my person. Can you see me through your reading glasses?

Will you tell me what you're doing, and in words I can understand?

Will you tell me when you don't know what to do? Can you face your own fear, your own uncertainty? When in doubt, can you call in help?

These are things to consider even if you don't deal directly with patients. If you're in research, administration, if you write—no matter what you do—eventually there is always going to be a patient at the other end of your decisions.

Now, of course, everyone is for this in principle. Who's against people?

But it gets harder when you get specific.

Will you be the kind of doctor who cares more about the <u>case</u> than the <u>person</u>? ("Nurse, call the gastric ulcer and have him come in at three." . . . "How's the fractured femur in Room 208?")

You'll know you're in trouble if you find yourself wishing they would mail you their liver in a plain brown envelope.

Where does money come on your list? Will it be the sole standard against which you reckon your success?

How much will it guide you in relating to your patients? Do patients in a clinic need less of your attention than private patients? Are they, for instance, less in need of having things explained to them?

Where will your family come on your list? How many days and nights, weeks and months, will you separate yourself from them, buried in your work, before you realize that you've removed yourself from an important part of your life?

And if you're a male doctor, how will you relate to women? Women as patients, as nurses, as fellow doctors—and later as students?

Will you be able to respect your patient's right to know and make decisions about her own body?

Will you see nurses as colleagues—or as handmaidens?

And if the day comes when you are teaching, what can young women medical students expect from you?

Questionnaires filled out by women at forty-one medical schools around the country have revealed a distressing pattern.

The women were often either ignored in class or simply not taken seriously as students. They were told that they were only there to find a husband and that they were taking the places of men who would then have to go out and become chiropractors. (Logic is not the strong point of sexism.)

They were often told that women just didn't belong in medicine. And at times they were told this by the very professors who were grading them.

They would be shown slides of *Playboy* nudes during anatomy lectures—to the accompaniment of catcalls and wisecracks from male students. And in place of discussions about their work, they would often hear a discussion of their appearance.

These are reports from forty-one different medical schools.

I'm dwelling on this because it seems to me that the male-female relationship is still the most personal and intense test of humane behavior. It is a crucible for decency.

I hope you men will work to grant the same dignity to your female colleagues that you yourselves enjoy.

And if you're a female doctor I hope you'll be aware that you didn't get where you are all by yourself. You've had to work hard, of course. But you're sitting where you are right now in part because way back in 1848 in Seneca Falls women you never knew began insisting you had a right to sit there. Just as they helped a generation they would never see, I urge you to work for the day when your daughters and their daughters will be called not "A woman doctor," or "My doctor, who's a woman . . .," but simply, "My doctor."

It may seem strange to rank the things you care about, but when you think about it, there isn't an area of your work that won't be affected by what you decide to place a high value on and what you decide doesn't count.

Decide now.

Well, that's my prescription.

I've given you kind of a big pill to swallow, but I think it'll make you feel better.

And if not—well, look, I'm only human.

I congratulate you, and please let me thank you for taking on the enormous responsibility that you have—and for having the strength to have made it to this day. I don't know how you've managed to learn it all.

But there is one more thing you can learn about the body that only a non-doctor would tell you—and I hope you'll always remember this:

The head bone is connected to the heart bone—don't let them come apart.

Thank you.

Title:		Author:	
Plot Summary:			
Author's views about	**Inferences from passage**	**Evidence from narrator's description of characters and situations**	**Evidence from your observations of society**
in society			
People's natures			
People's relationships			

Reading Critically

Introduction

35

You have practiced the reading skills that strengthen your comprehension: understanding and noting the most important ideas, recognizing the author's method of organizing those ideas, taking written notes, anticipating possible test questions, and inferring meanings the author intended you to understand. Another skill is the ability to judge or evaluate the way in which an author presents ideas. The following chapters will help you to develop this skill of critical reading.

Consider these advertisements and the accompanying questions:

Questions

1. What does this advertisement sell? _____

2. How many people are pictured in the advertisement?   0   1   2   3   many

3. The time of day is _____

4. The scene is _____

5. Your attention focuses on _____

Your answers are based on observable facts from the picture. In this magazine advertisement, a woman sits at a writing table in a "comfortably" furnished living room. You focus on the woman, the furnishings, and the words "investments" and "more thought." (The original ad is pictured in tones of gold, rust, and brown.) Now consider this question.

6. The mood of the advertisement is one of
_____ (a) friendship.
_____ (b) elegance.
_____ (c) sexuality.
_____ (d) adventure.

In order to answer question 6, you must consider the facts presented in the advertisement, and you must evaluate the picture. The mood is not directly stated in the picture, but rather is implied through the "facts" presented.

Now that your investments require more thought,

Kidder, Peabody offers you tax-free bonds that yield more than interest.

As one of the nation's leading underwriters of tax-free bonds, Kidder, Peabody is in a unique position to offer a vast selection of securities to investors. Whether they're seeking more interest, or more security.

And as one of the industry's leading innovators, many of our offerings are unique, designed to let investors take advantage of the latest economic trends. Our highly popular Compound Interest Bonds, for

instance, give investors tax-free interest on tax-free interest; and our equally popular Option Tender Bonds yield high tax-free interest with protection against downside market risk.

If your holdings are complex and you're not sure which bonds are right for your investment needs and tax considerations, call on a Kidder, Peabody stockbroker to help you think it through. Our brokers are accomplished professionals, skilled in assisting upper-income individuals, whatever their degree of sophistication. And, because of Kidder's extensive underwriting commitment, our brokers have access to more

municipals than most of their counterparts in the industry. In addition, they can give you the thinking of experts in our thirteen regional offices who specialize in local offerings throughout the country.

Whether you would like your securities to yield more interest or more security, Kidder, Peabody will give you a wide choice in tax-free bonds. Talk to one of our brokers at an office near you.

Kidder, Peabody & Co. INCORPORATED
Founded 1865
Members New York and American Stock Exchanges
—— over 60 offices worldwide / Member SIPC ——

Reprinted with permission.

Just listen to them. "She's the first!" "I knew it! I knew it!" "Have they set the date?" You want to tell the world. But first you have to share it with the gang. You've shared perfume and clothes, secrets and dreams—the silly and the serious. And this is serious. There it is, bigger than life, on the third finger of your left hand. Reach out to faraway family and friends. Big news or just a "hello," they love hearing from you.

Ⓐ Bell System

Reach out and touch someone.

Courtesy, AT&T Communications.

Questions

1. What does the advertisement sell? _____

2. How many people are pictured in the advertisement?   0   1   2   3   many

3. The time of day is _____

4. The scene is _____

5. Your attention focuses on _____

You can answer the questions based on facts in this picture. Each answer is provable according to information in the advertisement.

Now consider this question.

6. The mood of the advertisement is one of
_____ (a) friendship.
_____ (b) elegance.
_____ (c) sexuality.
_____ (d) adventure.

In order to answer question 6, you must consider the information presented in the advertisement, and you must evaluate the picture. The mood is not directly stated in the picture, but rather it is implied through the "facts" presented.

Additional Questions

1. How does the first advertisement try to influence you to buy the product? _____

_____

_____

2. How does the second advertisement try to influence you to use the product? _____

_____

_____

In order to analyze both advertisements critically and answer the questions, you must consider the facts.

	Setting	Number of people	Time of day	Focus	Mood
Ad 1 "Stock-brokerage firm"	living room	one	appears to be evening	woman "more thought" furnishings "investments"	elegance
Ad 2 "Telephones"	bedroom dormitory	five	evening	group of friends phone "touch" "share"	friendship

Advertisers use location, number of people, and time of day to help project certain moods. In addition, they use colors to enhance the moods. For example, gold, rust, and dark green often enhance the feeling of elegance. On the other hand, red, yellow, and bright blue often help create a sporty and lively mood. By projecting moods, advertisers not only sell their products, such as a brokerage firm or a telephone system, but also provide an image of you now or what you might become if you buy the products. For example, if you employ this brokerage firm, you may become more selective, elegant, and perhaps wealthier. Or, if you continue to use this phone system, you will share in lively, warm, joyous, and popular activities.

Just as advertisers use colors, setting, people, and times of day to create moods and to sell images, so authors use words to create moods and to sell images and viewpoints. Authors sell ideas through their words and styles of writing.

> **Critical reading** involves a judgment of the ways in which the author presents ideas in order to express a viewpoint. As you read critically, you are evaluating the manner and purpose of the author's presentation.

Here are several questions that will help you to evaluate a passage critically. Read the eight questions and the brief explanations that follow. Then practice asking these questions as you read passages in the next chapters.

Begin by noting why you think the author wrote the passage. Who is the author and how does his or her position or background influence or determine the purpose in writing the passage?

> 1. **Who is the author?**
> 2. **What is the author's purpose in writing the passage?**

In order to see how the author achieves a purpose, look at the words used in the passage. Select the words that describe an event or character, and see whether these words help to create a specific mood or feeling.

> 3. **What words does the author use to describe people, ideas, and events?**
> 4. **What mood or feeling does the author create?**

When you understand the author's purposes, you will begin to understand the author's views about people, events, or social issues. What are the author's viewpoints? Does the author present all aspects of an issue, or just one side of it?

5. What issue is being presented?
6. What is the author's viewpoint?
7. Does the author present all sides of the issue?

As you analyze the author's viewpoints, you should become concerned with the factual bases for those views. Are the author's viewpoints based on facts, opinions, or a combination? Does the evidence appear complete?

8. Does the author use facts or opinions or both to support a viewpoint?

Each of the questions focuses your attention on the author's style, intent, and accuracy of presentation. Your comprehension moves beyond the literal level to a critical judgment of the author and the material.

Determining the Author's Purpose

36

Previewing is a study technique that you apply to texts: you consider specific chapter sections, question what you know about the subject, and note which ideas the author emphasizes. Previewing can be adapted to nontext readings to help you read critically. First, consider who the author is and what the author's background or credentials are. By noting these points, you begin to understand the author's purpose for writing the passage.

Example

Author	Topic	Probable Purpose
Dr. John Block, Chairperson, American Society for Prevention of Cruelty to Animals	Spaying of Cats and Neutering of Dogs	To propose a spaying and neutering program to help control the stray animal population

In this example, the author's association with the ASPCA is closely linked with programs to help control the stray animal population. An understanding of the author's position, or title, along with a determination of the author's purpose in writing about the given topic will help you evaluate further statements made by the author.

Noting an author's background, title, or position helps you to determine the author's probable **purpose** for writing the passage.

Practice: Four authors have written articles on the same topic. In the space provided, briefly describe each author's probable purpose for writing the article. The first one is done for you.

Topic of the Article	**Authors**	**Probable Purpose**
1. Cleanliness of City Streets	City sanitation commissioner	To show the improvement in keeping the city clean since the commissioner took office
	Local resident	To show the need for more sanitation services in his or her neighborhood
	Mayor of the city	To show the improvement in city services since the mayor took office
	Political opponent of the mayor	To show the need for more efficient city services since the mayor has failed to provide them

Topic of the Article	**Authors**	**Probable Purpose**
2. Summer Rock Festival	Local businessperson	
	Town resident	
	Town sheriff	
	Concert promoter	

Topic of the Article	Authors	Probable Purpose
3. Environmental Pollution	Secretary of the Interior	
	Family living near an industrial site	
	Owner of a manufacturing plant	
	Member of the town council	
4. Centralized Computer Files on Every Citizen	Internal Revenue Service (IRS) agent	
	President of a credit company	
	Ex-convict	
	Citizen	

Topic of the Article	Authors	Probable Purpose
5. U.S. Atomic Energy: Plans for Future Use	**Anti-nuclear organization**	
	Nuclear Regulatory Commission (NRC)	
	President of a utility company	
	Residents living near a nuclear plant	

Topic of the Article	Authors	Probable Purpose
6. Farm Subsidies	**Textile manufacturer**	
	President of the Farmers' Organization of America	
	Independent business owner	
	President of the largest farm machinery manufacturer in the United States	

Topic of the Article	Authors	Probable Purpose
7. Use of Search Warrants	Conservative member of the Supreme Court	
	Sister of a known drug dealer	
	Police officer	
	Lawyer with the American Civil Liberties Union	

8. Medical Research	Head of the Food and Drug Administration (FDA)	
	Chairperson of the Society for the Prevention of Cruelty to Animals (SPCA)	
	Victim of a rare disease	
	Faith healer	

Topic of the Article	Authors	Probable Purpose
9. Admissions Procedures for Medical School	**Medical school admissions board**	
	Minority applicant to medical school	
	Parents of an applicant to medical school	
	American Medical Association	

10. Legalized Casino Gambling	**State gaming commission**	
	Owner of Casinos, International Hotel	
	Leader of local religious board	
	Chairperson, local Parent-Teachers' Association (PTA)	

Once you understand the author's purpose, you can begin to evaluate the ways in which the author achieves that purpose. What pictures, words, or symbols does the author use to create a mood or feeling?

Example

In each of the following advertisements, consider both the picture and the written text. Then complete the chart that follows.

Today's business world is a jungle. To survive, you've got to be strong. You've got to be tough. That's why smart business people travel with the Samsonite Accord® Attache. The Accord features a strong, yet lightweight frame, tough molded shell, sleek comfortable handle, and a durable three-wheel combination lock that opens only when right side up. Sure the business world is tough. But Samsonite's attaches are even tougher.

Samsonite®

Reprinted with permission.

Author	Purpose	Mood	Images and Words to create the mood
Time, Inc. ad			stronger, healthier, sexier, they question fundamentals, insight, understanding, MUSCLE, woman in leotard, warm-up tights, stares out at reader
Samsonite ad			jungle, survive, strong, tough, smart, sleek, durable, tougher, SURVIVOR, young business-man in traffic of city clutches paper, briefcase, "Clark Kent" look

The purpose of both ads includes more than the sale of a magazine or an attaché case. In one ad, the mood is one of determination and provocative strength. In the other ad, the mood is one of "heroic" determination. Both ads create these moods through pictures and words. The moods or "feelings" of both ads clearly represent the underlying purpose of the advertisers. The magazine ad emphasizes a sense of independence, strength, and total femininity in the potential subscribers. The luggage ad emphasizes a sense of strength, aggressiveness, and heroic daring in its potential buyers.

In each of the ads, you have seen how advertisers attempt to sell more than their products; they sell moods and feelings about the products through carefully chosen images and words. Authors similarly create moods or feelings about subjects. Authors, however, use only words to achieve their purposes.

> **Noting the words an author chooses to describe people, events, and issues can help you to evaluate the mood the author creates.**

Practice: Imagine that you are called upon to create an advertisement for a product such as a perfume or a car. Select a product you are familiar with and, in the space provided, complete each statement to show how you might develop the advertisement.

1. The purpose of this advertisement is to sell _____

_____.

2. I want people to feel that they will be (or they will have) _____

_____ if they buy this product.

3. To achieve my purpose, I will create a mood of _____

_____ about this product.

4. To create a mood of _____, I will use the following:

   number of people _____

   time of day _____

   setting _____

   colors _____   _____

   _____   _____

5. To develop the mood, I will use the following words:

   _____   _____   _____

   _____   _____   _____

Now try to evaluate the author's purpose and the mood of a selection through words alone.

Practice: Read each letter and answer the questions that follow.

1. To the Editor:

   Your recent editorial about raising the minimum drinking age is absurd. Young people are certainly stable and mature enough to decide whether they should drink and when they have had enough to drink. Today's honest, responsible teenagers make totally rational decisions. Raising the drinking age would limit the freedom of choice for the millions of level-headed, responsible youth of this country.

Sincerely,
John Smith, student
Community High School

1. The author is _____

2. The author's background is _____

3. The author writes this letter in order to _____

_____

4. The author creates a mood or feeling about teenagers that is _____

_____

5. The author uses the following words to achieve that feeling:

_____ _____ _____

_____ _____ _____

2. To the Editor:

   In response to your recent editorial denying this city's utility company the modest increase it recently requested, we wish to point out that the American Public Utility Company has always provided maximum efficient service to all customers. Conscious of this country's rising costs, the Company has maintained a policy of offering its subscribers low-cost, quality service and a constructive program of ever-expanding services to meet all needs. The goals and ideals of the American consumer are of utmost concern to the Company. We are merely asking for a fair increase needed to cover the cost of scientific development of products and services which ultimately benefit every customer of American Public Utility.

Sincerely,
Max Davison
Chairperson, Board of Directors
American Public Utility Company

1. The author is _____

2. The author's background is _____

3. The author writes this letter in order to _____

_____

4. The author creates a mood or feeling about the Company of _____

_____

5. The author uses the following words to achieve the feeling:

_____   _____   _____

_____   _____   _____

_____   _____   _____

_____   _____   _____

3. To the Editor:

   Recently, after hearing of a tragic accident, I became very aware of an urgent problem facing every community. The problem is drunk driving. Drunk drivers kill, maim, and disfigure innocent victims. Yet our laws do very little to deter or punish these drivers. The public needs to be aware that these drivers cause serious injury or death to innocent bystanders and get away with it. If arrested, these criminals are soon on the roads again and are often involved in other alcohol-related accidents. We must have much stricter legislation in order to stop these tragedies.

                                    Sincerely,
                                    Mrs. Elyse Robbins
                                    San Diego, California

1. The author is _____

2. The author's background is _____

3. The author writes this letter in order to _____

_____

4. The author creates a mood or feeling about drunk drivers of _____

_____

5. The author uses the following words to achieve the feeling:

_____   _____   _____

_____   _____   _____

_____   _____   _____

_____   _____   _____

4. To the Editor:

I was chagrined to discover that my seven-year-old son, who has a fairly mature facility with the English language, was not familiar with the concepts of the terms clockwise and counterclockwise. I found myself employing many words in order to convey the concepts.

The introduction and pervasiveness of digital timekeeping, apart from being esthetically less pleasant than the once-familiar clock face, with its big and little hands, is depleting the language of two valuable descriptive terms which have often facilitated communication.

Lengthier and perhaps less descriptive explanations of the movement conveyed by clockwise will result in future generations being deprived of the ability to conjure up an image of an arc moving toward completion of a circle in one or the other direction.

I intend to present my child with a traditional watch on his eighth birthday, assuming that I am able to locate one suitable for a youngster.

CHARLES I. FRISCH
Rockville Centre, L.I., Aug. 3, 1983

1. The author is _____

2. The author's background is _____

3. The author writes this letter in order to _____

_____

4. The author creates a mood or feeling about watches that is ____

_____

5. The author uses the following words to achieve that feeling:

_____   _____   _____

_____   _____   _____

Practice with Longer Passages: Read each of the following passages, and evaluate critically the author's purpose and use of words to create a mood.

1.   It was Thursday. I was sitting in the back of the room in a seat with a chalk circle drawn around it. The idiot's seat, the troublemaker's seat.

The teacher thought I was stupid. Couldn't spell, couldn't read, couldn't do arithmetic. Just stupid. Teachers were never interested in finding out that you couldn't concentrate because you were so hungry, because you hadn't had any breakfast. All you could think of was noontime, would it ever come? Maybe you could sneak into the cloakroom and steal a bite of some kid's lunch out of a coat pocket. A bite of something. Paste. You can't really make a meal out of paste, or put it on bread for a sandwich, but sometimes I'd scoop a few spoonfuls out of the paste jar in the back of the room. Pregnant people get strange tastes. I was pregnant with poverty. Pregnant with dirt and pregnant with smells that made people turn away, pregnant with cold and pregnant with shoes that were never bought for me, pregnant with five other people in my bed and no Daddy in the next room and pregnant with hunger. Paste doesn't taste too bad when you're hungry.

[*This passage is excerpted from* nigger, *an autobiography.*]

(Gregory, 44)

1. The author is _____

2. The author's background is _____

3. The author writes this passage in order to _____

   _____

4. The author creates a mood of _____

5. The author uses the following words or phrases to create the mood:

   _____   _____

   _____   _____

   _____   _____

   _____   _____

2.   And if you're a male doctor, how will you relate to women? Women as patients, as nurses, as fellow doctors—and later as students?

Will you be able to respect your patient's right to know and make decisions about her own body?

Will you see nurses as colleagues—or as handmaidens?

And if the day comes when you are teaching, what can young women medical students expect from you?

Questionnaires filled out by women at forty-one medical schools around the country have revealed a distressing pattern.

The women were often either ignored in class or simply not taken seriously as students. They were told that they were only there to find a husband and that they were taking the places of men who would then have to go out and become chiropractors. (Logic is not the strong point of sexism.)

They were often told that women just

didn't belong in medicine. And at times they were told this by the very professors who were grading them.

They would be shown slides of *Playboy* nudes during anatomy lectures to the accompaniment of catcalls and wisecracks from male students. And in place of discussions about their work, they would often hear a discussion of their appearance.

These are reports from forty-one different medical schools.

I'm dwelling on this because it seems to me that the male-female relationship is still the most personal and intense test of humane behavior. It is a crucible for decency.

I hope you men will work to grant the same dignity to your female colleagues that you yourselves enjoy.

And if you're a female doctor, I hope you'll be aware that you didn't get where you are all by yourself. You've had to work hard, of course. But you're sitting where you are right now in part because way back in

1848 in Seneca Falls women you never knew began insisting you had a right to sit there. Just as they helped a generation they would never see, I urge you to work for the day when your daughters and their daughters will be called not "A woman doctor," or "My doctor, who's a woman . . . ," but simply "My doctor."

It may seem strange to rank the things you care about, but when you think about it, there isn't an area of your work that won't be affected by what you decide to place a high value on and what you decide doesn't count.

Decide now.

[This speech was delivered by Alan Alda, actor and star of the former television series "MASH."]

(Alan Alda, Commencement Address)

1. The author is _____

2. The author's background is _____

3. The author writes his speech in order to _____

_____

4. The author creates a mood of _____

5. The author uses the following words or phrases to create the mood:

_____   _____   _____

_____   _____   _____

_____   _____   _____

_____   _____   _____

_____   _____   _____

Determining the Author's Viewpoint

38

When you analyzed passages, you inferred ideas that were not stated but implied by the author. Those ideas were based on statements made about characters, plots, and settings. Based on evidence, you drew conclusions about people and society in general and also applied those ideas to your society. When you applied inference skills, you were determining the author's viewpoint about the nature of people, their relationships, and society.

Authors often present a particular viewpoint about societal issues. You should be able to identify the issue and determine what viewpoint or side of the question the author supports.

Example

How can city administrators vote themselves pay increases when they are already earning substantial salaries? Moreover, they recently imposed a ceiling on pay increases for city employees.

Questions

1. What issue is being discussed? _____

2. What are the possible sides of the question? _____

_____

3. What is the author's viewpoint about the issue?

_____

_____

Example

City administrators have given up top-salaried positions in private industry in order to serve the public interest. It is therefore essential for these administrators to receive salaries that effectively compete with the private sector.

Questions

1. What issue is being discussed? _____

2. What are the possible sides of the question? _____

_____

3. What is the author's viewpoint about the issue? _____

_____

_____

Reading critically involves recognizing the issue, the sides of the issue, and the **viewpoint** the author presents. Recognizing the author's views about people, events, or societal issues provides a broader degree of understanding.

Practice: Read the following letters and answer the accompanying questions.

1. To the Editor:

In <u>The Times</u> for July 27 was a story relating the fact that Secretary Weinberger had called off the use of dogs for the study and teaching of war-wound care.

When a bullet or a fragment tears into a limb, it shreds and destroys muscle, breaks bones, divides nerves, tendons and arteries. Soldiers will be wounded thusly in the wars, actions, brushfires and maneuvers of this and coming decades.

When our son or grandson or nephew or just plain citizen soldier falls wounded, we want for him the best surgery the Army can provide. We want the most expert surgeon in the field to fix that limb and above all to repair those nerves, vessels and bones. With prompt, effective care the salvage rate is better than 90 percent; without it, there is amputation and permanent crippling, if not gas gangrene and loss of life.

How to learn? A protesting Dr. Donald Doyle is quoted in the article as stating that the learning process on living animal tissue has "absolutely no application" in combat-wound surgery. He is absolutely wrong. This is the only way to learn, unless we are to send green surgeons into combat for on-the-job learning. All three combat services have taught inexperienced surgeons to treat fresh wounds, in animals.

The animal is anesthetized; its operation has all the protection and precautions of clinical surgery. Why pick the dog for this ruling? If animal life is to be spared, what's the trouble with sheep and goats? Or is it merely the institutionalized sentimentality of the animal ethics group? What about human ethics?

Sure, Mr. Secretary, leave out dogs if you want. But for goodness' sake, do your job and say it out loud: Your responsibility is to our citizen soldiers and their care, not to dogs. Stand up and be counted for excellence in the "little things" that mean life and limb to the soldiers under you, as well as those great big things like missiles.

FRANCIS D. MOORE, M.D.
Boston, July 28, 1983

The writer is Moseley Professor of Surgery, emeritus, at the Harvard Medical School.

1. The author is _____

2. The author's background is _____

3. The author's purpose in writing this passage is _____

_____

4. The author creates a tone of _____

5. The author uses the following words to create this tone:

_____ _____ _____

_____ _____ _____

_____ _____ _____

_____

6. The issue being discussed is _____

_____

7. The possible sides of the issue are _____

_____

_____

8. The author's viewpoint is _____

_____

_____

2. High Mail Rates, Low Service

I recently sent a letter to New York City, one to Hauppauge and two others to Syracuse. It took six days for my letter to the city to arrive at its destination and the letter to Hauppauge has still not arrived. Both of the letters mailed on two separate occasions to the Syracuse area never arrived at their destinations.

A letter from one town here on Long Island to an adjacent town, unless you mail it at a main Post Office such as Freeport, Mineola or Hempstead, can take anywhere from two to three days to arrive. I can't for the life of me figure out why we continue to sit still and accept ever-increasing rates without any change in efficiency of service. What a passive society we have become!

Isn't there any way we, the public, can demand better service if we are to continue to pay surcharges and other annual increases in the cost of mailings. It is actually becoming cheaper (and certainly more certain) to make a phone call to our particular destination.

I am a businesswoman and recently I went to send a certified letter with a return receipt requested only to find out that half-ounce letter cost $1.40 via certified mail. It is time we got on the back of the postal service for their inefficient handling of each costly piece of mail.

Ellen Woodbury
Westbury

1. The author is _____

2. The author's background is _____

3. The author's purpose in writing this passage is _____

_____

4. The author creates a tone of _____

5. The author uses the following words to create that tone:

_____   _____   _____

_____   _____   _____

_____   _____   _____

_____   _____   _____

6. The issue being discussed is _____

_____

7. The possible sides of the issue are _____

_____

_____

8. The author's viewpoint is _____

_____

_____

3. TV Doesn't Kill; Guns Do

Elisabet Van Nostrand

The murder trial of 15-year-old Ronny Zamora, whose defense was television intoxication, has spawned a new bumper sticker. "TV Doesn't Kill People; People Kill People," it proclaims, in a takeoff on the old gun lobby slogan. In fact, the Florida case is a tragic illustration of why the gun lobby's version of the maxim, that asserts that guns don't kill, is wrong.

The gunners also have long proclaimed that, "If Guns Were Outlawed, Only Outlaws Would Have Guns." The implication is clear: Gun control would serve only to disarm the law-abiding citizens while leaving criminals free to shoot at will and without opposition.

Ronny Zamora did not own a gun. He was not an outlaw until the moment he broke into his elderly neighbor's house. His neighbor, 83-year-old Elinor Haggart, was clearly not an outlaw. She had a gun, for what purposes we can only surmise but pre-

sumably for self-defense. And it was with her own gun that she was slain.

Doesn't that gun bear the blame for her death in a far more immediate sense than the television programs watched by an impressionable youngster? Without it, Ronny couldn't have followed the example set by trigger-happy cops and robbers on the home screen.

The gun lobby is sure to argue, as it has argued before, he could have stabbed her or choked her or beaten her to death. Does that mean, the argument goes, we should also ban knives and ropes and baseball bats? Of course not. They serve other purposes as well. In fact, their main purposes have nothing to do with death or destruction. With the exception of those used for target shooting, guns serve no purposes except to kill or wound. And, in the case of handguns, their only victims are human beings; nobody goes deer-hunting with a Colt .45.

But more important in terms of the Florida tragedy is the question of whether or not Ronny would have killed the old woman next door if the task had been difficult, taken more time or brought him in direct physical contact with her. Guns kill suddenly and from a distance; the killer neither has to touch his victim nor spend any appreciable time in the act itself.

"Bang! You're dead!" is more than a childish exhortation. It's the literal truth. Many children have been killed by others playing with guns they didn't know were loaded or didn't know how to handle. People shoot themselves or others accidentally every day.

But they also shoot themselves or each other deliberately because a gun happens to be handy, not because it was obtained for that purpose. Friends shoot friends, husbands shoot wives and wives shoot husbands. After it's all over, they're victims along with those whom they've killed. Ronny was a victim all right—not so much of television but of a society that allows its citizens to keep guns at will, for whatever purpose. So was Elinor Haggart.

Elisabet Van Nostrand is a member of the editorial pages staff of Newsday.

1. The author is _____

2. The author's background is _____

3. The author's purpose in writing this passage is _____

   _____

4. The author creates a tone of _____

5. The author uses the following words to create that tone:

   _____   _____   _____

   _____   _____   _____

   _____   _____   _____

   _____   _____   _____

6. The issue being discussed is _____

   _____

7. The possible sides of the issue are _____

   _____

   _____

8. The author's viewpoint is _____

   _____

   _____

4. Video World—a Worthless Void?

John Rosemond

In the town where I live, a video arcade adjoins a restaurant I frequent for lunch. A few weeks ago, while waiting for a friend, I wandered inside this electronic carnival, curious to find out why the multitudes flocked here.

As I stood just inside the door, waiting for my eyes to adjust to the dim light, a maelstrom of noise swirled around me—groans, crashes, staccato beepings, sirens, roars, the rat-a-tat-tat of a machine gun, the zip-zipping of laser cannons, all mixed with loud, power-chord rock that blared from speakers hung high on the walls.

In the back corner, two people sat motionless in a lighted glass booth labeled "Get Your Change Here." The walls were lined with video games, about half of them manned by people peering intently into the screens. Their expressionless faces were awash with a harsh fluorescence, hands tapping buttons or wrapped around small control levers, bodies occasionally twitching as, I supposed, another Space Invader or Pac-Man—what's the electronic equivalent of biting the dust? Swallowing the void?

In the center of this audio-visual nightmare was a cluster of tables. Most of these, too, held video games. Hunkered over the one nearest where I stood was a young woman. Her left hand had a death grip on one side of the table top. Her eyes were locked, unblinking, on the screen, her expression intense, glazed. She was breathing loudly through her mouth. Except for her right hand, which jerked spasmodically under the table, she was motionless.

After lunch, my friend suggested a stop in this den of din. Reluctantly, I went along.

The first thing I saw when my sight returned was the same woman, sitting at the same table, with the same left-handed grip, the same blank expression on her face, her right hand still jerking. Had lunch been a dream or had time stopped in this place? I didn't stick around to find out.

Several weeks earlier, while visiting the grandparents during the holidays, I had watched my children become absorbed in an Atari game to the exclusion of all else. They said they were having fun. The tension on their faces as they "played" told me otherwise.

Video games bother me. I think they're not only worthless, but destructive as well.

"Destructive? Come now, John-boy, video games are a challenging way for children to occupy their time. They require thought, they stimulate the imagination and, besides, they build eye-hand coordination."

I think not. In the first place, video games do not qualify as play. Play is curious, exploratory, spontaneous. Play is open-ended, flexible, expansive. A child's play transcends the boundaries of space, time, materials and language. A child at play is transforming the commonplace into the extraordinary.

Video games do not compare. They are preprogrammed, closed electronic systems. They do not encourage or enable creativity. They require no initiative and even, I suspect, dampen it.

More than anything else, play is constructive. But when a video game is over, and your quarters have run out, you have nothing but eye strain to show for your efforts. Let's not kid ourselves, video games are hardly thought-provoking. They are mindless. In fact, I suspect that for the most part cerebral activity during video gaming is confined to the lower reflex-oriented areas of the brain.

As for the popular belief that video games strengthen eye-hand coordination, this is an impossible conclusion. First, video games require the hands to perform only simple, abbreviated movements. Second, the hands are remote from the field of vision.

More likely than not, video games damage developing eye-hand skills. Furthermore, because the action takes place within a small, rectangular, two-dimensional plane, the efficient perception of spatial relationships probably suffers as well.

But the most disturbing aspect of the video game craze is the obsessive, don't-bother-me attitude they induce. Watching that woman at the arcade, watching my children at their grandparents', I was reminded of compulsive gamblers, sitting for hours on end, pumping quarters into slot machines—the mentality is the same.

Video games are electronic drugs. And there is no such thing as a harmless addiction.

1. The author is _____

2. The author's background is _____

3. The author's purpose in writing this passage is _____

_____

4. The author creates a tone of _____

5. The author uses the following words to create that tone:

_____ _____ _____

_____ _____ _____

_____ _____ _____

6. The issue being discussed is _____

_____

_____

7. The possible sides of the issue are _____

_____

_____

8. The author's viewpoint is _____

_____

_____

Distinguishing Between a Fact and an Opinion

39

The skill of critical reading includes the ability to determine whether an author's views are supported with facts, opinions, or a combination. Distinguishing between facts and opinions is a basic skill of reading critically. Consider these examples of fact and opinion statements.

Example

FACT: Fish swim in the ocean.

OPINION: The best place to catch good-tasting fish is the ocean.

FACT: National pollsters collect information about the habits of television viewers.

OPINION: Television accurately measures viewers' habits.

FACT: Police belong to the civil service force of the city.

OPINION: Police are very careful not to arrest innocent people.

FACT: Department managers are responsible for the personnel they supervise.

OPINION: Department managers are supportive of their staff's professional and personal needs.

Each factual statement can be proved. For example, there is evidence to prove that "Fish swim in the ocean." The opinion statements are also known as viewpoints. They cannot be proved with objective evidence. For example, "The best place to catch good-tasting fish" may or may not be the ocean.

Authors can use facts, opinions, or both to support their viewpoints. A **fact** can be proved with written, stated, or observed evidence. An **opinion**, although it may be valid, is a statement that expresses a personal bias and cannot be objectively proved. You must distinguish between an author's use of facts and opinions to support a view. When you can do this, you will be able to evalute the strength of the author's views.

Practice: Read each of the following statements carefully. If the statement can be proved with unbiased evidence, write FACT. If the statement is an expression of a personal viewpoint, write OPINION.

———————— **1.** Scientists can divide the nucleus of an atom.

———————— **2.** California is known for its fine Mexican restaurants.

———————— **3.** Business partnerships involve at least two people.

———————— **4.** Dinosaurs are extinct.

———————— **5.** Television has a greater influence on children than on their parents.

———————— **6.** A best-seller is a book that leads sales records during a specific time period.

———————— **7.** Partnerships are more rewarding than sole ownerships.

———————— **8.** The first astronauts showed great courage.

———————— **9.** Scientific journals are usually boring.

———————— **10.** Children should not play with toy soldiers and guns.

Practice: Read each of the following statements carefully. Label each statement FACT or OPINION.

———————— **1.** Community colleges offer better educational programs than four-year colleges.

———————— **2.** Only law enforcement officials should carry guns.

———————— **3.** The first man to land on the moon was an American.

———————— **4.** Women are better cooks than men.

———————— **5.** Allergic people must be treated with allergy shots.

———————— **6.** Maritime law is enforced on the seas.

———————— **7.** More federal subsidies are needed for small businesses.

———————— **8.** Most restaurants employ male chefs.

———————— **9.** The mayor was elected by an overwhelming majority.

———————— **10.** Science courses are the most difficult courses in college.

———————— **11.** Malnutrition is the greatest worldwide problem.

———————— **12.** The country can expect an economic recession in the next few months.

———————— **13.** The earthquake was the largest ever recorded on the Richter Scale.

———————— **14.** Computers are an asset to most businesses.

———————— **15.** The nursing profession is open to both men and women.

Practice: Read the following four selections and answer the questions that follow each.

1. Puerto Rico: Home

J. L. Torres

Ironically, my stepfather died in a veterans' hospital. The sad day we went to claim his body, I could not help wondering that to his last day the man never truly was assimilated into the American mainstream. He passed away an American (indeed, he was born into citizenship), a survivor of World War II and the Korean conflict. Yet, he rarely spoke English, considered American food bland, and he could never understand football.

My stepfather was pure Puerto Rican. He ate Puerto Rican food, relived childhood memories of his island hometown, listened to Latin music, watched Spanish television, played dominoes and liked a shot of rum. He followed traditional Hispanic values and mores. In the way of all machos, he was serious and proud. But he died in a veterans' hospital in Manhattan.

They told us that his benefits entitled him to an American flag. My stepfather left the Army with three stripes and an honorable discharge. As he got older, though, he tore up his voter's registration card and never voted again. Most Puerto Ricans never really feel American. How can we, when we stubbornly embrace our culture and in the process remind ourselves of our differences? Years of alienation can change a man's heart. So in that roundabout manner in which older people come to talk about dying, he would often tell us that he didn't want "that rag" on his coffin. At the funeral parlor no one spoke up when the mortician placed the flag alongside his head. I felt as if we had betrayed him.

That incident, however, only touches the surface. My mother decided to lay his body to rest in Puerto Rico. And I thought: "God, all those years of struggling, working so hard to accumulate enough money to go back, and he never made it." You see, the Puerto Rican Dream is of returning home. Even the young people talk about going back and buying a home. In the funeral parlor in Puerto Rico I learned that many Puerto Ricans come back home dead. It's the last wish for the nostalgic who never made it back alive.

Another irony: Puerto Rico observes its 81st year as an American colony, while the United States celebrates 203 years of independence. Through some 81 years, Puerto Ricans have traveled freely between the States and the island. You would think that in that time some process would have evolved whereby Puerto Ricans "became" Americans. (Being born Americans isn't enough for us; we have to grow into it.) But I think of my stepfather and me, and I see little difference. I speak and write English better than he, but I eat Puerto Rican food, listen to Salsa and, having studied Spanish formally, I read Puerto Rican writers and thinkers lost to my stepfather's generation. I don't like dominoes and prefer Scotch to rum. I can only respect the memories older people have of Puerto Rico. But I do dream of going back. I want to write about it and its people. I struggle not to die before I accomplish my dream. I guess that remains the same. Perhaps the only major difference is that I wouldn't allow myself the dilemma of having to decide whether I wanted an American flag on my coffin or not.

J. L. Torres is a contributing editor to Latin N. Y. *magazine.*

1. The author is _____

2. The author's background is _____

3. The author's purpose in writing the passage is _____

_____

4. The author creates a tone of _____

5. The author uses the following words to create that tone:

_____ _____ _____

_____ _____ _____

_____ _____ _____

6. The issue being discussed is _____

7. The possible sides of the issue are _____

_____

_____

8. The author's viewpoint is _____

_____

_____

9. The author uses the following facts to support the viewpoint:

_____

_____

_____

_____

_____

_____

10. The author uses the following opinions to support the viewpoint:

_____

_____

_____

_____

_____

2. A Son Divided

William Colgan

My son, 10 years and one day old, waves gamely as the Greyhound pulls out. He is bound 150 miles south to spend the long Fourth of July weekend with his mother. I stand in the hot parking lot, waving back until the bus fades far down into the stream of traffic. My son has made this strange shuttle many times before. He is one of the new legion of suddenly old children, paying in part for their parents' failures.

I have stood here before and should not be too upset. Only this trip is different: His mother has remarried in the past month, and my son is going to live for the first time in a new house with a new, part-time surrogate father. The man is a complete stranger to me.

Some people advise that I should be content. After all, if his mother is happier, the wisdom goes, won't that make a better situation for my son also? Perhaps. But it still galls and burns in the gut.

My situation is better than most. Unlike nearly all divorced fathers, I enjoy joint custody: All major decisions regarding my son must be made by mutual agreement, and each parent is legally entitled to physical custody for half of each year. Because of school, the year is not split evenly: My son spends about 160 days each year with me, 200 with his mother. The summer, however, is nearly all mine, and the summer is the best of times. We have a good beach on Lake Champlain, a healthy garden, and my son plays centerfield for a baseball team of eight-to-10-year-olds that I coach. We won our opening game, and my son collected a double and a single. We celebrated at the local Pizza Hut. I should be satisfied, but I am not.

The 200 days away are 200 too many. More than half his year, more than half mine. And now there is a new man. Who is he? What is he like? Does that make any difference? By what right does he shelter my son under his roof more nights of the year than I do?

The Government statisticians measure every-

thing relentlessly. They tell us that one of two children born today will spend at least part of his life in a single-parent home. Most of these children will be reared by their mothers, since the courts still almost automatically, and unthinkingly, grant child custody in divorce to women. The fathers often become phantoms. They are limited to weekend visits, cut off from any role in vital choices of schooling, community and religion, vulnerable to termination of their visitation rights. American fathers, usually without much fuss, thought or evaluation, routinely surrender the most basic rights of paternity in divorce proceedings. I wonder if this is so in other cultures? Are the men of Greece, India, Japan, Brazil also so quick to yield their children? Why is the father's role and responsibility so diminished in America?

My immediate problem is that both his mother and I love our son. He is all we have to show for our marriage, except perhaps some aging photo albums from happier days, and our Solomon-like decision to split custody is really the best of a bad situation.

According to the practitioners of currently fashionable psychobabble, we live in the best of times because more and more people are "being up-front" about their feelings and "doing their own thing." A system in which nearly everyone eventually winds up married to someone else is welcomed as a positive development, a sign of a new maturity in our society. Perhaps.

I should be grateful that my son and I are together as much as we are. We are not strangers to each other, nor, I hope, will we ever be. We are involved in each other's lives, and we have many fine times together. I shouldn't mind that he now lives with another man. After all this will give him a new "relationship" to develop. Learning to develop relationships is a vital survival skill in the new world a-building in America. I shouldn't mind.

But the thing still seems wrong.

William Colgan is 35 years old. He has been separated and divorced for a total of three years.

1. The author is _____

2. The author's background is _____

3. The author's purpose in writing the passage is _____

4. The author creates a tone of _____

5. The author uses the following words to create that tone:

_____   _____   _____

_____   _____   _____

_____   _____   _____

_____   _____   _____

6. The issue being discussed is _____

7. The possible sides of the issue are _____

_____

8. The author's viewpoint is _____

_____

9. The author uses the following facts to support the viewpoint:

_____

_____

_____

_____

_____

_____

_____

10. The author uses the following opinions to support the viewpoint:

_____

_____

_____

_____

_____

_____

_____

3. Beating Runners at Their Own Game

David L. Smith, M.D.

The latest insanity to hit the American public is running. I just returned from Washington, DC, where instead of being mugged in Rock Creek Park, I was run over by joggers. The Mall looked like a gigantic amateur footrace: runners of all possible descriptions determinedly plodding up and down, from the Capitol to the cherry trees and back again. So many people have had heart attacks trying to run up the Washington Monument that everybody is now required to take the elevator.

Now all this is okay if not taken too far. Running is at least a halfway decent substitute for bicycling if for some reason you can't ride your bike. It is said to be good for the heart, and it might even help you lose weight. (Although I have always been able to eat enough to stay fat, with any amount of exercise.)

The trouble with it is too many runners have the idea there is no other exercise that is as good, not even bicycling. Some of these same runners go so far as to claim that running a marathon (26-plus miles) is the supreme athletic test. Those who do not run marathons, they imply, have not yet arrived among the elite.

All this is, of course, a lot of hokum. Although good runners can often outdo good cyclists on a treadmill, most runners don't know that good cyclists can outdo good runners on a bicycle ergometer. It takes just as much power to ride record times as it does to run them. The marathon can be dangerous. It leads frequently to injuries and even heatstroke. We can tell this to runners, but sometimes they may be hard to convince. They see cyclists in terms of the lady who rides her balloon-tired one-speed so slowly that she must have the balancing ability of a track rider, or the kid who rides the wrong way down the street on his high-riser, with his front wheel held up in the air. The typical runner may never have even met a real bike racer.

1. The author is _____

2. The author's background is _____

3. The author's purpose in writing the passage is _____

   _____

4. The author creates a tone of _____

5. The author uses the following words to create that tone:

   _____ _____ _____

   _____ _____ _____

   _____ _____ _____

   _____ _____ _____

   _____ _____ _____

6. The issue being discussed is _____

7. The possible sides of the issue are _____

   _____

   _____

8. The author's viewpoint is _____
_____
_____

9. The author uses the following facts to support the viewpoint:
_____
_____
_____
_____
_____

10. The author uses the following opinions to support the viewpoint:
_____
_____
_____
_____
_____
_____
_____

40

Evaluating Total Selections

Read the following selection and answer the questions that follow it.

Phenomena, Comment, and Notes

John P. Wiley, Jr.

Something deep within many of us wants not to be alone. We not only like movies about extraterrestrials, we secretly hope they will land in our neighborhood, arrive at our house. We are embarrassed by the more lurid UFO tales precisely because we want so much for the next one to be true.

More than once, standing in a field at night looking up at the stars, I have found myself thinking "Now would be a good time." I watch for a light that grows brighter, comes closer, swoops in for a landing all unseen by neighbors or military radar. Too many bad movies too long ago, perhaps. For a few minutes one night I thought I had my UFO. Driving along a busy interstate highway, I saw a light in the sky, moving slowly and exhibiting a pattern of brightening and dimming. I pulled over, stopped in a shower of gravel on the shoulder, and leaped out of the car. The light drew closer and closer, until I could see that it was a small plane, advertising the county fair with an array of lights on the underside of the wings.

Many people, I suspect, want the aliens to arrive for the sheer excitement and for the disruption of the routine of daily life. Even before we know the aliens' intentions, we are sure that tomorrow will not be like today and it is easy to feel that any change is good. The problems that weigh us down are suddenly insignificant, and we are caught up in a larger issue, the largest the world has ever faced.

We have a history of yearning for alien life. The popular response today to movies about lovable, or at least benign, aliens seems little different from the excitement of newspaper readers in 1835 over a phony report that Sir John F. W. Herschel had "discovered" batlike people living on the moon (*Smithsonian*, March 1982). The hoax could not have lasted as long as it did unless people wanted to believe it. (Herschel himself was in Capetown at the time and knew nothing about it.) Percival Lowell, seeing the canals he wanted to be there, was not alone in adamantly wishing for life on Mars.

And the yearning may be for more than simple excitement. As individuals and as nations we are not generally doing as well as might be hoped, and yet it is not clear how to do better. We live with a sense that we should be doing better, a kind of "divine discontent" once used as an argument for the existence of God. Extraterrestrials arriving in starships would be so far ahead of us technologically that we could hope, even assume, that they were ahead of us socially as well. At the very least they would have avoided destroying themselves and been able to cooperate well enough to travel the stars. Presumably they would have something to teach us about living together as well as about rocket engines.

On our better days, when we are pretty sure we can muddle through without any help from anyone, we can still prefer to believe that there is life elsewhere in the universe. Otherwise the waste is overwhelming. One hundred billion stars in our galaxy, 100 billion galaxies: a universe billions of light years across and just one inhabited planet? It just doesn't compute. (To fully appreciate this argument, step outside some dark, moonless night and slowly sweep along the Milky Way with a pair of binoculars. And that's just a small part of one galaxy.)

Not everyone, of course, is convinced. Lots of people would like nothing less than an alien spaceship landing in their backyard. And lots of scientists think they have the answer to Enrico Fermi's demand: Where are they?

It has been said that if intelligent life had arisen elsewhere, it would have spread through the galaxy and would already have arrived here, at least in the form of self-reproducing computer probes. None has arrived, again raising the question: Where is everybody?

So perhaps we are really alone after all. No one is coming to bail us out, no one is coming for a visit, no light will ever swoop down to my field in the night. No god will pop out of a strangely lit machine. Our future is entirely up to us. If we make it, we will have done it by ourselves, and will be able to take appropriate pride.

But there is another possibility. Suppose we are not the only, but the first? Suppose that in galaxies across all of space and time, as stars formed and synthesized heavy elements and exploded and died, as planets accreted out of the debris, as organic molecules became more complex in an evolution toward life, we were the first? Not in the whole universe, perhaps; modern cosmology weighs powerfully against any argument for the Earth's uniqueness. But suppose that, in the random order of things, life did arise first on Earth in this galaxy, or in this sector of the galaxy. And suppose there is life on lots of other planets around us, but it is a million or a hundred million years behind us.

Then we can imagine that someday in the distant future the life forms on those planets may find themselves discontented and yearning for something to happen, looking at the night sky and hoping for company. Starships will appear in their skies, and the aliens will land. They will have something to offer about rocket engines, and about how to make a go of life. They will be us.

1. The author is _____

2. The author's background is _____

3. The author's purpose in writing the passage is _____

_____

4. The author creates a tone of _____

5. The author uses the following words to create that tone:

_____   _____   _____

_____   _____   _____

_____   _____   _____

_____   _____   _____

6. The issue being discussed is _____

_____

7. The possible sides of the issue are _____

_____

_____

8. The author's viewpoint is _____

_____

_____

9. The author uses the following facts to support the viewpoint:

_____

_____

_____

_____

_____

10. The author uses the following opinions to support the viewpoint:

_____

_____

_____

_____

_____

The following letter was written by Dr. Paul Williamson, a Mississippi physician, to his son, Snap, who was about to enter Tulane University in New Orleans. At the time the letter was written, students on many campuses were vigorously protesting the American involvement in Vietnam. In many instances, the National Guard was called into action on college campuses.

Read this letter, and answer the questions that follow it.

A Doctor's Letter to His Son

Dear Nathan:

Of course you know that your mother and I love you deeply. There are limits to that love. Let me discuss one with you today.

You are going to Tulane. We are proud and happy for you. There are, however, awkward things that must be discussed. College kids over the nation are "protesting."

They use many beautiful phrases. What it often amounts to is a contest with the duly constituted authorities of the United States Government. The only term that could apply is revolution. People are quite rightly shot in revolutions.

I suppose there is the legal differentiation between a peaceful demonstration and breaking windows. One graduates into the other by such indifferent degrees; it is difficult to say where one ends and the other begins.

The duly constituted authorities have been merciful beyond belief—far too merciful, I think—

with students. Obviously, this patience is nearing an end. Snap, I have seldom heard of a student being shot at his study desk. When he goes in the open and contests the ground with the National Guard, he may very likely be shot—and very rightly.

Let us take, for example, the sweet little girl in Kent, Ohio. I feel nothing but sorrow that a beautiful young girl of great mental attainments be killed. Yet, Snap, if she had been studying—doing what her parents were paying for her to accomplish—would she have died?

She was helping contest the ground with duly constituted U.S. authorities. In this case, I back the U.S. I think it rather remarkable that they didn't shoot 200 more. In this case, the girl was a revolutionary and she got exactly what a revolutionary should expect.

The same, Snap, would be true of you. If you care to challenge the U.S. Government, this is your affair. If you get killed doing it, this is your affair. You see, there are constitutional ways to change the U.S. Government and I agree that it desperately needs changing. However, if you choose to try to change it by revolution, expect to get shot. Mother and I will grieve but we will gladly buy a dinner for the National Guardsman who shot you. You see, son, they pretty-up in definition all the things that you might want to do. When brought to its basics, it is still a revolution.

I am sorry for the colored boys who were killed at Jackson. But, son, I know a lot more about this than will ever be printed in national news media. There was sniper fire the night before as well as the night the police fired back. The students were given 15 minutes' warning to clear the area before the police fired. I thought the duly constituted authorities were most gentle to take only two. If you take part in something like this and get shot, Mama and I will back the U.S.

It may sound like great martyrdom to give your life for an ideal. Indeed, it may be when you are old enough to judge ideals. Trying to whip the National Guard or the Army appears to me as damned foolishness. Snap, I have been shot and it hurts like hell. It's funny, but you don't think of ideal over the pain.

Now use your head, son. Remember this country is getting tired of student demonstrations which lead to revolution. The National Guard can shove in a couple of clips and clean Tulane. I think they ought to when students disturb the peace and destroy property.

One thing of which you have probably not thought: Tulane is a non-profit corporation belonging to the public, which means one brick is yours. The National Guard is a public organization, which means that one bolt on one rifle may have been paid for with your tax.

It seems awfully foolish for you to pay for the bolt that snaps the cartridge home which kills you. It seems even more foolish to tear down the bricks you own.

When I went to Oklahoma City University, I always thought of it as my university. Ann and I probably own one bit of cement between the bricks. Believe me, sir, I was very careful of that bit of cement.

I, too, had ebullient spirits, but I used them for more practical purposes. Have you ever considered how many co-eds there are to be kissed? There is a much more worthy purpose than absorbing a bullet and not nearly so painful.

Think of these things.

Love,
Dad

Questions

1. Who is the author? _____

2. What is the author's purpose in writing this letter? _____

3. What mood does the author create about students? _____

4. What words does the author use to create the mood? List them.

_____ _____ _____

_____ _____ _____

_____ _____ _____

_____ _____ _____

5. What mood does the author create about the government? _____

6. What words does the author use to create the mood? List them.

_____   _____   _____

_____   _____   _____

_____   _____   _____

_____   _____   _____

7. What issue is being discussed? _____

_____

8. What are the possible sides of that issue? _____

_____

_____

_____

9. What position does the author take? _____

_____

10. Does the author use facts, opinions, or a combination to support his viewpoint? _____

11. Write one fact the author uses to support his viewpoint.

_____

_____

12. Write one opinion the author uses to support his viewpoint.

_____

_____

13. Does the author achieve his intended purpose (refer to your response to question 2) in the letter?

Explain. _____

_____

_____

_____

_____

The following letter appeared in a national newspaper one week after the doctor's letter appeared. Read this letter and answer the questions that follow it.

An Answer to the Mississippi Doctor

Joseph Kelner

What hath God wrought in our younger generation? Are the college kids mostly empty-headed swingers dedicated to pot and sex, long hair and smashing windows? Certainly not. They are the most idealistic, clear-thinking generation ever to come along. They ask penetrating and embarrassing questions about the status quo. Would we really prefer that they be otherwise?

In his letter advising his college son last week, Dr. Paul Williamson of Mississippi suggested that young men in college mind their own business and devote their time to kissing co-eds rather than to protesting injustices. Would we really prefer it that way, or can't they do both?

For every lunatic dynamiter there are a thousand serious-minded young people who really give a damn about American ideals and dreams. But hypersensitive high government officials have branded them as "bums" and "revolutionaries" because of their strident protests against continuance of an undeclared, unconstitutional and pointless war which disrupts their education, kills, blinds and cripples them by the hundreds of thousands.

We, the older generation, have much to answer for. We have allowed our country to decay and deteriorate. We were too permissive of our own government. We stood by passively while our elected officials inched us into the bottomless pit of Vietnam. While our land, water and air were polluted and fouled for decades by profit-hungry industry, we were reticent and compliant, each of us devoting our energies to the pursuit of happiness and material gain in the good Horatio Alger tradition. The college kids simply cannot see us spending hundreds of billions on Vietnams and ABMs while our cities rot and people are hungry. They see our priorities aborted and our principles perverted to favor a military-industrial complex.

So they protest. Some throw rocks and a few criminal extremists go much further. The Kent State massacre could have happened on any campus. Consider the setting. High government officials had attacked, atmosphere was already inflamed by our invasion of Cambodia. It set the stage for a self-righteous National Guard firing squad to execute defenseless students.

This is new in America. The constitutional right to protest and dissent was shattered by a volley of rifle shots at Kent State. The victims were hundreds of feet from the firing squad—too far away to make the most abject coward truly apprehensive for his own safety.

This was unjustifiable killing for the expression of words and ideas, not for self-defense or deeds. But the Ohio county grand jury, reflecting a callous community conscience, indicted everyone but those who pulled the triggers, and the blindfolded lady justice atop the country courthouse must have wept at these omissions.

Dr. Williamson professes to be a compassionate man. He expressed sorrow that "the sweet little girl in Kent was killed." She was on her way from one college building to another on her campus and stopped to see what was going on. A bullet from a National Guardsman over 300 feet away cut her down and ended her young life. The doctor ruefully says, "she got what the revolutionary should expect" and that, "it is remarkable that they didn't shoot 200 more." This, too, is new in America.

Jeffrey Miller was shot through the head over 250 feet from the execution squad. He died instantly. The picture of a young girl weeping over his lifeless body went around the world. Her tears were not for Jeffrey alone. They were for America's shame before the world that this could happen here. The scene somehow was out of focus. Its locale should have been against a wall in Castro's Cuba or near a ditch at Auschwitz.

Young Americans are a proud and sturdy lot who are not going to disappear. They are keenly aware of the current scene. To talk to them is to admire them. They think we can do better to put our values in order. They have the natural impatience of youth against decades of indolence and crusty traditions of inertia which have permitted America to deteriorate. Why their violent protests when we marched into Cambodia without

Congressional authority? To them this was an extension of Vietnam's horror, a compounding of the original felony.

What else bugs our youth? Racism and poverty and an establishment unresponsive to the need for real change. They resent the divisive hard line of government officials castigating dissent and dissenters in colleges or in our publicity media. But a growing number of uptight Americans seem willing to suppress minority views. We appear to be galloping toward a mass totalitarian intolerance of minority ideas.

The complaint of our youth is not against the Constitution but that its spirit is being ignored and circumvented by hypocrisy.

Joseph Kelner, a former president of the American Trial Lawyers Association, represents the estate of Jeffrey Miller in a lawsuit arising from the shooting of Jeffrey Miller at Kent State University.

Questions

1. Who is the author? _____

2. What is the author's purpose in writing this letter? _____

_____

3. What mood does the author create about students? _____

4. What words does the author use to create the mood? List them.

_____   _____   _____

_____   _____   _____

_____   _____   _____

_____   _____   _____

5. What mood does the author create about the government? _____

6. What words does the author use to create the mood? List them.

_____ _____ _____ _____

_____ _____ _____ _____

_____ _____ _____ _____

_____ _____ _____ _____

_____ _____ _____ _____

_____ _____ _____ _____

7. What issue is being discussed? _____

_____

8. What are the possible sides of that issue? _____

_____

_____

_____

9. What position does the author take? _____

_____

10. Does the author use facts, opinions, or a combination to support his viewpoint? _____

11. Write one fact the author uses to support his viewpoint. _____

_____

_____

12. Write one opinion the author uses to support his viewpoint. _____

_____

_____

13. Does the author achieve his intended purpose (refer to your response to question 2) in the letter?

Explain. _____

_____

_____

_____

_____

_____

_____

Acknowledgments

Adler, Ronald B., and George Rodman, from *Understanding Human Communication*. Copyright © 1982 by CBS College Publishing. Reprinted by permission of Holt, Rinehart and Winston, CBS College Publishing.

Alda, Alan, Commencement Address given at Columbia College of Physicians and Surgeons, May 16, 1979. Courtesy of Alan Alda.

Baker, Russell, "A Shocking Tale," *New York Times*, November 16, 1972. Copyright © 1972 by The New York Times Company. Reprinted by permission.

Baltake, Joe, "Most People Remember Their First Kiss," *New York Daily News*, August 12, 1983. Knight-Ridder Newspapers.

Berry, Adrian, *The Next Ten Thousand Years: A Vision of Man's Future in the Universe*, A Mentor Book, New American Library, Inc., 1974.

Boone, Louis E., and David L. Kurtz, from *Contemporary Business*, 2d ed. Copyright © 1979 by The Dryden Press. Reprinted by permission of Holt, Rinehart and Winston, CBS College Publishing.

Boone, Louis E., and David L. Kurtz, from *Contemporary Business*, 3d ed. Copyright © 1982 by CBS College Publishing. Reprinted by permission of Holt, Rinehart and Winston, CBS College Publishing.

Boylestad, Robert L., from *Introductory Circuit Analysis*, 4th ed., Charles E. Merrill Publishing Company, 1982.

Brown, J.M., F.K. Berrien, D.L. Russell, and W.D. Wells, *Applied Psychology*. Copyright © Macmillan Publishing Co., Inc. 1966. Excerpts reprinted with permission of Macmillan Publishing Co., Inc.

Carpenter, Kathleen, and Doris H. Calloway, *Nutrition and Health*, Saunders College Publishing, 1981.

Christian, James L., from *Philosophy: An Introduction to the Art of Wondering*, 3d ed., Holt, Rinehart and Winston, 1981.

Cole, Stephen, "Crime as the Cost of the American Creativity," *Newsday*, August 24, 1983.

Colgan, William, "A Son Divided," *New York Times*, July 18, 1979. Copyright © 1979 by The New York Times Company. Reprinted by permission.

Crispin, Edmund, *The Moving Toy Shop*, Penguin Books, 1946.

Curtis, Helena, *Biology*, 3d ed. New York: Worth Publishers, 1979.

Davis, William, *Business Data Processing*, © 1978, Addison-Wesley, Reading, Massachusetts. Pp. 332 and 333. Reprinted with permission.

Dintiman, George B., and Jerrold S. Greenberg, *Health Through Discovery*, © 1983, Addison-Wesley, Reading, Massachusetts. P. 72 and pp. 346–347. Reprinted with permission.

Doyle, Sir Arthur Conan, *The Hound of the Baskervilles*.

Excerpt published with the permission of the copyright owner of the Sir Arthur Conan Doyle literary estate.

Du Gas, Beverly Witter, *Kozier-Du Gas' Introduction to Patient Care: A Comprehensive Approach to Nursing*, 2d ed. Philadelphia: W.B. Saunders, 1972.

Ewbank, Henry L., Jr., *Meeting Management*, Dubuque, Iowa: Wm. C. Brown, 1968.

Freedman, Jonathan, *Introductory Psychology*, © 1978, Addison-Wesley, Reading, Massachusetts. Pp. 204, 320, and 467. Reprinted with permission.

Frisch, Charles, "Letter to the Editor," *New York Times*, August 3, 1983. Copyright © 1983 by The New York Times Company. Reprinted by permission.

Gabler, Robert E., Robert Sager, Sheila Brazier, and Jacqueline Pourciau, from *Introduction to Physical Geography*. Copyright © 1975 by Rinehart Press. Reprinted by permission of Holt, Rinehart and Winston, CBS College Publishing.

Grawunder, Sr. Mary Redempta, from the book *Practical Nursing Review*. Published and copyright © 1980 by Arco Publishing, Inc., New York.

Gregory, Dick, with Robert Lipsyte, *nigger*. Copyright © 1964 by Dick Gregory Enterprises Inc. Excerpts reprinted by permission of the publisher, E.P. Dutton.

Haviland, William A., from *Cultural Anthropology*, 3d ed. Copyright © 1981 by Holt, Rinehart and Winston, Inc. Reprinted by permission of Holt, Rinehart and Winston, CBS College Publishing.

Hess, Beth B., Elizabeth W. Markson, and Peter J. Stein, *Sociology*, Macmillan Publishing Company, Inc., 1982.

Hickok, Robert, *Music Appreciation*, 2d ed., © 1975, Addison-Wesley, Reading, Massachusetts. Pp. 49 and 50 and p. 430.

Horton, Paul B., and Chester L. Hunt, *Sociology*, 3d ed. Copyright © 1972, McGraw-Hill Book Company. Excerpts used with permission of McGraw-Hill Book Company.

Hyde, Stuart W., *Television and Radio Announcing*, 2d ed. Copyright © 1971, 1959 by Houghton Mifflin Company. Excerpts reprinted by permission of the publisher.

Insel, Paul M., and Walton T. Roth, *Core Concepts in Health*, 3d ed., Mayfield Publishing Company, 1982.

Insel, Paul M., and Walton T. Roth, *Health in a Changing Society*. Copyright © 1976 by Mayfield Publishing Company. Excerpts reprinted by permission of Mayfield Publishing Company.

Johnson, Willis H., Louis E. DeLanney, Thomas A. Cole, and Austin E. Brooks, from *Essentials of Biology*, 2d ed. Copyright © 1969, 1974, by Holt, Rinehart and Winston, CBS College Publishing.

Jones, Kenneth L., Louis W. Shainberg, and Curtis O.

Wiley, John P. Jr., "Phenomena, Comment and Notes," *Smithsonian*, January, 1983.

Williamson, Paul, "A Doctor's Letter to His Son," *New York Times*, November 11, 1970 (Op-Ed). Copyright © 1970 by the New York Times Company. Reprinted by permission.

Willis, Edgar E., from *Writing Television and Radio Pro-grams*. Copyright © 1967 by Holt, Rinehart and Winston, Inc. Reprinted by permission of Holt, Rinehart and Winston, CBS College Publishing.

Woodbury, Ellen, "High Mail Rates, Low Service," *Newsday*, July 18, 1979. Copyright 1979, *Newsday*, The Long Island Newspaper. Reprinted by permission.

Index